BIG-BLOCK CHEVY PERFORMANCE

Modifications and Parts Combinations for High Performance Street, Racing, Marine and Off-Road Use

DAVE EMANUEL

HPBooks

HPBooks
are published by
The Berkley Publishing Group
A member of Penguin Putnam Inc.
375 Hudson Street
New York, New York 10014

First Edition: August 1995

© 1995 Dave Emanuel
10 9 8

The Penguin Putnam Inc. World Wide Web site address is
http://www.penguinputnam.com

Library of Congress Cataloging-in-Publication Data

Emanuel, Dave, 1946-
    Big-block Chevy performance : modifications and parts combinations
for high performance street, racing, marine, and off-road use / Dave
Emanuel. — 1st ed.
        p. cm.
    Includes index.
    ISBN 1-55788-216-9 (pbk.)
    1. Chevrolet automobile—Motors—Modification—Handbooks, manuals,
etc. 2. Chevrolet automobile—Parts—Handbooks, manuals, etc.
3. Chevrolet automobile—Performance—Handbooks, manuals, etc.
I. Title
TL215.C48E4 1995   95-8128
629.25′04—dc20   CIP

Book Design & Production by Bird Studios
Interior photos by the author unless otherwise noted
Cover photos by Steve Reyes

NOTICE: The information in this book is true and complete to the best of our knowledge. Some of the information is derived, excerpted or based upon the author's previous work, *Small-Block Chevy Performance*. Such information is generic and applicable to both the big- and small-block Chevrolet engines, and is included here for the benefit of the reader. All recommendations on parts and procedures are made without any guarantees on the part of the author or The Berkley Publishing Group. Tampering with, altering, modifying or removing any emissions-control device is a violation of federal law. Author and publisher disclaim all liability incurred in connection with the use of this information.

ACKNOWLEDGMENTS

One of the most difficult aspects of writing a book about engine performance modifications is finding solid, valid information. Many engineers and engine builders have their own agendas and very often swap fact and fiction as if there's no difference between them. Fortunately, I've been able to find a group of people who have worked diligently to determine what works and what doesn't. Even more important, they're willing to share their findings with me.

My sincerest gratitude to Garry Grimes, Grimes Automotive and Marine Machine; Mike and Chad Hedgecock, Eagle Racing Engines; Jim Oddy, Oddy's Automotive; Norm Wizner, Wizner Performance Products; Howard Stewart, Stewart Components; Randy Dorton, Hendrick Motorsports; Fred Roland, Vibratech Performance; Scooter Brothers, Competition Cams; Harvey Crane, Crane CamDesign; Myron Cottrell, TPI Specialties; Roger Allen, Chevrolet Race Shop; Jack Underwood, Chevrolet-Pontiac-Canada Group; Chuck Maguire, GM Powertrain; Ron Sperry, GM Powertrain.

Then there's the matter of Michael Lutfy, HPBooks automotive editor. Although he has yet to master the art of turning wrenches, Michael has an uncanny knack for knowing precisely how to put an automotive book together. He consistently improves upon whatever an author submits to him. In spite of his tendency to nag a bit like a mother-in-law, his efforts are sincerely appreciated and they have brought many improvements to *Big-Block Chevy Performance*.

—

CONTENTS

INTRODUCTION

Several years ago, I wrote a book entitled *Small-Block Chevy Performance*. Following its publication, it seemed only natural to begin processing the words that would comprise a book entitled *Big-Block Chevy Performance*.

The two engines have much in common, and consequently, so do these two books. However, each engine has a distinct personality and lineage, so there are also distinct differences. Those differences have become greater and more significant in the past few years, especially since the advent of the Gen V big block. Even more changes are on the horizon.

Although the Gen V engine addresses some of the shortcomings inherent in the Mark IV version, it also introduced many of its own unique wrinkles. Then there's the matter of compatibility. In typical myopic fashion, some of the engineers working on the Gen V focused exclusively on current production and gave no consideration to compatibility between Mark IV and Gen V blocks and heads. Thankfully, those engineers have since retired or found other employment and many of the wrongs of the Gen V will be fixed when the Mark VI version, known inside GM as "Mark Fix," is introduced, sometime before the end of the decade.

Like the small block, Chevy's "Rat" motor has been amply covered in magazines and other books. But *Big-Block Chevy Performance* covers some new ground and also explains in detail many procedures and philosophies that are usually glossed over. Much of the information you'll find in the following chapters comes directly from engineers in GM's Powertrain Division, and from some of the top engine builders in the country. They certainly didn't give away all their secrets, but they were surprisingly candid and did supply a wealth of practical, usable data on parts selection, machining and set-up procedures. So even experienced engine builders will find something useful in the following chapters.

While reading through this book, be aware that you may come across sections containing information that doesn't agree with some common practices. The primary reason that the big-block Chevy continues to grow (in displacement) and produce more horsepower per cubic inch than any other engine of its size is that even though the basic design is over 30 years old, it is inherently sound and engine builders are therefore able to easily apply the latest technological improvements. So in the 1990s, just as it was in the 1960s, the Chevy big block is still the large displacement powerplant by which all others are measured. ∎

Are the days of the mighty big-block coming to an end? Naysayers and environmental critics have been predicting the big block's demise for two decades now, but time and again, it has beaten the odds to not only survive, but flouish. For maximum, stump-pulling high performance, nothing quite compares to Chevy's venerable rat motor.

BIRTH OF THE BIG BLOCK

Chevrolet's revolutionary small block V-8 was only three years old, but it had already become apparent that a powerplant of larger bore and stroke dimensions would be required to keep pace with Ford and Plymouth. So when the 1958 Chevrolets were unveiled, the 283 cid small block wasn't the only option for buyers with V-8 tendencies. An entirely new engine with unusual scalloped valve covers and a displacement of 348 cubic inches was also available.

Known as the "W" engine, the 348 ultimately grew into the infamous 409. Although immortalized in song, and feared on the drag strip and the street, the 409 had inherent limitations. As a performance engine, it was a step-child, an overgrown sibling of the 348, which was originally designed to serve in Chevy's full-sized trucks. The 409 performed admirably for a number of years, blowing away the competition more often than not, but its basic design placed severe limitations on its potential as a race engine.

Mystery Engines

That fact had not been missed by Chevrolet engineering and in 1963, a new Chevrolet big block sent heads spinning and lips flapping when Junior Johnson blasted around Daytona Speedway at the then-unprecedented speed of 166 mph.

The Chevrolet big block began life with a displacement of 396 cubic inches in 1965. The next year, it was also available as a 427-incher. As if the garden variety 427 didn't have enough going for it, Chevrolet developed a limited production high output version that could be ordered as RPO L-88. With aluminum cylinder heads and a cornucopia of high performance internals, the 425-horsepower rating was a joke. Actual gross horsepower was well over 500.

The 1966 SS-396 Chevelle was Chevy's first widely available muscle car. It was available with either a 325-, 360- or 375-horsepower 396 engine. In stock form, these cars would turn 13-second quarter-mile times. As the Ed Roth T-shirt design says, "Hell hath no fury like a Chevy SS-396."

The powerplant that propelled Johnson's '63 Chevy to such an incredible speed had a displacement of 427 cubic inches and was possessed of unique cylinder heads with canted valves. Such cylinder heads had never been seen before and caused the new big-block Chevy to be tagged a "Mystery Engine." Officially known as a Chevrolet Mark II engine, the new big block quickly faded from sight when GM pulled its support of racing.

Mark IV—But two years later, the "Mystery Engine" reappeared. It had gone through several generations of change, as denoted by the switch from a Mark II to a Mark IV designation, and it was released in a 396 cid rather than 427 cid form. However, the lineage was unmistakable.

Introduced in the middle of the 1965 model year, the 396 had a 4.094" bore, 3.760" stroke and horsepower ratings of 325 when installed in full-sized Chevrolets, and 425 when tucked beneath the hood of a Corvette. It was also available in a limited number (201) of 1965 Chevelles in 375-hp form as part of the optional RPO Z16 package.

It didn't take long for Chevy to bump the displacement of its new big block. For the 1966 model year, a 427-cid version of the Mark IV engine was available in full-sized cars and Corvettes with horsepower ratings of 390 (RPO L36) and 425 (L72). The 396 was the largest engine available in regular production Chevelles and Camaros and at the beginning of the

The L-88 was a serious engine and Chevrolet wanted to be sure it was fed properly. A warning tag regarding fuel octane was posted on the console of L-88 Corvettes.

model year, only 325-hp (L35) and 360-hp versions (L34) were available. Later, a 375-hp 396 was introduced (L78). This was essentially the same solid lifter engine that had appeared in the 1965 Corvette rated at 425 horsepower. (The 375-hp 396 installed in 1965 Z16 Chevelles had hydraulic lifters.)

RPO L71/L88—The next high water mark for the Chevy big block came just a

In the early days of Pro Stock, big-block Camaros, especially those from Malvern, Pennsylvania, gave Chevy lovers plenty to cheer about. Bill Jenkins in his "Grumpy's Toy" Camaros kept big blocks in the spotlight for many years.

Corvettes and big blocks used to go together like horsepower and torque—back in the days before politicians were involved in the automobile business. Perhaps the most infamous Corvette/big-block combination was the 1969 ZL1, which featured aluminum block and heads. Only two were produced.

year later. For the 1967 model year, RPO L71 featured three Holley two-barrel carburetors and a rating of 435 horsepower. If that wasn't enough to satisfy power maniacs, aluminum cylinder heads could be added, or the box next to RPO L88 could be checked. The L88 was a full-on race engine thinly disguised as a full-on race engine. It included aluminum heads, an 850-cfm Holley four barrel, high-rise aluminum intake manifold, mechanical lifter cam and 12.5:1 compression ratio. With tongue firmly implanted in cheek, specification writers listed horsepower as 430. "Informed sources" of the day stated that a stock L88 actually produced 550-560 horsepower.

ZL1—The L88 continued as the ultimate big block until 1969 when the ZL1 was released. With its aluminum block, the 427-cid ZL1 weighed about 150 pounds less than an L88, but the weight reduction wasn't cheap; the ZL1 option for a 1969 Corvette was priced at $4,718. By comparison, an L88, which had aluminum heads and a cast-iron block, cost $1,032. Considering that the base price for a 1969 Corvette coupe was $4,781, it's not surprising that only two

ZL1 Corvettes were built. However, a total of 69 ZL1 Camaros were also built, primarily to humble the Boss 429 Mustang.

Although the ZL1 and L88 engines were designed primarily for racing, their creation had a significant effect on future passenger car big blocks. Specifically, the "open" combustion chambers used in the aluminum heads eventually found their way into iron head castings. That's significant because the open style chamber delivers a significant improvement in air flow capacity that translates directly to increased horsepower.

454—In 1970, big-block displacement was increased again, this time by way of a 1/4-in. increase in stroke. With the same 4.251" bore as a 427, and a 4.00" stroke, the 454 is the largest big block Chevy ever installed in a standard passenger car or pickup truck. Also in 1970, the 396 had its bore dimension increased .030" to 4.126" which raised displacement to 402 cubic inches. In spite of the displacement

In 1970 displacement was bumped to 454 cubic inches, which was the largest big block installed in passenger cars. The 502 cubic inch big block brought new grandeur to the displacement charts, but it's available only through GM Performance Parts.

3

There have even been a few big-block-powered fuel Funny Cars over the years. Back in the late '60s, "Rapid Ronnie" Runyon put away quite a few Hemi entries in his 427-powered Corvair.

increase, Chevelles with 402-cid engines were still labeled SS-396.

LS6—But there was no mistake in badging when a Chevelle was equipped with a 454 engine. 1970 marked the first time that an engine larger than 400 cubic inches could be ordered in a standard production Chevelle. Not only did

This photo, from Chevrolet Engineering, shows a 435-horsepower 427 engine with three two-barrel carburetors being readied for testing. The blur on the right is an engineer doing some last minute wiring.

Chevrolet pull the stops out on displacement, the division also raised the roof on horsepower. As might be expected, a mild version of the 454 engine (RPO number LS5) with hydraulic lifter cam, 10.25:1 compression ratio and 360 horsepower appeared on the option chart. But so did RPO LS6. This engine was rated at 450 horsepower and featured 11.25:1 compression ratio, mechanical lifter camshaft, 800 cfm Holley four-barrel, rectangular port cast iron heads, forged pistons and four-bolt main caps.

With the 1971 model year, compression ratio was reduced in all GM-produced engines and the LS6, by virtue of a drop to a 9:1 compression ratio was rated at 425 horsepower. That was the last hurrah for high horsepower, factory-installed big blocks. Additional detuning for the 1972 model year, elimination of killer engines like the LS6 and a switch from gross to net horsepower figures dropped the 454's. By 1975, a 454 engine could no longer be found beneath the hood of a Corvette and the next year, the venerable big block

Big blocks like to breathe, and nothing helps them breathe better than a blower. Although Hemi Chryslers were the most popular engines in supercharged classes, a number of racers built Chevy-powered Double-A Altereds.

appeared only as an option on trucks.

The Legend Lives On

For a time, it appeared as though big blocks were destined for a future of obscurity. Pro Stock drag racing had shifted its focus to small blocks as did NASCAR's Winston Cup division. Big blocks were unavailable in passenger cars and unwanted in race cars. But after contrived oil shortages and energy crises subsided, cubic inches once again became fashionable and popularity of the Chevy big block began to surge. Although its use in new vehicles was and is still restricted to trucks, the big block became the mainstay in many classes of racing, in high performance street machines and in the marine industry.

Gen V—The big block's resurgence ultimately prompted an updated version in 1991. Known as the Gen V (the engine should have been known as the Mark V, but a pre-existing copyright forced a designation change), it features significant changes to the block and cylinder heads. Specifically, Gen V

It may say "Oldsmobile" on the valve covers, but it's really a big-block Chevy. In the late 1980s, Oldsmobile and Pontiac developed cylinder heads and other hardware specifically for racing. Ultimately, Olds developed its own block, but it's strongly based on the Chevy big block.

blocks feature a one-piece rear main seal, oblong coolant holes in the deck surface, no mechanical fuel pump and relocation of the main oil gallery from the oil pan rail area to a position alongside the camshaft. Cylinder heads also have the same oblong coolant holes and incorporate non-adjustable rocker arms.

The big blocks found in current race cars bear little resemblance to their predecessors of the '60s. This Pro Modified engine features a dry sump oiling system, dual Holley Dominators on a fabricated aluminum ram manifold, crank-triggered ignition and enough nitrous oxide to produce about 1600 horsepower.

By comparison, a 454 as installed in a late-model truck is a rather sedate affair. However, throttle body fuel injection and electronic ignition, both controlled by a computer, enable late-model 454s to deliver exceptional fuel economy and excellent torque.

Current emissions and fuel economy requirements have all but eliminated the possibility of a big block ever again being installed in a production passenger car.

But the Chevrolet big block (now produced by GM Powertrain division) will continue to live a vibrant life, as it continues to be factory installed in trucks and boats, and owner installed in street vehicles and race cars. GM has demonstrated its intention to continue production of the big block through its 1991 introduction of the Gen V version and the soon to be released (or possibly already released) Mark VI.

There are also several aftermarket sources for big-block cylinder blocks. Even if production of the engine were to cease, GM Performance parts would likely continue offering complete 454 and 502 cid big blocks and individual components as over-the-counter parts. Outside the world of GM, World Products offers a cast-iron Mark IV compatible block and aluminum blocks are manufactured by Keith Black, Donovan and Rodeck.

Call it what you will—Mark IV, Gen V, Rat Motor or corporate large block—the engine that was christened the Chevrolet big block has been making history for three decades. With a heritage like that, bolstered by the fact that there's no substitute for cubic inches, its future is secure. ■

Although big blocks haven't been available in passenger cars since the mid-Seventies you can still find them beneath the hoods of pickups. The SS-454 pickup carries on the sporting big block tradition started by the SS-396 Chevelle and has become something of a cult vehicle amongst performance-oriented truck enthusiasts.

2

SHORT BLOCK

CYLINDER BLOCK

"If some is good, more is better and too much is just enough." Although it reflects the government's philosophy on budget deficits, that old adage is also popular with racers, performance enthusiasts and boaters when the topic at hand is engine displacement. In Chevyspeak, nothing says cubic inches like a big block and fortunately, all the parts required to turn philosophy into reality are readily available.

Production and over-the-counter big blocks have been available in a variety of displacements (see chart on page 8 for bore and stroke).

Although bigger is typically equated with better, there seems to be a direct correlation between engine displacement and building costs. Consequently, it may be more appropriate to build a 396 or 427 rather than a 454 or 502. And if an engine is destined to reside in a restored vehicle, the option of changing blocks may not be possible because you may be crucified by Corvette and muscle car purists.

A cylinder block is the foundation of

Nobody has squeezed more power out of a production-based big block than Charles Carpenter. Often called the "Father of Shoebox Racing," Carpenter began on a low budget, with an all-steel '55 Chevy and not very many exotic engine parts. His original cars turned in spectacular performances, but as the appearance of this car demonstrates, he ultimately stepped up to state-of-the-art equipment.

Gen V Bow Tie blocks have round, rather than oblong, cooling holes in the deck surface, accept crankshafts designed for a one-piece rear main seal, and have no provision for a mechanical fuel pump. Seal adapters that allow the use of older style cranks (designed for a two-piece rear main seal) are available, as are oil pans for each type of seal. Mark IV Bow Tie blocks have many of the same structural features as the Gen V version, and may be the better choice if you have a garage full of Mark IV cranks and oil pans.

CID	BORE	STROKE
396	4.094	3.76
402	4.125	3.76
427	4.250	3.76
454	4.250	4.00
502	4.466	4.00

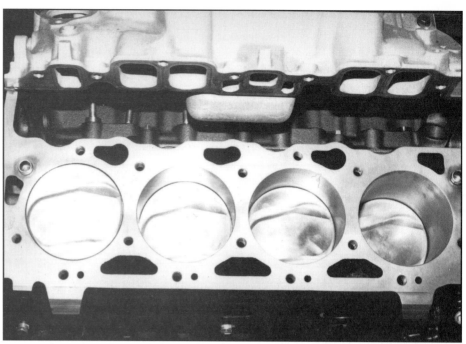

A Gen V production block is easy to identify by its oblong coolant holes. These holes can cause sealing problems if Mark IV heads are installed—sometimes they leak, sometimes they don't. It depends on production tolerances.

Nothing succeeds like excess, which is one reason for the popularity of the 502 cubic-inch (8.2 liters) big block (part no. 10185085). The complete engine assembly includes a Gen V production marine block (part no. 14096817), rectangular port open chamber heads and heavy-duty components throughout. Bore and stroke dimensions are 4.447" x 4.00".

any performance engine. No great revelation there, but a point that seems to be missed all too frequently is that you don't build a killer engine on a poor foundation. The quality of machine work is of vital importance. Although the block itself has little effect on horsepower (unless it's completely butchered) it does influence the ability of other parts to perform at maximum efficiency. It also plays a big role in determining durability.

If you're building a high performance engine, be sure to take your parts to a machine shop that can provide the required level of quality. Some traditional shops are perfectly capable of achieving the finish quality and tolerances that are required, others simply are not. Don't believe all that you read. Get recommendations from people who have experience dealing with local shops. And don't trip over dollar bills to pick up pennies. Many of the shops that do

Casting date format varies depending on the year. This block was manufactured on 12/21/72. (The "L" denoting the twelfth month is to the left of "21.")

Casting numbers, also cast into the bellhousing flange, are another clue as to a block's identity. Casting number and date will usually be all that's required for a positive identification. Since only one "8" is included, it sometimes requires a bit of detective work to determine the decade.

Late-model big blocks are easy to identify because their displacement is cast into the sides. This is a 7.4-liter block; translated into English, that means 454 cubic inches.

High performance blocks are supposed to have "Hi-Perf Pass" cast into the surface just below the camshaft boss. However, as this photo indicates, that's not always the case. This block has all the required high performance attributes, but has "Pass Perf" as an identifier.

Big blocks aren't used in many forms of oval track racing, but they predominate on the Super Modified circuit. Weighing only 1800 pounds, these cars typically use alcohol-burning, fuel-injected 468-cubic-inch engines mounted 18 inches to the left of the car's centerline. They absolutely fly around a race track.

quality work charge a little more than average. That's because it takes more time to do things right. What is the advantage of saving $25 on machine work and then grenading the engine because something wasn't machined accurately enough?

Playing with Blocks

When selecting a block for high performance or race usage, a good rule of thumb is to begin with a thorough visual inspection and a sonic check of the cylinder walls. If the block is acceptable, remove the casting flash in the valley and add trash screens over all the openings. Although it may seem like overkill to install trash screens in a street engine, it's cheap insurance. Too many engines have been lunched because a piece of a broken rocker or valve spring worked its way down and destroyed a camshaft, crank or block.

As for the block casting itself, all production short deck 4-1/4-in. bore blocks are pretty much the same. Some early "Hi Perf" blocks had provisions for an external oil cooler (two threaded outlets directly above the oil filter), but

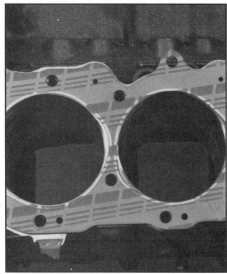

Big-block head gaskets contained scalloped areas around each cylinder. These areas are typically beveled in the block for additional valve clearance.

Two-bolt blocks are much more readily available than four-bolt versions and will take a surprising amount of abuse. If four-bolt main caps are required, they can be retrofitted. These steel caps contain provisions for splayed outer bolts and include studs in place of the inner bolts.

The Bow Tie big block's reputation for strength isn't without foundation. Hefty four-bolt main bearing caps, generous webbing and plenty of cast iron in all the necessary places makes for excellent durability under racing conditions. Bare Bow Tie blocks weigh 269 pounds.

these were deleted in the early 1970's. You'll find "Hi Perf Pass" or some derivative thereof (see photo) on virtually all 427 and 454 blocks. However, neither this marking nor the casting number assures you that the block will be drilled for four-bolt main caps. There are cases where the same casting number has been used on two-bolt and four-bolt blocks, so if you're buying a used engine, the only way to tell is to pull the pan and look. All the blocks have provisions for four main cap bolts, it's just that on some passenger car blocks, these holes aren't drilled and tapped. Supposedly, the 512 casting is the hot number because it's rumored to have thicker cylinder walls, but some experts haven't been able to find any difference. There have been a lot of plain vanilla blocks that have cylinder walls that are over .300-in. thick. What you've absolutely got to do is have a block sonic-checked before you spend any money on it. That holds true whether you're starting with a brand new block or a used one. Core shift can be a problem, especially if you're going to overbore it .060-in. or more.

Although having four-bolts holding the main caps in place is nice insurance, there's no structural difference between a standard Mark IV two-bolt and four-bolt block (aside from the obvious additional bolt holes). For general performance use as well as bracket or street/strip drag racing and autocrossing, a two-bolt block is entirely adequate unless an absurdly sized nitrous system is installed. Grimes Automotive has built many 600-horsepower engines using two-bolt blocks and cast iron crankshafts. These engines frequently enter the Twilight Zone above 7000 rpm yet durability is never a problem. The secret to making a two-bolt block live is precise machine work and the installation of top quality main studs in place of bolts.

Block Options

If a new block is to be used, the most common choice is part number 1404480, which includes a 4.250-in. bore, four-bolt main bearing caps and a deck height of 9.80-in. (measured from crankshaft centerline to the deck surface). It also features cylinders that are relieved at the top to unshroud the intake valves.

Another option is part number 14103151, which is the heavy-duty truck version of the standard passenger car block. (Pickup trucks are equipped with passenger car blocks.) The only

difference between the two blocks is a .400-in. higher deck height; the truck block measures 10.200-in. from crankshaft centerline to deck surface. For high performance engines, the advantage of the additional deck height is that it allows the use of longer-than-stock connecting rods, which reduces rod angularity and will also accommodate longer strokes. (Truck blocks were

The production two-bolt block is no slouch either. Although it doesn't have the strength of its Bow Tie cousin, this block has more than enough strength for high performance and bracket racing use. There is additional material that's cast into the block at the front and rear to accommodate the holes required for four-bolt mains. Structurally, two-bolt and four-bolt production blocks are identical except for machining.

Chevrolet isn't the only company producing beefy big blocks. World Products offers its Merlin blocks in three deck heights—9.800", 10.200" and 11.625". The tallest version can accommodate a 4.625" bore and 5.600" stroke, which translates to 750+ cubic inches.

MARK IV VERSUS GEN V

There are a number of differences between Mark IV and Gen V blocks, many of which aren't obvious. At first glance, it may not be apparent that the Gen V block has no provision for mounting a mechanical fuel pump, and that a one-piece, rather than two-piece rear main seal is used. Gen V blocks are designed to accept a one-piece oil pan gasket, so even though the timing covers bolt patterns are identical between Mark IV and Gen V blocks, timing covers aren't interchangeable. However, water pumps are.

Of more significance is the difference in oiling systems. In Mark IV engines, the main oil gallery is located just above the oil pan rail on the left (driver's) side. This location presents a major problem if main caps with splayed outer bolts are installed-- the bolt holes run right into the gallery. The possibility of cutting into this passage when machining for crankshaft clearance or boring the cylinders also exists.

In Gen V blocks, the main oil gallery has been relocated alongside the camshaft. Oil is routed directly from the main gallery directly to the four front main bearings; the rear main is fed from the oil filter outlet.

Oil reaches the cam bearings through passages that intersect the bearing bores at an angle that results in an oval hole. To ensure adequate cam oiling, cam bearings must be installed so that their holes line up with the oval openings. This is accomplished by installing the cam bearings with their holes at "2-o'clock" when viewed from the front of the block.

Compared to a production Gen V block, the Bow Tie version contains more material at the bottom of the cylinders. This can cause interference with long stroke crankshaft assemblies and with the distributor, and chamfering may be required to obtain adequate clearance. Also note that some aftermarket distributors may not seal the passenger side lifter gallery without special machining. ∎

originally given the additional .400-in. in deck height to accommodate pistons with four, rather than three rings.) If an engine is to have stock bore, stroke and connecting rod length, a standard passenger car block should be used.

Bow Tie Blocks—If you're planning to build a "take no prisoners" big block, whether it be supercharged, fed a dose of nitrous or simply naturally aspirated, the wise choice is to begin with a Bow Tie block. Mark IV Bow Tie blocks are available in both short (9.800-in.) and tall (10.200-in.) deck heights, as part numbers 10051106 and 14044808 respectively. Both have semi-finished bore diameters of 4.250-in. and will accept finished bore diameters as large as 4.560-in.

Another alternative is a Gen V Bow Tie block (part no. 10185049 for short deck, 10134367 for tall deck). Like their Mark IV counterparts, the Gen V Bow Tie blocks feature siamesed cylinder walls (no water jacket between cylinders) and four-bolt main bearing caps, but have the new style one-piece rear main seal.

Unlike production Gen V blocks, the Bow Tie versions have round rather than oblong coolant holes in their deck surfaces. Consequently, Mark IV cylinder heads can be installed using standard

head gaskets.

Yet another option is a race-prepared Gen V Bow Tie block. The short deck version (part no. 24502500) is supplied with 4.125-in. diameter cylinders while the tall deck model (part no. 24502502) has 4.250-in. cylinders. As with standard Gen V Bow Tie blocks, the race-prepared versions will accept bore sizes up to 4.600-in.

Race-prepared Bow Tie blocks feature steel main bearing caps and a Mark IV-style rear main seal, thereby allowing Mark IV-type oil pans to be installed. These blocks also feature eight head bolt bosses located in the lifter valley, so four extra head bolts can be installed in each head. The additional head bolts improve head gasket sealing.

Irrespective of the block chosen, trash screens should be installed. In the event that something breaks up top, the screens prevent unwanted pieces from causing damage down below.

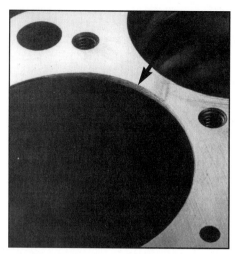

Chamfering the top of the cylinders isn't a major operation because not much material has to be removed—just enough to unshroud the valves. Both intake and exhaust sides should be chamfered.

World Products has also gotten into the act of manufacturing cast-iron Chevrolet cylinder blocks. World offers its Merlin block in three deck heights—9.800-in., 10.200-in. and 11.625-in. (part nos. 8010, 8011 and 8012 respectively). On all three versions, cylinder walls are at least .400-in. thick at a bore diameter of 4.625-in. Other features include billet steel main caps with splayed outer bolts and inner studs, eight head bolt bosses in the lifter valley and dual oil pan bolt patterns (stock and Olds DRCE). These blocks also incorporate a fuel pump boss and .625-in. thick deck surfaces.

Block Machining

But before any machine work is begun, each block should be sonic-checked for adequate cylinder wall thickness. Any block that has less than .300" thickness on the thrust surfaces—before boring and honing—should be rejected unless the engine will see only occasional mild abuse.

Align Honing—Once a suitable block is located, it should be align honed to assure that the main bearing saddles are of the proper diameter and in perfect alignment. Following align honing, it's wise to install the main bearings and check to verify that the holes in the upper

halves are properly aligned with the oil supply holes in the block. Any misalignment can usually be corrected by simply elongating the saddle holes as required.

Many machinists either overlook or disregard the importance of align honing. But every critical block dimension is taken off main bearing saddle alignment, so align boring and/or honing should be the first machining operation and it must be done accurately. When a block is align honed, you absolutely must have the oil pump installed and the bearing caps tightened to the required torque, using the same fasteners (either studs or bolts) that will be installed when the engine is assembled. This is critical because when you tighten the main cap bolts or studs, or the oil pump bolt, it distorts the cap.

Deck Height—After align honing, the next step is to mathematically figure out deck height. Many engine builders use a BHJ True Deck plate to determine deck height and squareness and deck the block as required. Then they move on to the boring bar and use a deck plate, rather than the existing bores, to locate the boring bar. This operation is necessary because in a production block, the bores may be off center by .010" to .015".

Cylinder Boring—Cylinder wall

finish is always a controversial topic, but a straightforward procedure always works best. The biggest concern is cylinder wall movement so the use of torque plates during boring and honing is mandatory. Rather than using "trick of the week" honing procedures, the real trick is to stick with the basic stones that provide the desired finish, as determined by the type of rings being used. (See piston ring section for specific recommendations.)

CRANKSHAFTS

The aspiring big-block builder has a choice of two stroke dimensions in production crankshafts—3.76-in. as found in 396, 402 and 427 engines and 4.00-in. as found in 454s. Although the 396/402 and 427 crankshafts have the same stroke, they're not identical; the 427 shafts have a heavier counterweight. Viewed from the front, the third counterweight back on a 396/402 crank is about 7/16-in. wide while on a 427-crank, it's 7/8-in. wide.

Both nodular cast iron and forged steel crankshafts have been used in big blocks over the years. The cast crankshafts have plenty of beef and will stand up to a surprising amount of abuse. But cast cranks do have their limitations, so the

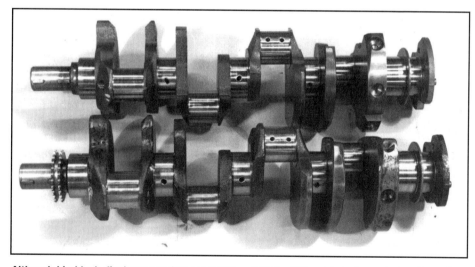

Although big block displacement has ranged from 396 to 502 cubic inches, stroke dimensions are either 3.76" or 4.00". Although cranks of the same stroke are seemingly interchangeable, they actually aren't, because counterweights vary depending upon the bore size of the engine for which the crank was intended.

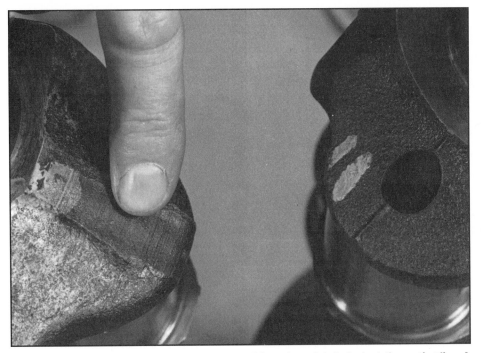

The easiest way to distinguish between a cast and forged crank is to look at the parting line. A broad surface (rather than a line) like the one on the left indicates a forging, a thin line identifies a casting. If the parting line has been ground away, tap the crank with a hammer. A forged crank will ring like a bell, a casting will respond with a dull thud.

If you're rummaging through used crankshafts and come across this number, you may have struck gold. Casting number 3987416 corresponds to part number 3963523, which is a 4.00" stroke shaft forged of 1053 steel. It was originally used in LS-6 and LS-7 engines and it is nitride-treated to increase hardness and is also cross drilled. It can also be used with Mark IV 502 engines.

forged varieties are generally preferred for high output engines—for peace of mind if no other reason.

Crank Options

For 396, 402 and 427 engines, the crankshaft part numbers of interest are 3967811 (Mark IV) and 10114186 (Gen V as used in 427 truck engines). If you're dealing in used components, the Mark IV crankshaft can be identified by forging number 7115. Its equivalent in the world of 4.00-in. strokes is part number 3963523, which will have either a 3520 or 7416 forging number. (Originally used in LS-6 and LS-7 replacement engine assemblies.) In the land of Gen V crankshafts, part number 14096983 pertains to the 454-cid version while part number 10183723 corresponds to a 502-cid powerplant. Both crankshafts can be

Big block cranks have plenty of beef, so if the journals have to be machined .010" or .020" undersized, the crank is still usable. However, all crankshafts should be checked for straightness and indexed.

Stick a blower on top of a big block and with the boost cranked up, strange things begin to happen to the bottom end. Jim Oddy developed this support for his 1800+ horsepower Pro Modified engines. It significantly improved crankshaft and bearing life.

Sometimes, even four main cap bolts aren't enough. After blowing the bottom out of a few blocks, Oddy designed a girdle to support the three center main caps. This type of support is required only for supercharged engines producing obscene amounts of power.

This is the type of bottom end usually seen on a big block. Four-bolt caps, a forged crank and beefy connecting rods are more than adequate for most engines.

identified by a 7044 forging number and are virtually identical, except that the latter is balanced for the heavier 502 rotating assembly.

From a practical standpoint, all Mark IV forgings are identical, so they're essentially interchangeable. However, not all cranks are the same. Sounds like you're reading something written by a politician, doesn't it? But it's not double-talk. Forgings originally destined for LS-6 or LS-7 and other high performance engines are nitrided and cross-drilled. Cranks installed in truck engines are not. Nitriding is a "good news, bad news" proposition. It does make the crankshaft harder and more durable, but it also makes it more brittle.

Used forgings are still available, but they're not particularly plentiful, so choices can be limited. Rather than worrying about nitriding, the smart play is to make sure a crank is straight and free of cracks. So before any machine work is begun, a newly acquired crankshaft should be Magnaflux inspected and checked for straightness (even if it's a brand new out-of-the-box GM part). If everything looks good, have the mains cross-drilled and the journals ground and/or polished as required and chamfer the oil holes.

Also note that all big-block cranks, which have 2.75-in. diameter main journals and 2.20-in. rod journals, can be machined up to .020-in. undersized without causing any substantial weakening. One benefit of grinding the journals undersized is that a generous (as opposed to stingy) fillet radius can be added where the journal meets the flank. (A fillet radius eliminates the stock straight-line intersection, which is a fertile ground for the growth of stress risers.) On the flip side, with a nitrided crankshaft, grinding the journals undersized removes the case-hardened surface. That shouldn't be a problem because nitriding isn't really necessary in most engines. In any event, the journals can be retreated if a case-hardened surface is required.

Crank Bearings

Bearings should be fit with .002-in. to .0025-in. clearance, and to ensure that they have a happy future, a top quality synthetic motor oil should fill the crankcase following engine break-in using a conventional mineral oil. As a general rule, most engine builders prefer to install a high volume oil pump in a big block. Additionally, before installation, an oil pump should be disassembled and the gear-to-housing clearance checked; it should measure .0025" at the front and the back. Irrespective of the type or brand of pump installed, it's *vital* that the pickup be welded or bolted to the pump body.

CONNECTING RODS

Any number of aftermarket rods are available, but stock Chevrolet rods are

The rod on the left has 7/16" bolts, the one on the right, 3/8" bolts. But bolt size obviously isn't the only difference. Along with larger bolts, the 7/16" rod has more material throughout, making it considerably stronger.

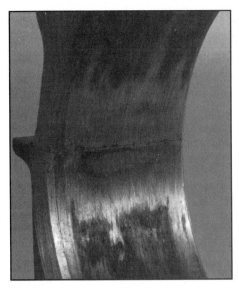

A stock production connecting rod is adequate for mild performance engines, but should be detailed. Note the junction where the cap and rod meet.

LS-7-style rods are beveled at the cap/rod junction to minimize shaving the back side of the bearings when they're installed. It also prevents the bearings from being pinched when the rod stretches at high rpm. Standard rods should have this bevel added for performance use.

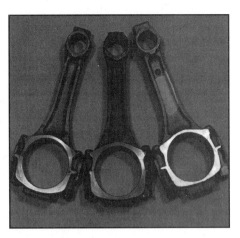

From left to right--a standard passenger engine connecting rod, a truck rod and an LS-7 rod with 7/16" bolts. Notice the difference in structure and beam width between these types of rods.

An alternative to Chevrolet rods is an "H"-beam rod from an aftermarket supplier. Manley is one of the companies offering this type of rod in standard and optional lengths.

suitable—and usually a bunch cheaper. You've got a choice of two basic types; both have a 6.135-in. center-to-center length, but one has 3/8-in. bolts, the other has 7/16-in. bolts. Standard passenger car and truck rods are the most common of the 3/8-in. bolt variety. Although the beefier 7/16-in.-bolt rods are obviously stronger, 3/8-in. bolts are suitable for most high performance and some race applications. The truck 3/8-in. forging is usually preferred because it's wider and has more material around the big end. Shot-peening may not be necessary, but it never hurts.

Rod Options

If you're in the market for new rods, Chevrolet part number 10198922 (color code white) will get you the same rods as used in LS-6, LS-7 and HO 502 engines. These rods feature 7/16-in. bolts, are Magnaflux-inspected, shot-peened and designed for a pressed pin. The same forging is available for full floating pins as part number 3969804 (color code green).

There's another rod that you sometimes hear about—it's the original high performance rod used on 1965-69 big blocks. (Part number 3856240.) Nobody uses these rods because brand new, they cost just as much as an LS-7 rod with 7/16-in. bolts, and used, they're as rare as a legitimate ZL-1.

One piece of advice if you're using 3/8-in. truck rods—bevel the rod and cap at the parting line (see photo). The 7/16-in. bolt rods are prepared this way at the factory; the bevel reduces the amount of material shaved from the back side of the bearing when it's inserted and also prevents the bearing from being pinched at the parting line when the rod stretches.

In recent years, there has been an outbreak of forged steel connecting rod manufacturers. Manley, Total Seal, Eagle, Childs and Albert, and Carrillo offer connecting rods in a variety of center-to-center lengths. Aluminum rods are another option, but their use is typically

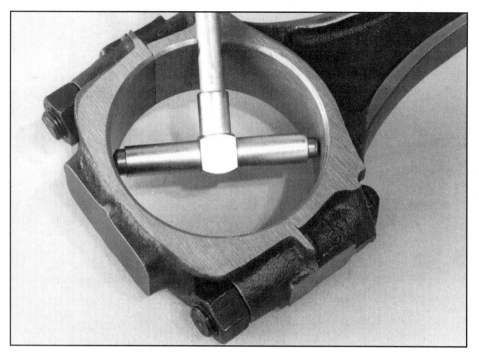

Some big-block pistons have very deep valve reliefs requiring that the top ring groove be located a good distance down from the deck. This isn't the ideal position for maximum power, but it's often necessary.

Whenever rods are reconditioned, they should be checked for proper big end diameter and roundness. Nothing should be taken for granted.

restricted to maximum effort drag race engines.

PISTONS

The best deal in town on big-block pistons can be found in the Keith Black and Speed-Pro catalogs. Both companies offer hypereutectic pistons which are ideal for high performance street (and some race) engines. These pistons are typically cheaper than their forged counterparts and are actually better suited for long-term operation in a high performance street engine. Both flat-top and domed varieties are available, so just about any compression ratio can be achieved.

For 454 race engines, the forged piston of choice is usually an LS-7 replacement (TRW part no. L2307AF, Speed-Pro part no. 7040PA) which has a 1/16-in., 1/16-in., 3/16-in. ring combination and a .580-in. tall dome. For 427 engines, the equivalent part numbers are L2308F and 7041PA (for open chamber heads) and 7011P (closed chamber heads). If you're trying to achieve a compression ratio of approximately 12.5:1 with a 396, suitable

pistons are listed in the TRW and Speed-Pro catalogs under part numbers L2308AF and 7021P respectively. Manley also offers an LS-7-style piston for engines with a 4.250-in. diameter bore in .030-in., .060-in., .100-in. and .125-in. oversized. The company also offers off-the-shelf pistons for engines with 6.385-in. long connecting rods (.250-in. longer than stock). Of course any number of piston manufacturers can supply custom pistons with just about any dome configuration desired.

Depending upon combustion chamber volume and deck clearance (which should be between .000-in. and .005-in.)

Big-block pistons are available in a variety of configurations, depending on combustion chamber size and the compression ratio desired. LS-7 forged replacement pistons are relatively low priced, but their large dome (right) makes them inappropriate for most street engines. However, the dome is thick enough that .200" can be milled off (left).

Custom piston manufacturers have developed special machining procedures to precisely shape piston domes. This eliminates a lot of the hand finishing that is often necessary to fit a dome to a combustion chamber.

Bow Tie blocks will accept a healthy amount of over-bore and that calls for appropriate pistons. As indicated by the number stamped on top, this piston is designed for a .090" overbore. Its small dome and lack of an exhaust valve relief indicates it was installed in a relatively mild engine. It was. On the dyno, it only produced 625 horsepower.

all of the previously referenced "off-the-shelf" pistons will pinch compression ratio to approximately 12.5:1 in combination with a 120cc combustion chamber, tight deck and Fel-Pro "blue" head gasket (which has a .0385-in. compressed thickness).

A few caveats regarding pistons:

• If a piston has a dome designed for closed chamber heads, it can be used with open chamber heads, but not vice versa.
• Piston-to-wall clearance with forged pistons is typically .006-in. to .0075-in., whereas cast and hypereutectic pistons require .002-in. or less clearance. That makes for quieter operation and longer ring life.
• Before "massaging" a set of pistons, check to make sure they're of the proper diameter and have the correct compression height. If you're installing full floating-type wrist pins, make sure the pinholes are machined to accept retaining rings.

Piston Rings

Most performance and race engine builders have very strong opinions regarding the brand and type of piston ring and the required cylinder wall finish. However, for long-term durability in any type of engine, a Total Seal ring set with a plasma moly top ring, gapless second and stainless-steel, low-tension oil ring is tough to beat.

At many high performance machine shops, the standard cylinder preparation for this ring combination includes boring the block to within .005" of desired finished bore size then traveling the rest of the way with a hone. The typical procedure involves rough honing with 220-grit (500 series) stones, followed by a few passes with 280-grit stones (600 series). A final finish is then applied with 400-grit (800 series).

Ring Gaps—For optimum sealing, rings should be inserted in their individual cylinders and end gaps filed to fit. In lieu of manufacturers' recommendations otherwise, the top ring should be given .020-in. to .022-in. end gap with forged pistons and .026 in. to .028 in. with hypereutectic pistons.

A 5/64 in., 5/64 in., 3/16-in. ring configuration is preferred for street and recreational marine engines. (Wider rings deliver better long-term durability.)

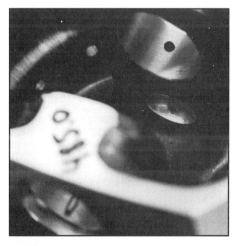

Pistons that are balanced by a high quality machine shop will show very little evidence. The best method of removing material to equalize weight is with a ball mill on the inside of the piston pin towers. Holes drilled in the underside of the dome indicate a second-rate job.

17

Although a 1/16-in., 1/16-in., 3/16-in. ring combination will provide improved ring seal at high rpm, such considerations are unwarranted in a street or recreational marine engine because the engine doesn't spend enough time in the tachometer's "Twilight Zone" to justify the trade-off of reduced ring life. Another consideration is that with a 1/16-in., 1/16-in., 3/16-in. ring package, oil consumption tends to be higher than with wider rings.

Other ring options include .043-in. or Dykes-type top rings. Both of these ring types are intended strictly for racing and while they do offer exceptional ring seal, they tend to wear very quickly.

According to Joe Moriarty of Total Seal, Inc., the main reason to use a narrow ring is to reduce ring mass—the lighter the ring, the less it tends to hammer the ring groove. This is only a consideration at high rpm, so there's no need to use anything narrower than a 5/64-in. ring if an engine isn't going to be used exclusively for racing.

Piston rock is another factor that

The ends of the rings are filed until the desired amount of end gap is achieved.

influences ring selection. With forged pistons, piston-to-cylinder wall clearance is greater than with cast or hypereutectic pistons, so the piston rocks more in the bore and that has a negative influence on ring seal—the wider the ring, the worse the effect. Cast or hypereutectic pistons usually require clearances of .002-in. or less, so piston rock isn't a major factor and there's little advantage of running a narrow ring.

Moriarty also noted that .043-in. and Dykes rings are strictly for full-tilt race applications where gas pressures are high and the engine is regularly disassembled for maintenance. With a .043-in. top ring, there is much less mass, which helps high rpm sealing. However, there is also a reduced contact face. As a result, heat transfer to the cylinder wall is reduced and the rings wear faster. With a Dykes ring, sealing at low rpm and low gas loads isn't very good and may result in oil getting up into the combustion chamber. Since a Dykes ring only seals well with heavy gas loading, it's only real application is for drag and similar types of racing where you're on the throttle all the time you're racing; Dykes rings are inappropriate for oval track and road racing because you're on and off the throttle.

Low Tension Rings—The latest trend in oil rings is low tension. The oil rings are the most significant contributors to ring drag, so reducing tension significantly lowers internal friction. In a low tension oil ring, improved ring

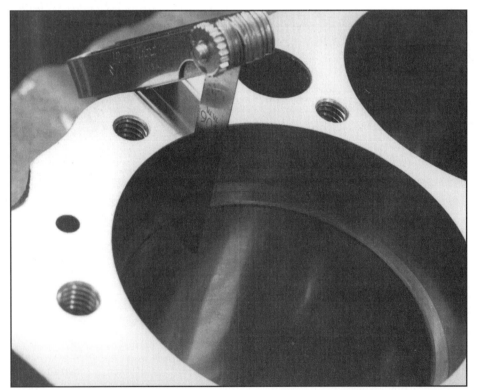

Thousands of engines have been built with rings that are taken out of the box and installed. But for optimum ring performance, you should use .005" oversized rings and individually fit each one to its respective cylinder by filing and checking end gaps.

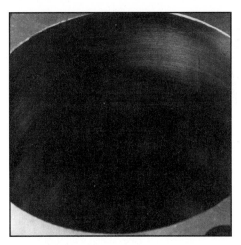

No ring can seal properly if the cylinder walls aren't prepared correctly. This textbook cross-hatch pattern is what you should see before you start assembling an engine.

It's not essential, but when file-fitting rings, a squaring tool should be used to ensure that the rings are properly positioned in the cylinders. Squaring tools are available for just about any cylinder diameter.

conformability (the ability of the ring to stay in contact with the cylinder wall) is achieved by manufacturing the oil rails from material with reduced radial thickness. Some companies are also experimenting with rails that are .015-in. thick rather than .024-in. in thickness.

As might be expected, the optimum ring package varies according to the type of life an engine is going to lead. What works best in a Pro Mod big block won't even be close to the optimum ring set-up for a 454 street engine. But having read this chapter, you're undoubtedly aware of the best ring combination for your short block. ■

COMPONENT WEIGHTS
(in pounds)

Cast iron heads, bare:	61
with valvetrain:	65
077 Aluminum head, bare:	27.5
Dart aluminum, bare:	38
fully assembled:	42
Aluminum intake manifold:	24
Forged crankshaft:	71
Water pump (iron):	13.5
Vibration damper:	15.5
Camshaft:	10
Steel valve covers:	3.5

For maximum ring seal, nothing beats a Total Seal Gapless ring set. These sets contain a ductile iron, plasma moly top ring, two-piece gapless second and stainless steel oil ring. This combination holds cylinder leakage to less than 2%.

3

INDUCTION SYSTEMS

CARBURETORS

Between 1965 and 1976, big-block Chevy passenger car engines were factory-equipped with a variety of Rochester and Holley carburetors. Following the "Fuel Crisis Era," big blocks survived only in trucks and had either Rochester QuadraJet or electronic fuel injection.

By far, Holley four-barrels have been, and continue to be, the most popular carburetors for high performance and race applications. However, aftermarket electronic fuel injection systems have become the induction systems of choice on ultra high performance and state-of-the-art street and marine engines. In racing, use of electronic fuel injection is lagging because it is not allowed in most categories of competition.

Holley Carburetors

Models 4150, 4160 & 2300—The 4150 and 4160 four-barrels and the 2300 two-barrel are closely related. All are members of the same family with the model 2300 two-barrel being nothing more than the primary two-barrel section of a 4150 four-barrel. The 4150 and 4160 models are virtually identical to each other with the exception of the hardware used to meter fuel in the secondary idle

Gordy Faust's "World's Fastest '66 Chevelle" Pro Modified car is a far cry from an original SS-396, but both it and its stock counterpart are fine examples of big-block power performance potential.

Standard flange Holley four-barrel carbs (models 4150 and 4160) have become the fuel mixers of choice for high performance big blocks. With air flow ratings ranging from 600 to 850 cfm, there's a 4150/4160 for just about any imaginable engine combination.

Holley's Spread Bore four-barrels are designed to be direct replacements for original equipment QuadraJets. Available with air flow ratings of 650 and 800-cfm, many Spread-Bores are 50-state legal for emissions-controlled engines.

and main circuits. Rather than employing a block with removable jets (as used on the primary side), 4160 carburetors are fitted on the secondary side with a metering plate that contains non-replaceable fuel metering restrictions. Model 4150 carburetors have metering blocks with replaceable jets in both the primary and the secondary circuits. Holley four-barrel models are available in a variety of configurations including: dual accelerator pumps and mechanical secondaries; single accelerator pump and vacuum secondaries; single "center squirter" accelerator pump with mechanical secondaries; adjustable idle screws on primary only; adjustable idle screws on primary and secondary; center inlet fuel bowls; standard idle mixture adjustment; and reverse idle mixture adjustment. The combination of items seems to be endless in this series, which offers various air flow capacities ranging from 390 to 855 cfm.

Models 4165 & 4175—These "Spread-Bore" carburetors, while very similar in appearance to the 4150/4160 models, differ considerably in construction, and share surprisingly few components with their relatives. This in spite of the fact that fuel metering circuits are conceptually identical. Power valves,

jets, fuel bowl vent accessories, secondary diaphragm springs, floats, needles-and-seats and some accelerator pump hardware are the only items that will successfully interchange between the 4150/4160 and the 4165/4175 series.

The reasons for the uniqueness of 4165/4175 components are both logical and straightforward. These carburetors were designed as direct bolt-on replacements for the Rochester QuadraJet and Carter Thermo-Quad, and as such must function in an emissions-sensitive environment. Therefore, carburetor components for the 4165/4175 family were designed to provide improved driveability while holding exhaust emissions within acceptable limits. They are offered in either 650 or 800 cfm versions; all have 1-5/32 in. diameter primary venturi, 1-3/8 in. primary throttle bores and 2-in. diameter secondary throttle bores. The 800 cfm model's extra air flow capacity is derived from 1-23/32 in. secondary venturis, as compared to the 1-3/8 in. venturis used on the smaller 650 cfm carb. Some 4165s use the reverse-idle system and two types of float bowls are also available. These are the only major differences between the Spread-Bores.

Model 4500—Model 4500 Holleys

and big block Chevy engines constitute a marriage made in high performance heaven. These "Dominator" carburetors are essentially a model 4150 on steroids. Their primary distinguishing feature is their size; although their fuel metering circuits are virtually identical to models 4150/4160, Dominators are physically much larger than other Holleys and have significantly greater air flow capacity. They were designed strictly for racing, but at least one model is suitable for use on high performance street engines.

All Dominators flow air and fuel through 2-in. diameter throttle bores and either 1-11/16-in. or 1-13/16-in. venturis.

Although Dominators are typically associated with air flow capacities of over 1000 cfm, Holley offers one rated at 750 cfm. Designed for street use, this "baby" Dominator has four-corner idle adjustment, but no choke. Obviously, it's not designed for daily driven cars in cold climates.

Part number 0-80186 is rated at 750 cfm and is designed for street engines; all others are primarily used for racing and rated at either 1050 or 1150 cfm.

Models 4010 & 4011—The latest additions to Holley's line-up of high performance four-barrels are the 4010 and 4011 series. Rather than having modular construction like other Holleys, these carburetors have a more simplified construction with only two major castings. These carburetors are also cast in aluminum rather than zinc and have a polished appearance. Depending on part number, a model 4010 carb will rely on either vacuum or mechanical secondary activation; the dual accelerator pumps are included on carburetors with mechanical secondary linkage. Model 4010 carbs are available in flow ratings of either 600 or 750 cfm and all have a square mounting flange, making them direct bolt-on replacements for Holley 4150/4160 and Carter AFB/AVS carburetors.

The 4011 models are cousins of the 4010. They feature a Spread-Bore mounting flange and are intended as direct replacements for the Rochester QuadraJet and Carter Thermo-Quad carburetors. The 4011 models are available in either 650 or 800 cfm flow capacities.

Rochester Carburetors

Rochester carburetors were manufactured by a division of General Motors, so it's not surprising that they have been installed on Chevrolet big blocks ever since the "rat motor" first bared its teeth. By 1973, QuadraJets became the only original equipment four-barrel carburetors used on Chevrolet big blocks.

Although they were designed with emissions and fuel economy in mind, Rochester QuadraJets function quite well on high performance engines. In fact, when properly modified, they deliver surprisingly strong performance. Their main drawback is price as replacement

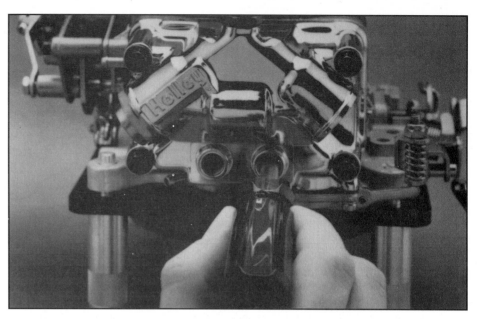

Changing jets on a Holley is a relatively simple task, which is one of the reasons that Holley carbs are so popular. Accessing the jets requires removal of only four fuel bowl screws. This Quick Change float bowl makes an easy job even easier. It's available for model 4150/4160 and 4500 Holley carbs in standard and chrome finish.

The latest additions to Holley's line of high performance carburetors are the Model 4010 (standard flange) and 4011 (Spread-Bore) four-barrels. These carburetors employ an aluminum rather than zinc main body and have significantly fewer sub-assemblies than the traditional Holley four-barrel. They're available with air flow ratings up to 800 cfm.

carburetors, especially late-model versions with electronic controls, are very expensive.

Beginning in 1993, Edelbrock Corporation began marketing "Edelbrock Performer" QuadraJet replacement carburetors. These carbs are manufactured by Weber USA and are actually brand new QuadraJet model 4MV, M4MC and M4ME carburetors. All can be used as direct Q-Jet replacements and each carburetor has all

Rochester's QuadraJet was factory-installed on more big blocks than any other carburetor. Although it doesn't have much of a performance image, a Q-Jet is more than adequate for stock and lightly modified big blocks.

Edelbrock is now the sole marketer of brand new QuadraJet carburetors. Four models are available and all are 50-state legal. Service parts and rebuild kits are also available.

the necessary connections for the model year engines it's designed to fit.

CARB SELECTION

When awareness of carburetor air flow capacity became commonplace, bigger was typically equated with better, and "too much" was barely enough—even the largest available four-barrel was not capable of over-carbureting a highly modified big block. Then conspicuous consumption came into vogue and the situation changed dramatically.

The largest standard-flange Holley four-barrel currently available flows 850 cfm and the larger square-flange "Dominators" flow up to 1150 cfm. Obviously, with the general availability of such grandiose carburetors, bigger no longer necessarily equals better. In fact, more often than not, a smaller four-barrel is preferable to an extremely large one. While a 600 cfm unit with vacuum secondaries is too small for most big blocks, it should be noted that the 325 and 360-horsepower 396 engines offered in 1966 were factory equipped with 585 cfm Holley four-barrels.

In the overall scheme of things, these were relatively mild engines and they didn't suffer too badly at the hands of the "pee shooter"-sized carbs with which they were equipped. But unless you're restoring a classic muscle car and want to stick with the original carb, a big block will breathe much easier with a carburetor having an air flow rating of at least 750 cfm.

Air Capacity

Choosing a performance carburetor therefore amounts to somewhat more than purchasing the largest model your budget allows. The first step is to determine the maximum air flow potentially demanded by the engine that is to receive the carburetor. On the surface, this appears to require no more than converting cubic inches (engine size) to cubic feet, multiplying by maximum rpm (to determine the engine cfm requirement), and selecting a carburetor that offers a corresponding air flow capacity. However, intended usage, engine efficiency, engine operating range and the total number of throttle bores must also be taken into consideration.

The basic mathematical formula for relating engine size and rpm to carburetor

air flow capacity is:

$$cfm = \frac{\text{Engine cid x Maximum rpm}}{3456}$$

By way of example, consider a 454 cid powerplant with a maximum engine speed of 7000 rpm. By working it through the above equation, the cfm works out to 920 cfm. Therefore, an 850 cfm double pumper would appear to be slightly too small and a 1050 Dominator would be a bit too large. What should you do?

Volumetric Efficiency—Consider volumetric efficiency (V.E.). Simply stated, volumetric efficiency is the percentage of the theoretical maximum amount of air and fuel that can be consumed by an engine every two revolutions. Theoretically, at wide open throttle, a 454 cid engine with a 100% V.E. will consume 454 cubic inches of air and gas every two revolutions. However, except for well-prepared race engines, few big blocks reach 100% V.E. Volumetric efficiency is not constant throughout the rpm range, although it is usually highest at the engine speed where

Holley four-barrels installed on big block race engines are typically reworked to optimize air flow. Removal of the choke housing is the most obvious modification, but equally important is assuring that the secondaries open fully. Note that the small link connecting the primary and secondary throttle levers has been bent to achieve this. On new carburetors, this link is usually straight.

Carb spacers can be valuable tuning aids. Open spacers significantly increase plenum volume, which has the same effect as installing a larger carburetor. Four-hole spacers also increase plenum volume but tend to increase the velocity of the mixture entering the intake manifold. Four-hole spacers are typically used to bolster mid-range torque, open spacers emphasize top end horsepower.

maximum torque is produced. According to Mike Urich, former vice president of engineering at Holley Carburetors and co-author of HPBooks' *Holley Carburetors, Manifolds and Fuel Injection*:

"An ordinary low-performance engine has a V.E. of about 75% at maximum speed; about 80% at maximum torque. A high-performance engine has a V.E. of about 80% at maximum speed; about 85% at maximum torque. An all-out race engine has a V.E. of about 90% at maximum speed; about 95% at maximum torque. A highly tuned intake and exhaust system with efficient cylinder head porting and a camshaft ground to take full advantage of the engine's other equipment can provide such complete cylinder filling that a V.E. of 100%—or slightly higher—is obtained at the speed for which the system is tuned."

As a general rule, you can assume a V.E. of 85% for high-performance street engines and a V.E. of 110% for all-out, highly tuned racing engines. As an example, consider a 468 cid race engine (a 454 bored .060") running at 8000 rpm:

$$cfm = \frac{468 \text{ cid} \times 8000 \text{ rpm}}{3456} \times 1.1 \text{ V.E.}$$

$$cfm = 1191$$

Theoretically, a carburetor with an 1150 cfm capacity would be ideal. (The 1.1 VE factor in the equation above is 110% converted to a decimal. To calculate the street carb cfm, use the above equation but multiply by .85—85% converted to a decimal—rather than 1.1. to arrive at a theoretical cfm).

These percentages of volumetric efficiency really mean that instead of consuming 454 cubic inches of air and gas every two revolutions, a 454 cid engine will actually pump a percentage of its total displacement through its cylinders. A 454 operating at 85% V.E. will only use 386 cubic inches of air and gas every two revolutions (454 x .85 = 386). Don't forget that VE varies somewhat with rpm and the highest VE usually occurs at or just above the rpm at

which an engine produces maximum torque.

The laws of physics prevent these percentages from changing very dramatically. Intake manifold efficiency, valve and port size, camshaft timing and exhaust manifold configuration are a few of the more readily identifiable factors affecting the volume of intake charge that will reach a cylinder prior to the power stroke. Since the low pressure created by a piston moving downward in a cylinder (during the intake stroke) is not sufficient to draw in 100% of the volume required to completely fill that cylinder (with the piston at the bottom of its travel), the effect of inertia is needed to keep the incoming air/gas mixture flowing after the piston has started moving upward (during the initial stage of the compression stroke). The inertia or "ram" effect increases with rpm, which is one of the reasons that internal combustion engines produce maximum horsepower in the upper rpm ranges.

Vacuum vs. Mechanical Secondaries

The only other basic consideration with four-barrels is how the secondary throttle

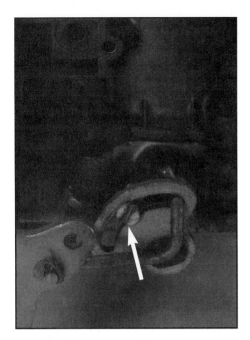

One way to convert a Holley four-barrel from vacuum to mechanical secondaries is to install a screw in the secondary throttle lever. Unfortunately, with no secondary accelerator pump, this will result in a huge stumble when the secondaries are smacked open. A far better arrangement is to select the appropriate secondary diaphragm spring.

is activated. Vacuum control offers potentially smoother operation and in theory "sizes" the carburetor to the needs of the engine. If a vacuum actuating mechanism is properly tuned, maximum air velocity through the carburetor will be maintained at all operational levels. This is theoretically possible because secondary throttle opening responds to engine demands. Therefore, a 780 cfm carburetor may never flow more than 650 cfm, if that's all the engine requires.

Mechanical secondaries offer the advantage of allowing the driver to control precisely when the secondary throttles are opened. This is especially important in oval track and road racing where performance "coming out of the corners" is critical. In drag racing, positive secondary throttle control is also advantageous so use of vacuum secondary carburetors is uncommon except in Stock and Super Stock classes where rules dictate retention of the original equipment carb. Therefore,

vacuum control is typically advised for street, R.V. and recreational boat use, while mechanically operated secondaries are found in virtually all competition applications. The notable exception is off-road racing, because the inconsistent terrain doesn't allow the driver to maintain a smooth, constant application of power.

Recommendations

Regardless of horsepower figures produced on a dyno, engineering theory or mathematical formulas, the bottom line is the ability of a carburetor to function in a real world environment. In many cases a carburetor is expected to compensate for inadequacies in the intake system. Some people mistakenly believe switching carburetors will correct certain problems (poor low-speed response or lack of top-end power) that are actually caused by other factors.

For example, the combination of a big-port intake manifold, large-diameter headers and a super-lumpy camshaft will not allow any carburetor to meter fuel with optimum efficiency. Not only will fuel economy be poor, reduced vacuum at idle (created by long cam overlap and weak low-rpm exhaust scavenging) will delay activation of fuel flow through the main nozzles. This makes for poor low-speed throttle response, disappointing torque and possibly an off-idle stumble. Switching to a smaller carburetor is frequently viewed as a means of improving low-speed operation. The reasoning is that velocities will be higher if venturi and throttle bore diameters are reduced. That's true at wide open throttle, but at part throttle, the effect is minimal. About the only advantage offered by a smaller carb is quicker activation of the main metering system. This may reduce the size of the performance "hole" but it will still be there.

Consequently, there is more to carburetor selection than mere size consideration. In spite of all the theories

and reasoning behind proper carburetor selection, in the real world things usually boil down more to a matter of price and availability. With Carter and Edelbrock carburetors, only a few models are available, so it's pretty much a matter of selecting the carb that provides the desired air flow capacity. With a Holley, the selection process is more involved, but not much. Part number 0-1850, which is rated at 600 cfm, and part number 0-3310, which is rated at 750 cfm, are "universal" carburetors that are produced in large volumes. Consequently, they're cheaper than other carburetors with similar air flow ratings. Other Holley carburetors with identical air flow capacities differ only in air/fuel calibration, linkage arrangement or choke mechanism. Since these carbs are tailored for engines of specific model years, they're easier to install and rarely require a change of jets. Emissions-type carbs will also clean up exhaust pollutants compared to a universal carb. The only real drawback is price: carburetors designed for specific applications are produced in relatively low volumes so they're more expensive than a universal

Holley's two-piece diaphragm lid (part no. 20-59) greatly simplifies changing of secondary springs. Rather than removing and disassembling the housing, all you have to do is remove the two screws attaching the lid.

One of the reasons that model 4150/4160 and model 4165/4175 carburetors are called "modular" is that so many subassemblies can be removed and interchanged. As a means of increasing air flow and the intensity of the signal that reaches the venturis, an original base plate is often replaced by a larger one and the bottoms of the venturis are blended to match.

carb of similar specifications.

Just about any street-type big block of 402 cubic inches or less will be well-carbureted by a 750 cfm four-barrel; big blocks of 427 cubic inches or greater displacement are equally well-served by a 750 cfm carburetor if they're mild mannered; aggressively tuned engines should be equipped with an 850 cfm four barrel. Super-high-performance and race engines usually benefit from one or more Dominator carburetors with cfm ratings of 1050 or 1150 cfm. A variety of other carburetors are also available for specific applications.

However, before selecting a carburetor, check the emissions regulations that pertain to your vehicle so you don't run into problems if a governmental agency decides to check your vehicle's emissions levels.

INTAKE MANIFOLDS

The application for which an engine is designed dictates the specific rpm range in which power must be concentrated. Selection of intake manifold type should

therefore be predicated upon a given design's ability to enhance performance at specific engine speeds.

All intake manifolds perform the same basic function, specifically that of providing a passageway between the carburetor and the intake ports of each cylinder. The configuration of the Chevy big block, like that of most V-8s, dictates that the passage connecting the manifold plenum to the cylinder head either travel a rather tortuous winding path, or take the shortest, most direct route. Both arrangements provide advantages and disadvantages which to some degree determine specific performance characteristics. In essence, each intake manifold configuration offers the potential for increased power within a particular rpm range while sacrificing performance somewhere else along the horsepower curve.

Dual-Plane Manifolds

Since passenger car engine designers are primarily concerned with low-speed driveability, they have always utilized the dual-plane design. Such manifolds are

essentially two-in-one affairs, each plane or manifold half routing air and fuel from a separate plenum area to an individual group of four cylinders. With each half of the manifold isolated from the other, runners are grouped so that 180 deg. of crankshaft rotation separates the intake cycles of cylinders fed by the same half of the manifold—hence the label "180-deg. manifold." The 180 deg. separation of cylinders, and relatively long runners, which are required to snake around obstacles (like other runners), are the dual plane's greatest virtues. They are also the reasons that the design is conducive to the production of ample low-speed torque. At higher engine speeds, however, these assets become liabilities as the manifold runners are too restrictive to handle the volume of air required to produce maximum horsepower at 5500+ rpm. The high-rise design alleviates some restriction problems by allowing the runners to curve more gently, but it can't completely eradicate the inherent characteristics of the dual-plane configuration.

Single-Plane Manifolds

Conversely, a single-plane manifold is ideally suited to supplying great volumes of air to the cylinders. With eight large runners connected by the most direct route to a single plenum, this design offers comparatively little air flow restriction. The large open plenum offers an additional advantage in that it supplies a large reservoir of air/fuel mixture (the open plenum) from which the cylinders may draw, and this has the same effect as installing a larger carburetor. For high rpm operation, this arrangement is ideal, but the large plenum/short runner combination intensifies the problems of low air velocities at lower engine speeds; with insufficient velocity, cylinders don't fill with intake charge as well as they do with a dual-plane manifold, so low-speed torque is significantly reduced.

Another problem with the single-plane

design is "mixture stealing" by adjacent firing cylinders. In the Chevy big-block V-8, at least two cylinders positioned next to each other fire in one-two succession. An example is number 7 cylinder firing immediately after number 5 cylinder. The first cylinder of the adjacent pair "steals" some of the intake charge that should go to the second, and at low engine speeds this can significantly reduce power output. At higher rpm levels, air velocities are such that each cylinder receives a full charge, but with the inherent low-speed problem, a single-plane manifold can lead to objectionable off-idle performance, especially in heavy vehicles and those that are geared for good economy on the highway.

Choices—With big-block Chevrolet engines being used in so many types of competition, the selection of single-plane intake manifolds is rather extensive. Brodix, Dart, Edelbrock, Holley, Offenhauser and Weiand all produce variations on the single plane theme. In addition to different runner lengths and plenum volumes, carburetor flanges may also differ; most manifold manufacturers offer two series of manifolds, one that accepts model 4500 Dominator carbs, the other for use with standard Holley flange carburetors.

For street and even some race engines, a dual plane manifold is the hot lick. Holley's 300-42 contains a standard carb flange, part no. 300-43 incorporates a Model 4500 Dominator flange. Both manifolds are designed for oval port heads.

Reducing Plenum Volume

One method of bolstering low-speed performance, both for a single- or dual-plane manifold, is to divide the plenum in half with an aluminum or steel plate. The resultant decrease in plenum volume reduces the air/fuel reservoir and intensifies the fuel metering signal that reaches the carburetor. The carb remains as the ultimate controller of air flow, but without a large open plenum between the carburetor and the runners, air flow velocities inside the manifold increase (which improves low-speed operation) but maximum flow volume decreases (which limits top-end power). In many instances, inserting a plenum divider will elevate manifold vacuum by one or two inches, and tremendously improve low-speed tractability. But the fuel metering signal received by the carburetor will also be intensified, resulting in a reduction in fuel economy unless the carburetor is rejetted.

As a general rule, reducing plenum volume has the same effect as reducing carburetor size; increasing plenum volume has the opposite effect. Adjusting

Edelbrock offers a wide variety of intake manifolds for Chevrolet big blocks with either oval or rectangular port cylinder heads. The Performer RPM Q-Jet is available for both types of heads. It's obviously designed for Q-Jet and Spread Bore models with an operating range of 1500 to 6500 rpm.

Dart Machinery (manufacturer of Dart heads) also offers a variety of big block intake manifolds. Most are serious race pieces such as this single plane model which features a large open plenum and a Dominator carburetor flange.

plenum volume does alter the rpm at which peak power occurs, but it isn't the only factor.

Some engines may respond best to a dual-plane manifold with a portion of the plenum divider removed. Prior to the advent of single-plane manifolds, this was a common modification for improving top-end horsepower. In the case of a dual-plane manifold, removing the plenum divider increases plenum volume, but there is an accompanying loss of carburetor signal. That can easily be overcome by rejetting. However, if competition class rules allow a single-plane manifold, that's the better choice.

If a dual-plane manifold is required, the term "cast iron" is probably in the same paragraph in the rule book. Surprisingly, many cast-iron four-barrel intake manifolds for big blocks aren't all that bad up to about 4500 rpm. In fact, some stock manifolds will produce more power than aftermarket high rise models in the off idle to 4500 rpm range. Conversely, some very low-rise intake manifolds have been produced for the big block to afford adequate hood clearance in Corvettes and Camaros. These manifolds should be avoided (if possible) as they choke an engine at anything above 4000 rpm.

Intake Runners

Runner length also enters the picture and determines the rpm at which optimum efficiency is reached. Intake manifold runners are said to be tuned when their length and cross-sectional area

are selected (based on the speed of sound) so that air movement is positively influenced. As with anything that moves, a column of air flowing into an engine has inertia. Movement of the air column is initiated when the intake valve opens and exposes the air in the intake manifold to a partial vacuum in the cylinder; pressure in the intake manifold is higher than in the cylinder, so the air naturally moves from an area of higher pressure to an area of lower pressure, thereby filling the cylinder. But when the intake valve closes, air movement does not stop immediately; the inertia of the air column keeps it moving and packs the runner with more air than it could otherwise accommodate. The inertia of the air column "rams" air into the runner's ports and has a slight pressurizing or supercharging effect. When the intake valve opens again, the pressurized air in the manifold rams itself into the cylinder, filling it with an extra dense air/fuel charge, which translates into increased power. This effect isn't constant at all engine speeds, but it's significant within a defined rpm band. Longer runners lower the speed at which optimum ram effect occurs; shorter runners have the opposite effect.

One drawback of an intake runner that's tuned to produce peak torque below 4000 rpm is that total air flow capacity is compromised. The runners are too long, and of too small a diameter to permit sufficient air flow to support engine requirements at high rpm.

Runner sizing plays a significant role in establishing the rpm band in which an intake manifold is most effective and the premise of shrinking runner area to improve low speed operating characteristics is also employed in single-plane manifolds designed for street operation. By altering runner cross-sectional area and plenum volume, a manifold designer can tailor a manifold to optimize performance at specific rpm levels. This accounts for the difference between street and race manifolds; they may appear quite similar externally, but there is a significant difference in internal dimensions, and the resultant effect on engine performance.

Single vs. Dual

Other considerations aside, a dual-plane manifold's relatively long runners make it less than the optimal design for high rpm use. By comparison, the shorter runners of a single-plane manifold are

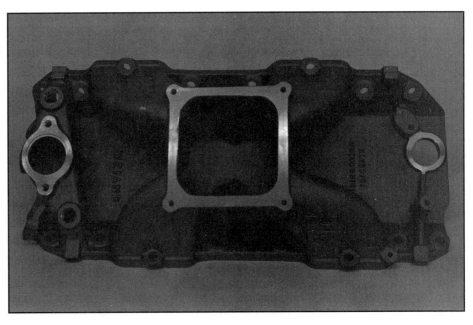

Weiand's Team G big block manifold sports a single plane design and a Dominator carburetor flange. This manifold produces excellent top end power.

"tuned" to maximize the ram effect at higher engine speeds (above 5500 rpm). As previously noted, single-plane manifolds predominate on race engines and dual-plane manifolds get the job done on the street.

Alternate Designs

Tunnel Rams—While single- and dual-plane manifolds are most commonly associated with a lone two- or four-barrel carburetor, the tunnel-ram type design is linked to dual four-barrels. With long, gently curving runners topped off by a generous plenum area, a tunnel-ram manifold is strictly a high rpm, maximum horsepower affair. Various manufacturers—Edelbrock, Holley, Offenhauser and Weiand—each have their own ideas as to optimum runner size and shape, and plenum volume, but all ram type manifolds are primarily designed for full-tilt race engines such as those used in race boats and drag cars. Single four-barrel tops are available for some models, but they generally prove unsatisfactory as fuel distribution is very erratic.

A tunnel-ram intake manifold *can* be run successfully on a street engine, but it usually requires some carburetor massaging. Edelbrock offers a street tunnel-ram manifold for big-block engines, with oval port heads, but warns that it is, "For applications where low-end torque is not a prime factor." This manifold has its runners sized to match stock and slightly modified ports. Runner length and cross-sectional area is also tuned for a lower operating range than a race tunnel ram. Although Holley and Weiand do not have ram manifolds specifically designed for street engines, their race manifolds have been used with some success on street engines.

If you're planning to run a tunnel-ram manifold on a street engine, keep in mind that most carburetors are designed for single four-barrel applications, the exception being a few race carbs that are calibrated for twin four-barrel manifolds. As such, the idle and main metering circuits may have to be recalibrated to avoid an excessively rich mixture. Vacuum secondary carburetors should also have their secondary diaphragms tied together so that they open at the same rate. Holley offers a special diaphragm cover (part no. 20-28) which incorporates a hose fitting for this purpose.

Long runners should make a tunnel ram manifold ideal for street use, so why do most manufacturers recommend not using this design on a daily driver? It has to do primarily with plenum volume and configuration. With the relatively large plenum that typifies tunnel ram design, the metering signal that reads the carburetors is diminished sufficiently to make air/fuel calibrations a chore. On the other hand, if port fuel injection is used in place of carburetion, a tunnel ram can turn a mild engine into a torque monster. That effect is demonstrated by the factory Tuned Port Injection system installed on

Intake manifold plenums differ considerably from one model to another. This view is of a dual-plane manifold that's designed to accommodate both standard Holley flange and Q-Jet/Spread Bore carburetors. These types of carb flanges occasionally present installation problems with carbs having large throttle bore diameters.

1985-1992 small blocks and the aftermarket "Tuned Ports" that are available for big blocks.

To date, a tunnel ram manifold designed for port fuel injection has not been commercially produced. However, a number of creative engine builders have modified standard tunnel ram manifolds with excellent success.

Also available from Holley is a Pro Dominator Tunnel Ram manifold (part no. 300-45). Two different tops sections are available–part number 300-204 accommodates two standard flange carbs, part number 300-206 is designed for dual Dominators.

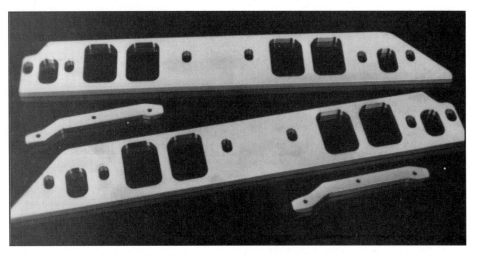

Different manifolds are required for standard deck and tall deck engines because the distance from one cylinder head to the other isn't the same. However, spacers can be used to make up the difference if it's necessary or desirable to install a standard manifold on a tall deck engine.

Recommendations

Laying down specific manifold selection guidelines is a job requiring a politician's skill with double-talk. With the number of variables pertaining to engine/chassis combinations being virtually unlimited, and with expectations equally diverse, making hard and fast rules is about like legislating a national 55-mile-per-hour speed limit—it just doesn't make sense. However, there are some broad guidelines that will keep you out of trouble. Edelbrock, Holley, Chevrolet and Weiand offer dual-plane high-rise manifolds that are ideally suited to stock and modified engines. These models produce strong low- and mid-range power and allow an engine to pull strongly up to about 6000 rpm. They represent the best all-around choice for any high performance street engine, and many boat engines. More exotic race type manifolds can be used successfully on the street but since they are designed to deliver maximum power at higher rpm (above 5000) they tend to compromise driveability and torque below 4000 rpm. Another drawback of a race-type single-plane manifold is lack of heat at the base of the plenum. This is a particular problem with certain models that have an air gap between the bottom of the plenum and the manifold base because it takes so long for the manifold to reach normal operating temperature. This isn't an insurmountable problem, but one you should be aware of when selecting an intake manifold.

Remember, you will have to live with the manifold you choose. An engine that talks back every time you attempt to accelerate away from a stop light is about as much fun as driving in stop-and-go traffic. If you're not prepared to make all the changes and some of the sacrifices necessitated by a race type manifold, stick with something tamer. Your car will be easier to drive, and a lot more fun. It will also run faster.

Most street engines run out of camshaft, cylinder head or carburetor before they ever get to the rpm at which a single-plane manifold makes maximum power. There are exceptions, but every time I've run a single plane versus dual plane dyno comparison test, the dual plane outperforms the single plane up to about 5000 rpm. If you shift at 5500 rpm, that doesn't give you much of an rpm range to take advantage of the increased top-end power.

One other word of advice—when purchasing an intake manifold, keep in mind that big blocks are produced in standard and tall deck form. A manifold designed for a tall deck block will not fit between the heads when they're mounted on a standard block and vice versa. Spacers can be used to adapt a standard manifold to a tall deck block, but a far better solution is to purchase the proper manifold.

Another caveat—if you're new to big blocks, it may escape your notice that two distinctly different types of cylinder heads exist. While it's physically possible to install a manifold designed for oval port heads on rectangular heads (and vice versa) the resulting performance will be less than stimulating.

ELECTRONIC FUEL INJECTION

Electronic fuel injection easily does things that a carburetor and intake manifold would never even dream of doing. EFI represents the best method of achieving maximum performance while keeping exhaust emissions as low as possible. While the myriad of electrical, computerized components of EFI may seem intimidating, this really isn't so. Although certainly more sophisticated than a Holley four-barrel, EFI still performs the same basic function—mixing fuel and air. These systems are intimidating at first because they're so different. But after working with one for a short time, you'll find that most of the same rules apply.

In general, electronic fuel injection systems are classified as either mass air or speed/density. Mass air systems (as found on 1985-1989 small-block Tuned Port Injection systems) incorporate a sensor to monitor the volume of air entering the manifold. A heated wire serves as the actual sensing device and air flowing past the wire cools it, altering its electrical resistance. Higher air flow has a greater cooling effect. The ECM monitors the resistance and adjusts fuel flow accordingly. Other sensors feed input to the computer so adjustments can be made for changes in manifold air temperature,

You can drag your vintage big block into the '90s by installing a Holley Pro-Jection system. With an air flow capacity of 900 cfm, the four-barrel Pro-Jection system is a perfect match for a deep breathing 427 or 454.

acronyms that is part and parcel of any electronic fuel injection system really does make sense. Each acronym pertains to a component that performs a specific and often times logical function.

ECM—Stands for Electronic Control Module. This is the brains of the outfit. Essentially, the ECM receives all sensor input and performs all the calculations required to establish fuel flow rates. The ECM also controls ignition timing.

PROM—The letters stand for Programmable Read Only Memory, which means that once programmed, a computer can read it, but can't alter it. The PROM or chip holds all the data that the ECM needs to match a given set of sensor inputs to fuel and ignition control outputs. The data inside a PROM is arranged in a multi-dimensional array that looks like a topographical map. The reason that computer-controlled engines don't always respond well to modifications is that if the ECM can't match the sensor input to the data in the map, it can't come up with the proper output data. The computer continues to "hunt" for a recognizable combination

throttle position and engine coolant temperature. When the system goes into "closed loop" operation, an Exhaust Gas Oxygen (EGO) sensor is used to monitor the oxygen content of the exhaust. Based on input from the EGO sensor, the ECM makes the adjustments required to keep the air/fuel mixture correct.

Speed/Density systems rely on computation, as opposed to measured air flow, to establish fuel flow with the actual control being established by values in a table. The ECM receives input from a variety of sensors, then matches each combination of inputs to a predetermined output. Speed/Density systems therefore have less ability to adapt to changes in engine configuration because the ECM never really "knows" how much air is entering the engine. It can only compute the amount of air based on sensor inputs. If it guesses wrong, the oxygen sensor will allow some corrections to be made, but the range is limited. Consequently, speed/density systems aren't as tolerant of performance modifications as their mass air counterparts— unless they are blessed

with a custom PROM or are programmable.

Primary Components

Believe it or not, the alphabet soup of

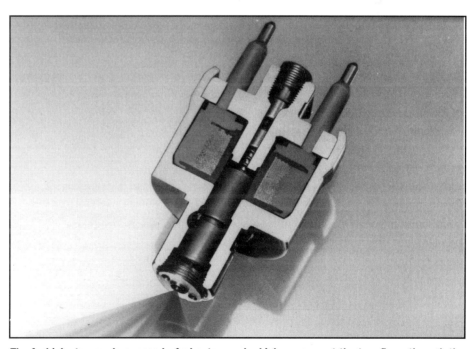

The fuel injector nozzle exposed—fuel enters under high pressure at the top, flows through the injector body and exits at the spray tip. Current passing through the coil that surrounds the injector controls the amount of time the injector stays open which in turn affects fuel delivery. This cut-away is of a throttle-body type injector as used on late-model, fuel-injected big blocks.

input data, and does the best job it can in coming up with proper output data—which makes for erratic engine operation. However, aftermarket PROMs can be programmed to include conditions not recognized by a standard PROM. All it takes is the right programming to make computerized controls capable of handling just about any engine requirement. In fact, with correct calibrations, electronic fuel injection can tame even the most radical big block, making it surprisingly tractable at low speeds, without compromising power.

EGO Sensor—The letters stand for Exhaust Gas Oxygen. This sensor measures the amount of oxygen in the exhaust and alters fuel flow so that the air/fuel ratio is maintained at stoichiometric, which is the chemically ideal ratio of 14.7:1. One of the problems with standard EGO sensors is that they must be located relatively close to the heads so they reach operating temperature. Heated EGO sensors are the solution and are used on many original equipment and custom installations. A heated EGO sensor is mandatory when an engine is equipped with some types of headers because the sensor is too far downstream and the exhaust is too cool for proper operation.

MAT Sensor—The letters stand for Manifold Air Temperature. As its name implies, this sensor keeps track of the air temperature within the manifold. This information is sent to the ECM so that calibrations can be finely tuned.

TPS—This is the Throttle Position Sensor. It doesn't take a rocket scientist to figure out that the TPS tells the ECM the position of the throttle. What isn't so apparent is that this sensor also sends data concerning the rate of throttle opening. This rate is used to calculate the degree of air/fuel enrichment required for acceleration (in a carburetor this function is handled by the accelerator pump). TPS position is physically adjustable, and a volt meter is normally used to determine

the proper position. Rotating the TPS counterclockwise increases the voltage, which results in a richer air/fuel ratio and usually crisper throttle response. But too much of a good thing is still too much and if the sensor is moved too far, the "Check Engine" light will come on during idle. This condition can usually be avoided by keeping TPS voltage close to original specifications.

Coolant Temperature—The name for this sensor is self-explanatory and the output of this sensor has a pronounced effect on performance. Both air/fuel ratio and ignition timing are altered depending upon coolant temperature. Lower temperatures result in richer mixtures and more aggressive spark timing. High temperatures have the opposite affect.

Knock Sensor—This device protects the engine from itself and from drivers with more money than intelligence. The sensor itself is like a small microphone and when it "hears" detonation, it sends a distress signal to the ECM instructing it to temporarily retard timing. If detonation continues, timing is retarded further; when the rattling stops, timing is returned to its original setting.

IAC—Stands for Idle Air Control. This device incorporates a small electric motor that controls a valve in the throttle body. If idle speed is too low, the motor pulls back, allowing more air to pass into the engine (thereby raising idle speed). If idle speed is too high the valve moves inward to further restrict the flow of air through the idle air port. With this device, the ECM can alter idle speed according to the demands of any operating conditions.

MAP Sensor—Manifold Absolute Pressure. This is another way of stating manifold vacuum. The MAP sensor is essentially an electronic vacuum gauge that tells the ECM the amount of load under which an engine is operating. The ECM alters air/fuel ratio to accommodate varying load conditions, just as a power valve or metering rods perform this function in a carburetor. Speed/Density

One of the reasons that electronic fuel injection is so precise is that a number of sensors are used to monitor temperatures and pressures. Intake air temperature is an important consideration for establishing proper air/fuel ratio, so a high quality sensor is essential.

systems (such as the stock TBI systems on big blocks) rely heavily on MAP sensor input to calculate the fuel curve.

Mass Air Flow (MAF) Sensor—In a speed density system, fuel flow is calculated, and the computation is based largely on throttle position and engine load as indicated by the TPS and MAP sensors; the ECM has no way of knowing how much air is actually passing through the engine. With a Mass Air system, the MAF sensor actually measures the amount of air entering. GM MAF sensors typically use a heated wire positioned in the air stream. As air flow increases, it cools the wire so voltage stays high; at wide open throttle, voltage through the wire (not voltage drop) will be close to the five volt maximum. At idle, voltage will be about .4 volts. A mass air flow system allows the ECM to accommodate a wider range of operating conditions than a speed/density system because it actually measures the air flowing into the engine. However, because of the added expense and complexity inherent in sensing mass air flow, most aftermarket

EFI systems are speed/density types.

Limp Home Mode—Of course, with all these sensors, something can very well take a wrong turn so electronic fuel injection systems incorporate what's known as a "Limp Home" mode. In the event of a major system or sensor malfunction, the ECM automatically slides into "Limp Home" mode where upon it holds timing to about 22 deg. and establishes a relatively rich air/fuel mixture. The whole idea of "Limp Home" mode is to protect the engine from damage while it is being driven a short distance. Some custom wiring harnesses (designed to allow installation of electronic systems in vehicles not originally so equipped) force activation of "Limp Home" mode. This isn't desirable, nor is it necessary. Proper harnesses are available from a variety of sources including Howell Engine Developments of Clinton Township, MI (810/791-6400).

Throttle Body Injection

Throttle body injection (TBI) systems position the injectors within the throttle body, rather than in each individual port. A TBI unit is similar to a carburetor in that it can be bolted directly to a four-barrel intake manifold. However, unlike a carburetor, which requires air flow to draw fuel through it, a TBI unit injects fuel under pressure.

Since the age of electronic engine controls dawned well after assembly line installed big blocks had been relegated to truck duty, throttle body injection has been the only factory installed system. In their standard form, original equipment throttle body systems aren't suitable for high performance use.

Holley Pro-Jection

One throttle body system that is suited to a high performance big block is Holley's Pro-Jection 4. Featuring a 900 cfm, four-barrel throttle body that can be installed on any four-barrel intake

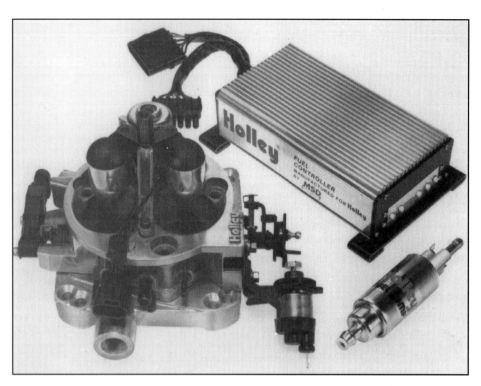

Surprising as it might seem, a two-barrel Pro-Jection system is suitable for some big blocks. With an air flow capacity of 670 cfm, it's obviously not designed for killer engines, but it is suitable for mildy reworked powerplants.

manifold, the system is relatively easy to install. It also offers a combination of power, throttle response and fuel economy unmatched by any carburetor.

How It Works—Pro-Jection systems (which are also available in two-barrel form) rely primarily on throttle position and engine rpm to determine fuel flow. As such, they lack the sophistication of an original equipment system, but are much easier to calibrate, especially on a radically cammed engine. Fuel flow is regulated by five adjustment screws on the system's Electronic Control Unit (ECU). ECU adjustments, which include choke, acceleration enrichment, mid-range, idle and power enrichment, are conceptually similar to the conventional fuel metering circuits in a carburetor. However, rather than changing jets or power valves, adjustments are made by simply turning a few screws.

Like all fuel injection systems, Holley's Pro-Jection incorporates a bypass circuit that routes unused fuel back to the fuel tank. Typically, plumbing a return line is the most troublesome aspect of a fuel

injection installation because it's often necessary to drop the fuel tank. However, proper return line installation is critical to the success of any fuel injection installation, so all the steps necessary should be taken to ensure it's done correctly.

Calibration—Calibration of Holley's Pro-Jection system is relatively easy, requiring only a little time and some experimentation to determine the optimum settings. But Holley's Closed Loop kit makes the process even easier. Sold as an option for use with any Pro-Jection system, the Closed Loop Kit (part no. 534-27) relies on an oxygen sensor mounted in the exhaust system to monitor air/fuel ratio and the control unit makes the appropriate adjustments. Closed loop operation is functional only after an engine has reached normal operating temperature and at less than 2/3 of maximum throttle opening. During engine warm-up and while at or near wide open throttle, fuel calibration is determined by the settings of the ECU adjustment screws.

The HP/TBI system from Howell Engine Developments utilizes a 900-cfm Holley Pro-Jection throttle body, GM ECM and custom wiring harness. This system allows big block owners to take advantage of the benefits of electronic fuel injection at a reasonable price. Full diagnostic capabilities are maintained, so custom calibrating and troubleshooting are simplified.

Port type fuel injectors operate under the same principles as their throttle body counterparts, but they're considerably smaller. This port injector is manufactured by Rochester Products and is available through MSD Fuel Management. It's available in a variety of flow rates, many of which are suitable for custom electronic fuel injection systems designed for big blocks.

Howell HP/TBI

A more sophisticated throttle body system is available from Howell Engine Developments. Bill Howell, a retired Chevrolet engineer, founded this company as a manufacturer of wiring harnesses for installing late-model, computer-controlled engines in older vehicles. Development of the HP/TBI system, which marries a modified Holley Pro-Jection throttle body with a GM ECM, was a natural outgrowth of the harness business.

Howell's HP/TBI is the only true high performance throttle body system that incorporates the precise fuel control advantages of an original equipment-type computer. And since Howell individually calibrates PROMs for each system, even radical engines can be accommodated. Of course, the key to making the Holley throttle body and the GM ECM communicate is a Howell harness.

The HP/TBI system is available with or without spark control. By including a computer-controlled distributor, knock sensor and electronic spark control module, the ECM controls ignition timing and makes adjustments when spark knock is detected. If a standard distributor is used in conjunction with the appropriate harness, the Howell system controls only fuel flow.

Port Injection

Although Chevrolet has never released a production Tuned Port System for the big block, several aftermarket companies, including Accel, TPI Specialties and Arizona Speed and Marine offer a variety of TPI-type systems and components that can be retrofitted to the big-block.

These systems are based on unique two-piece manifold castings and utilize a 1000 cfm throttle body. Like the Tuned Port system found on small blocks, the big-block manifolds incorporate long runners (approximately 15 inches) leading to each port. The system can be driven by a stock GM ECM designed for a speed/density system or by an aftermarket ECM. Typically, 30-lbs/hr. injectors are used with engines displacing 454-468 cubic inches.

Custom Systems—Several options are also available in the realm of custom fuel injection systems. Programmable fuel controllers, some of which also have ignition control capabilities, are available from Motec Systems (Huntington Beach, CA), EFI Technologies (Torrance, CA) and Accel/DFI. These controllers allow the fuel curve to be customized using a PC or laptop computer, so the fuel demands of virtually any type of big block can be accommodated—provided a properly sized fuel delivery system is plumbed.

Modifications to Stock Fuel Injection

With an electronic fuel injection system, semiconductors, rather than hard parts typically are responsible for determining maximum performance potential. And the brains of the outfit is the PROM, which contains the data that the ECM uses in making decisions. As such, within a system controlled by a GM ECM, the key to maximizing power is having the right PROM.

Unfortunately, obtaining a properly calibrated PROM isn't always easy. Late-model vehicles are required to meet emissions regulations and high performance equipment produced for those vehicles must meet either Federal

EPA or California ARB requirements. Those requirements stipulate that original calibrations for idle and part throttle operation must be maintained. Consequently, the calibrations used by companies like Hypertech, Inc. of Memphis, TN, the largest supplier of aftermarket PROMs, alter fuel flow and ignition timing ONLY at or near wide open throttle.

As such, a standard "Power Chip" will not improve the idle quality or throttle response of a highly modified engine. That can be accomplished only with a custom PROM that's calibrated for a specific engine. Installation of such PROMs is legal only if a computer-controlled engine is installed in a vehicle that is not subject to emissions regulations (pre-1966 in California, pre-1968 in the remaining 49 states).

In the case of a 396, 402, 427 or 454 installed in a vehicle, in which a big block was never offered, requirements are often blurred. As the law is generally interpreted, exhaust emissions levels must be consistent with whichever is later, the engine or the chassis. From a practical standpoint, emissions requirements can often be difficult to determine because a late-model or custom fuel injection system can be installed on an engine originally produced in the Sixties and installed in a chassis dating from the Seventies or Eighties. The best bet is to check local emissions requirements and make sure there are no blatant violations. Properly calibrated, an electronic fuel injection system will deliver lower emissions levels than any carburetor.

Pulse Width and Fuel Pressure

With electronic fuel injection, fuel flow is primarily governed by three factors—injector flow rate, system fuel pressure and pulse width. Pulse width refers to the length of the electronic pulse that tells the injector nozzle to stay open. Increasing

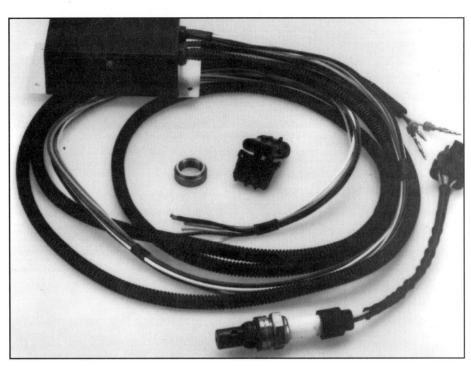

Although not as sophisticated as the Howell system, Holley's closed loop kit improves Pro-Jection system operation. It includes an oxygen sensor and the circuitry required to tell the main controller what it needs to know to keep air/fuel ratio at 14.7:1.

pulse width keeps the nozzle open longer so fuel flow is greater. Injector flow rate refers to the amount of fuel a nozzle is capable of flowing (usually expressed in pounds per hour). A richer air/fuel mixture may be achieved by lengthening pulse width, switching to larger capacity nozzles, increasing fuel pressure or some combination of all three. However, if the mixture is too rich, power will drop, just as it does in a carbureted engine.

When a pressure increase causes a drop in power, the air/fuel ratio is simply too rich. Installing a new PROM can correct the situation by shortening the pulse width so the ratio is brought back to the optimum setting. Extremes in fuel pressure can adversely affect fuel atomization, so the key is to achieve the proper combination of pressure, pulse width and flow rate, as opposed to using pressure adjustments to compensate for deficiencies elsewhere. It takes quite a bit of experimenting to determine the most desirable fuel pressure/pulse width combinations, but most fuel injection specialists have figured out most of the answers.

Replacement Injectors—It would seem that the hot tip for a big block with electronic fuel injection is to install super high capacity injectors. However, this is one instance where less is frequently more. Depending on an individual engine's maximum fuel flow requirements, smaller injectors (in combination with higher fuel pressure) may produce more horsepower and better fuel economy—if fuel pressure and pulse width are correctly set—because of improved atomization. The one caveat is that it takes fuel to make horsepower so maximum injector flow rate must be consistent with engine demands at maximum power. At part throttle, the computer reads the EGO sensor input and adjusts injector pulse width so that the proper air/fuel ratio is achieved. When fuel pressure is increased, the computer automatically shortens pulse width to compensate. However, at wide open throttle, the system switches from closed loop to open loop and ignores EGO sensor input. When this occurs, it relies totally on the calibrations stored in the PROM.

Fuel injection is continually making inroads under the hoods of race cars. Holley's 2x2 Projection system includes two 670 cfm throttle bodies mounted on a Tunnel Ram intake manifold. It's designed for engines with rectangular port heads producing over 400 horsepower.

Any big block port injection system that relies on a GM ECM incorporates saturated circuit-type injector nozzles. Most custom ECMs are designed to be compatible with either saturated circuit or peak and hold nozzles. The terms refer to the electronic method by which the injectors are controlled, and the point to be aware of is that nozzle type must be specified according to system requirements. Peak and hold nozzles can't be installed in a system designed for saturated circuit nozzles and vice versa.

One of the most easily accessible sources of electronic fuel injection nozzles is MSD Fuel Management (a division of MSD Ignitions) of El Paso, Texas. The company's catalog lists both type of injectors in various flow ranges so it shouldn't be too difficult to accommodate a big block's thirst for fuel. Saturated circuit nozzles are available in flow ratings of 19, 21, 22, 38 and 50 lbs/hr; peak and hold nozzles with flow ratings of 26, 34, 72 and 96 lbs/hr.

As a general guideline, a fuel flow of 50 lbs/hr is required for every 100 horsepower. That being the case, a 550-horsepower big block requires injectors that can deliver a total of 275 pounds of fuel per hour. Since the engine has eight injectors, each one must be rated at a minimum of 34.375 lbs/hr , a requirement that can be met by a set of 38 lbs/hr nozzles.

BSFC—If you're used to dealing with carburetors, you'll find that total fuel flow numbers seem to be a bit off— for good reason. Fuel injection is so much more efficient that it takes measurably less fuel to produce the same amount of power. This is reflected in the Brake Specific Fuel Consumption (BSFC) numbers which relate fuel consumed to horsepower produced (BSFC= Fuel Flow/Horsepower). EFI-equipped engines typically produce BSFC readings of .40 to .43 at peak power while a carbureted engine will usually have readings in the range of .46 to .50. ∎

Whether a big block is equipped with a carburetor or fuel injection, maintenance of adequate fuel pressure is essential for top performance. These Volumax pumps from Holley provide fuel delivery rates of 160 and 250 gallons per hour and are delivered with pressure preset at 15 psi. They're designed for use with carburetors. Fuel injection systems typically operate at higher pressures and require their own types of fuel pumps.

4

CYLINDER HEADS

Cylinder heads are understandably a vital ingredient in any recipe for "porcupine" horsepower pie, so whether a big block is being built for street performance, drag racing, oval track, road racing, marine or off-road applications, the heads must be properly matched to the pistons, camshaft and intended engine usage if maximum power is to be extracted. Countless numbers of big blocks have had all visions of glory destroyed by misdirected "experts" who either selected the wrong cylinder heads, or took a wrong turn while modifying them. Such mistakes aren't difficult to make because ego and poor judgment frequently win out over common sense.

STOCK IRON CASTINGS

In spite of the vast array of cylinder heads produced by Chevrolet and a host

One of the most infamous big block-powered cars of the late 1980s was Rob Vandergriff's Pro Mod '57 Chevy. One of the first Pro Mods to top 200 miles per hour, Vandergriff demonstrated the mass quantities of air that will flow through a modified big block cylinder head.

BIG BLOCK CHEVROLET PRODUCTION CYLINDER HEADS

Casting Number	Application yr/cid	Chamber cc	Intake cc	Exhaust cc
Oval Port				
336781	'74, 454	110	256	114
353049	'73, 454	110	255	119
3999241	'71-'72 402, 454	105	252	116
3993820	'71-'72 396, 402, 454	105	255	114
3964290	'70, 454/390, 402/330,		262	115
Rectangular Port				
6272990	'71, 454/425	118	323	127
3994026	'71, 454/425			
6258723	'71, 454/425			
3946074	'71, 454/425 al	114.8	308	122
3946074	'70, 454/465 al	114.8	308	122
3964291	'70, 454/450 402/375	108c	327	122

Types

From the time the big block was introduced, Chevrolet has offered a variety of cylinder heads. Low and medium performance big blocks are topped off with cylinder heads having oval-shaped intake ports; high performance big blocks derived increased breathing capacity from heads with rectangular intake ports. The word "Pass" cast into a big-block head identifies it as being of the oval port persuasion; "Hi-Perf" cast into a head denotes rectangular ports. Early models of both oval and rectangular port heads have a bathtub-shaped closed chamber; 1971 and later castings are usually of the open chamber design.

Plug Hole—Another characteristic that distinguishes early- from late-model cast-iron heads is the spark plug hole. 1969 and earlier heads are machined for gasketed 3/4" reach plugs (Champion "N" type) with a 13/16" hex; 1970 and

ordering new heads from a Chevrolet dealer's parts department. However, once a cylinder head is out of its original box, a part number is of no use because the only identifying marks on the head itself are the casting numbers.

of aftermarket manufacturers, there are usually only a few models that are truly applicable for an engine of a particular personality. Just as passenger car heads rarely provide the ultimate power levels on a race engine, race heads usually provide less than impressive results when installed on a true street engine. It all has to do with combustion chamber volume, port size and casting integrity.

Identification

Chevrolet big-block cylinder heads are most commonly identified by their casting numbers, which may be found in a variety of locations, depending upon the particular head. The complete casting number is located beneath the valve cover, usually above an intake port. Additionally, either the last three digits of the casting number or the complete number can usually be found beneath one of the intake ports when a head is viewed from the combustion chamber side.

Only the last three digits are commonly used when referring to cylinder heads. As an example, in machine shops, bench racing parlors and other houses of high performance, casting number 6272990 is called simply a "990" casting. In the real world, the first four digits are virtually meaningless, as is the actual part number (6260482), which is used only when

Casting number 14096188 identifies this head as a high performance model with rectangular intake ports. It's interchangeable with the 990 casting. This head is the only Mark IV cast iron open chamber model still available from GM Performance Parts.

Casting numbers are usually located beneath, as well as on top of, one of the intake ports. On some castings, the complete number is included, on others, only the last three digits. Pass indicates oval intake ports.

The combustion chamber in this truck head shows the reason these castings are not well suited to high performance applications. Note the vast expanse between valve seats, an indication of the relative small valve diameters.

The intake ports in truck heads are almost round. They're matched by small valves which make the truck castings unsuitable for use on a high performance engine.

later heads require a tapered seat 1/2" reach plug with 5/8" hex. All GM aluminum heads installed on production engines were machined for 3/4" reach 13/16" hex spark plugs.

Truck Heads—A third type of big-block head is the one used on truck engines. These heads have almost round intake ports and very small valves. They're about as applicable as a one-barrel carburetor in performance applications.

But the permutations and combinations don't end there. In addition to open and closed chambers with either rectangular or oval intake ports, big-block Chevy heads are also available in either cast iron or aluminum. As might be expected, only rectangular port designs have been cast in aluminum.

Gen V Heads

In 1992, the world of big-block Chevy heads got even more diverse with the introduction of the Generation V engine. Although many parts are interchangeable between Mark IV and Gen V engines, cylinder heads are not—at least not without some modification. (See next chapter for conversion and modification

details.)

Non-Adjustable Valvetrain—One of the Gen V's major departures from big block tradition was inclusion of a "net lash" or non-adjustable valvetrain. As opposed to screw-in rocker studs, which allow valve lash or lifter preload to be adjusted, Gen V heads employ a non-adjustable shouldered bolt, with 3/8" threads, to keep each rocker in place.

Another drawback to the Gen V rocker arm arrangement is the sleeve that fits over the rocker bolt. The outside diameter of this sleeve requires an equally large slot in the rocker arm. Consequently, there isn't much surface area left for the pivot ball to contact. In addition to inviting outright rocker arm breakage, this configuration is prone to galling at the pivot ball/rocker arm interface because there's so little surface area.

Additionally, the stock valvetrain will not safely accommodate much more than .500" valve lift, so if Gen V heads are to be used in any engine that prides itself on horsepower, the rocker stud bosses should be drilled and tapped to accommodate traditional Mark IV-style 7/16-14 studs and guideplates.

Open vs. Closed Chambers

The term "open chamber" refers to

39

heads with combustion chambers having a nominal volume of 118cc's while "closed chambers" are nominally rated at 108cc's. In spite of these "official" specifications, real world combustion chamber volumes vary somewhat according to casting.

Regardless of intake port configuration, all big-block heads produced from 1965 to 1969 had closed chambers. The first open chamber appeared in 1969 ZL-1 aluminum heads. Cast-iron heads with open chambers first appeared in late 1970 for the 1971 model year.

Without question, a big block will produce more power with open chamber cylinder heads. In fact, the improved air flow and combustion efficiency offered by the open chamber design is frequently sufficient to more than offset the power loss caused by a drop in compression ratio (which can be over a full point) produced by the increased combustion chamber volume.

Oval Port Castings

For anything less than a full-tilt, take-no-prisoners race engine, oval port heads are actually the hot lick. Such a statement may seem to arise from a softening of brain tissue, but it is in fact true. While there's no question that rectangular port heads unquestionably offer greater maximum horsepower potential, it is also true that an extremely aggressive engine (super high compression ratio and fender-shaking cam) spun at high rpm is required to take full advantage of the air flow potential.

At less than tach-warping engine speeds, the smaller cross-sectional area of the oval-shaped intake port promotes higher velocities which results in superior cylinder filling. Depending upon the degree of port rework, this advantage extends up to approximately 6500 rpm with a 454, and somewhat higher with smaller engines. Above that speed, the ports become restrictive, whereas rectangular ports are just starting to get

Gen V cylinder heads have the same port configurations as their Mark IV counterparts, but unfortunately have a "net lash" rocker arm system which is non-adjustable. Note that bolts, rather than studs, hold the rocker arms in place.

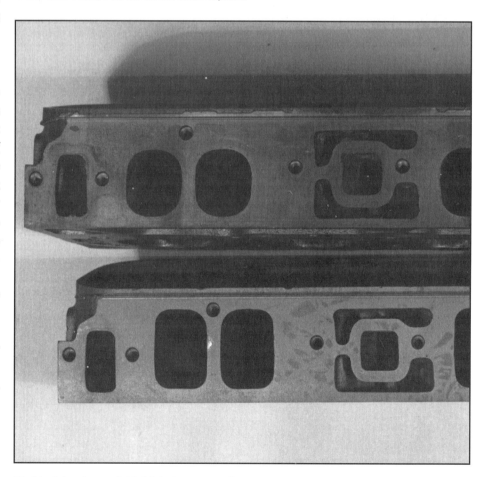

Big block heads are divided into two categories—oval port (top) and rectangular port (bottom). Although rectangular intake ports were once considered essential for optimum performance, they're actually appropriate only for large displacement, high revving engines. Oval port heads flow a healthy amount of air—enough to produce over 600 horsepower.

with the program.

Dyno tests by numerous engine builders have repeatedly proven the horsepower prowess of properly prepared oval port heads. A 468-cid engine, equipped with a single Holley 1050 Dominator four-barrel, will easily pump out over 615 horsepower and 540 lbs-ft. of torque with the appropriate roller camshaft (approximately 278/282 degrees of duration @ .050" lift) and compression ratio (12.5:1). Wearing a milder suit of armor—10:1 compression ratio and a cam with a duration of 255 degrees at .050" lift—a 468 will easily push its horsepower curve to the 575 level and put torque over 520 lbs-ft.

The oval port casting numbers of interest are 336781, 353049, 3992241 and 3993820, which were originally installed on 1971-1974 396, 402 and 454 cid engines. These castings were originally equipped with 2.06" intake and 1.72" exhaust valves. For high performance use, these heads are routinely fitted with 2.19" intake and 1.88" exhaust valves.

Rectangular Port Castings

The definitive rectangular port big-block head has become casting number 6272990 (or 14096188), which is still available through GM Performance Parts dealers as part number 6260482. Originally released in 1971, on 425-hp 427 engines, these castings feature open-style 118cc combustion chambers, 2.19" intake and 1.88" exhaust valves and Texas-sized intake and exhaust ports. This casting is very similar to 3994026, which originally brought exceptional breathing capability to 1971 LS-6 engines.

Mark IV—Although there are numerous other Mark IV rectangular port castings, most are of the closed chamber persuasion, which, as previously mentioned, are inferior in their ability to produce horsepower.

These two heads illustrate some of the subtle differences between oval and rectangular port heads. Both castings have open combustion chambers, but notice the difference in the shape of the boss around the spark plug holes. The 990 casting on top is identified by three digits on the underside of one port, and "Hi Perf Pass" beneath another. The 049 head on the bottom is similarly identified with "049" and "Pass" cast into the bottoms of the ports on the left.

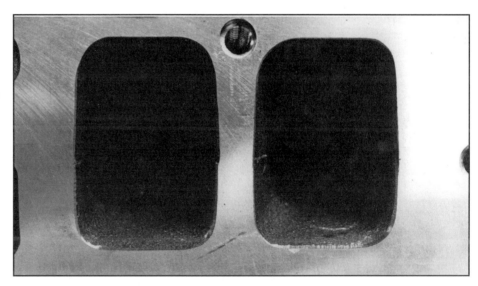

This closeup really shows the extremely generous dimensions of rectangular ports. Approximate dimensions are 1-3/4" by 2-1/2". Oval port heads measure approximately 1-3/4" by 2".

Gen V—Chevrolet also offers Gen V heads with rectangular intake ports. Released as a service replacement for HO 454 and HO 502 engines, these heads feature 118cc open combustion chambers, 2.19" intake and 1.88" exhaust valves and 325cc intake ports. In essence, they're the Gen V equivalent of the 990 head.

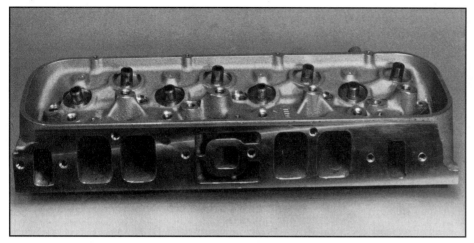

Aluminum 077 heads are based on the 1969-71 aluminum heads but feature a number of improvements, including a revised intake port floor. These heads are suitable for street and race usage.

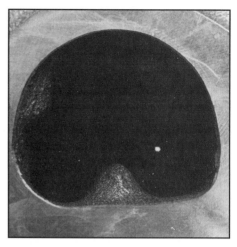

The vane in the exhaust ports of 077 heads turn a "D"-shaped outlet into a "C". These vanes were added to reduce turbulence and improve flow. However, many engine builders choose to remove them in their quest for increased horsepower. Note the light at the end of the tunnel.

CHEVROLET ALUMINUM HEADS

Almost since the inception of the big block, Chevrolet has offered aluminum cylinder heads that are more appropriate for racing than for mundane service on a passenger car engine. As early as 1967, aluminum castings were supplied on the infamous L-88 Corvette engines. As time progressed, so did demands for horsepower and several editions of big-block aluminum heads were released to meet those demands.

In late 1968, a second design L-88 head was released and brought the term "open chamber" to the lexicon of big block Chevy engine builders. Service replacements are still available for both versions with casting number 3919842 matching up to closed chambers and 14011077 pertaining to open chambers.

Proliferation of big-block aluminum head designs proceeded at a feverish pace when the "Bow Tie" high performance parts program kicked into high gear. Along with a myriad of head configurations came an alphabet soup of exhaust port shapes—"C", "D", "W" and "O"—which can be more than a little confusing.

077 Head—The 077 head was a ground-breaker, because it included a vane in the exhaust port flow that was designed to reduce turbulence. This vane, which is frequently removed by head porters, gives the port a "C" shape as opposed to the "D" shape it would have without the vane. So the same port configuration is alternately described as a "D"-port with a vane or as a "C" port. (It's known only as a "seaport" when used in marine applications.)

Rectangular Ports—Bow Tie aluminum heads with rectangular exhaust ports and vanes in the floor are often said to have "W" ports. However, the "W" may look like a "C" to some people so the question then becomes is a "C" port a

As this old Chevrolet Engineering photo demonstrates, when Chevy first tooled up for aluminum big-block heads, both open and closed chamber designs were evaluated. By 1969, the open chamber design had conclusively proven its superiority.

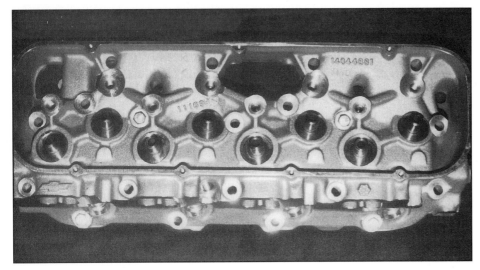

This Bow Tie aluminum head is intended for serious competition applications. It features 380cc intake ports, 105cc open combustion chambers and a rectangular "W"-shaped exhaust port. Intake ports are raised .100" and exhaust ports are raised .750" compared to a production head.

"D" port with a vane or a rectangular port with a vane? Typically, the "C" designation applies to the production heads while the "W" is reserved for "Bow Tie" heads.

Introduced in 1984, casting number 14044861 incorporates a number of significant changes that require alterations in intake and exhaust system components. As compared to production cylinder heads, the 861 castings feature intake ports that are raised .100" and exhaust ports that are raised .750". The rocker rail is also .750" higher (stock valve covers will fit) and valves with stems .200" longer than their stock counterparts are required.

128 Casting—Another variation on the Bow Tie theme was introduced in 1987, in the form of casting number 10051128, which features symmetrical intake ports. Designed specifically for Pro Stock drag racing, this casting eliminates the dual personality of previous big-block intake ports. Like the 861 head, the 128 casting requires an intake manifold and headers with the appropriate port configurations.

In standard configuration, a big-block head has two long (for cylinders 1, 4, 5 and 8) and two short (for cylinders 2, 3, 6 and 7) ports. The different lengths and resultant port volumes translate to a measurable difference in air flow capacity. In turn, power output of each cylinder may vary significantly, depending upon whether it's served by a long or short port. The symmetrical port head eliminates the Dr. Jekel and Mr. Hyde personas by routing air and fuel of every cylinder through ports of the same length and volume.

Why didn't they do that before? Because with a symmetrical port layout, two runners in each head are located directly above a head bolt. Each of these ports has a hole in its floor to accommodate an Allen-headed cap screw. There is also a threaded hole in the port roof to allow access to the cap screw.

Along with 400cc intake ports and large, round exhaust ports, the 128 casting features a unique combustion chamber. Referred to as a "semi-open" design, the relatively shallow chamber has a volume of only 72 cc's. Other unique characteristics include intake valve and exhaust valve angles of 18 and 10 degrees respectively (compared to 26 and 17 degrees for conventional big-block heads). Valve inclination (or compound angle) was also changed from 4 to 2.5 degrees.

Perusal of the accompanying cylinder head chart will reveal a raw, unmachined version of the 128 casting listed as 10051129. At first glance, this would appear to be a misprint because the casting number should be the same between unfinished and fully machined castings. However, 128 heads are cast of 356-T6 aluminum alloy while the 129

This race-ready head features 2.25" intake and 1.88" exhaust valves, which have proven to be an ideal combination for high output big blocks. Both rectangular and oval port heads will accept valves of these sizes.

GM PERFORMANCE PARTS BIG-BLOCK HEADS

Casting No.	Part No.	Intake Port Volume/Type	Combustion Chamber	Valve Dia. In/Ex	Notes
CAST IRON					
	14096802	325/R	118 (o)	2.19/1.88	G5 HO replacement, bare casting
	14096801	325/R	118 (o)	2.19/1.88	4096802 complete assembly
6272990	6260482	325/R	118 (o)	2.19/1.88	LS6/LS7 replacement
3964291	3919839	325/R	108 (c)	2.19/1.88	Closed chamber replacement head
ALUMINUM					
3919842	3919838	325/R	107 (c)	2.19/1.84	L89 1st design service replacement
14011077	14011076	295/R	118 (o)	2.19/1.88	L89 2nd design, C-port
14011077	14011004	295/R	118 (o)	2.19/1.88	Same, but solid casting, no water jacket
14044861	14044862	380/R	105 (o)	2.19/1.88	Bow Tie, rectangular exhaust port with vane (W-port)
14044861	14044861	380/R	105 (o)	2.19/1.88	Machined 861 casting, no valve seats or guides
14044876	14044861	380/R	105 (o)	2.19/1.88	Raw 861 casting, unmachined
10051128	10051128	400/R	72 (so)		Bow Tie symmetrical port, no valve seats or guides, round exhaust ports
10051129	10051129	400/R	72 (so)		Raw, unmachined version of 128 casting,355-T6 material
10049875	10049875	376/R	83 (o)	2.28/1.88	Pontiac small port head
10045427	10045427	460/R	91 (o)	2.40/1.90	Pontiac large port head
	10093386*	365/R1	61	2.40/1.90	Pontiac head with spread intake ports

Note: R- rectangular; R1- rectangular with rounded roof; (o)-open chamber; (c)-closed chamber; (so)- semi-open chamber
*10093386 is fully machined, part number 10093385 is an unmachined version

heads are cast of 355-T6 alloy which is slightly harder and easier to weld. The 129 castings also have somewhat smaller ports and a slightly different combustion chamber shape.

Used Heads

Although some of the heads described here have been out of production for some time, they are included because used castings are still available. Sometimes a pair of used castings can be a real bargain, but they can also turn out to be over-priced boat anchors. Mike Hedgecock of Eagle Racing Engines in Knoxville, TN, offers some advice if you intend to purchase used castings at a swap meet or similar venue:

"Inspect them very carefully. Don't ever accept a pair of heads that have been completely assembled because the closed valves can be hiding damage around the valve seat or in the port. Valve springs and seals may also be hiding a cracked valve guide. The best bet is to purchase bare castings and be sure you know where to find the seller in the event that the heads don't check out. Many times cracks are almost impossible to find until a head is pressure-checked. Reputable suppliers of used cylinder heads will usually guarantee basic casting integrity, meaning that the heads are free of cracks and other damage that can't be repaired through normal repair practices. Even if everything looks good, have the heads Magnafluxed and pressure-checked before having any work done on them. The only thing worse than buying a bad set of heads is finding out they're bad after you've spent money modifying them."

AFTERMARKET CYLINDER HEADS

Considerable expense is involved in bringing a cylinder head from concept to reality, so prior to the 1970s, Chevrolet Motor Division was the only reliable source of cylinder head castings. But since that time, the demand for other than factory-produced cylinder heads has grown to the point that companies like Brodix, Dart and World Products have jumped in with a variety of cast-iron and aluminum heads designed specifically for high performance and race applications. Even Pontiac Motorsports offers aluminum castings for big-block Chevy engines. They are available through the GM Parts Performance Catalog. Virtually all aftermarket heads are designed for Mark IV blocks.

Brodix big-block heads are available as bare castings or as complete assemblies. The -1 castings are suitable for street and race engines and feature 280cc intake ports and raised exhaust ports.

Pontiac Heads

Pontiac heads identified by casting numbers 10045427 and 10049875 are known as large port and small port respectively. The large port version is intended for engines with displacements ranging from 450 to 600 cubic inches and features 460cc intake ports, 91cc combustion chambers and seats for 2.40" intake and 1.90" exhaust valves. The valve angles are 18 degrees and 9 degrees for intake and exhaust respectively, representing an 8-degree "roll" compared to conventional big block valve angles.

The small port version of the Pontiac head shares most dimensional specifications with its big port brother, the exception being valve sizes and port volumes. Designed for engines of 450 cubic inches or less, casting number 10049875 includes seats for 2.28" intake and 1.88" exhaust valves, has 376cc intake ports and 83cc combustion chambers.

Both of these heads are supplied with bronze valve guides packaged separately (not installed) and require extra-long valves and special valvetrain components. A special water manifold (part no. 10045450) which equalizes cylinder head temperatures and eliminates coolant flow through the intake manifold should be installed on

Brodix -1, -2 and -3 castings look similar externally, but port configurations differ significantly. Each head is designed for engines of particular performance levels.

either large- or small-port Pontiac heads.

Brodix

Brodix has been manufacturing big block cylinder heads for quite some time and offers a variety of castings. One of the latest additions is an oval port head designed for mild engines up to 454 cubic inches. Brodix oval port heads have stock-sized exhaust ports and 250cc intake ports. This head is designed to promote high port velocities for improved low speed and mid-range torque.

For engines requiring greater air flow capacity, Brodix offers big block -1, -2 and -3 head castings. The -1 includes raised D-shaped exhaust ports, 280cc rectangular intake ports and 119cc combustion chambers. Brodix -2 castings are similar to -1s, for the intake ports which have a volume of 310 or 327cc's.

The next step up in flow capacity is the -3 "Big Brodie" casting which has huge 370cc intake ports and is typically fitted

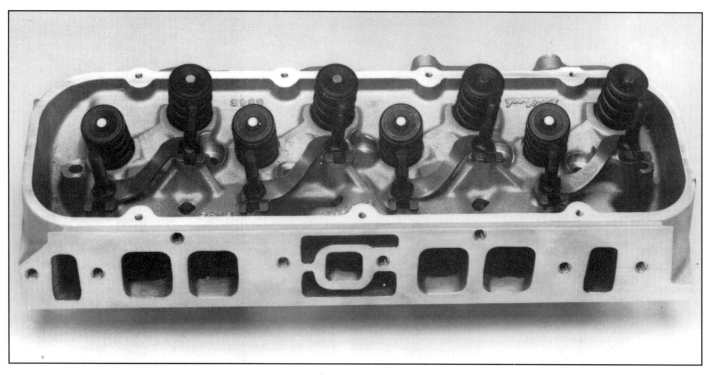

Edelbrock's approach to Chevrolet big-block aluminum heads is to combine the best of features found on stock heads. The Edelbrock intake ports are "rectoval"—a rectangular shape that is dimensionally similar to a standard oval port.

with 2.30" intake and 1.88" exhaust valves. Like the -1 and -2 heads, standard combustion chamber volume is 119cc's; the -1 and -2 heads can be angle milled to drop chamber volume to 95 cc's, but minimum suggested chamber volume for -3 castings is 110cc's. Brodix -1, -2 and -3 castings are available with or without water jackets.

Another group of castings available from Brodix is the EB Series which is designed for Pro Stock type engines. These castings include extremely large ports capable of meeting the air flow requirements of 500+ cubic inch engines.

Edelbrock

In the beginning, the only choice in big-block heads was between oval and rectangular intake ports. Then the plot thickened with the introduction of raised ports and symmetrical ports. Then Edelbrock added a new twist by introducing an aluminum head with "rectoval" ports.

Intended for moderate performance applications, the Edelbrock aluminum head (part no. 6045) incorporates a unique "rectangularized" version of the traditional oval-shaped intake port. This

design was developed as a means of combining the air flow capacity of a conventional rectangular port with the higher velocity air movement that

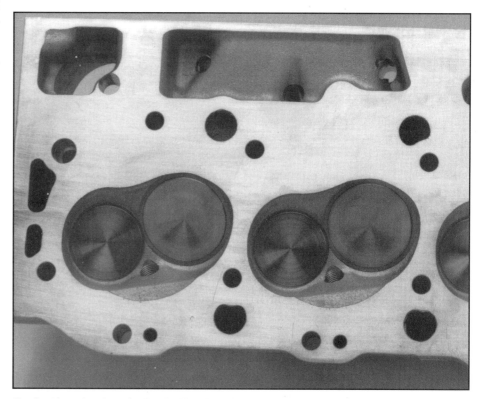

Combustion chambers in the Edelbrock heads are "semi-open," a design which is said to improve combustion efficiency. Standard valve sizes are 2.19" and 1.88".

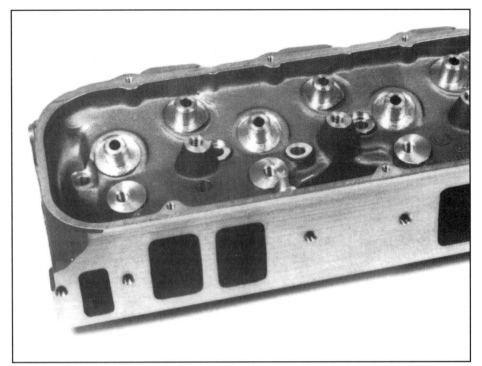

Dart's "Bolt-On" big block heads are available with a variety of intake port configurations—265cc oval, 320cc or 365cc rectangular. Irrespective of intake port configuration, the exhaust ports are raised and as-cast combustion chamber volume is 140cc's. With that volume, these heads can be used on supercharged engines, or they can be milled to build high compression.

characterizes oval port heads.

Other features include 110cc semi-open combustion chambers, 280cc intake ports and 2.19-in. intake and 1.88-in. exhaust valves with 11/32-in. stems. Edelbrock states that the deck surface was specifically designed to be compatible with both Mark IV and Gen V blocks. Although the intake ports are uniquely shaped, they're compatible with intake manifolds designed for oval port passenger car (not truck) heads.

Dart Machinery

Dart was co-founded by long-time Pro Stock racer Dick Maskin, so it's not surprising that its catalog lists three unique styles of big-block aluminum heads. The standard Dart head is a bolt-on replacement; part no. 6002 features 320cc intake ports and part no. 6003 sports 360cc intake ports. Both part numbers have 119cc open-style combustion chambers and include valve seats that accept 2.19-in. intake and 1.88-in. exhaust valves, but larger valves can

be installed. Dart's Kevin Feeney notes that most engine builders machine Dart big-block heads to accept 2.250" intake valves.

These castings differ somewhat from their standard Chevrolet counterparts. The intake and exhaust valves have been "rolled" two degrees for increased air flow and the rocker arm studs bosses were relocated to accommodate the change in valve angles so standard rockers and guideplates can be utilized. However, intake valve length must be .250-in. longer than stock and the four head bolts that are positioned near the exhaust ports (which are raised) must be 1-in. longer than stock. Although supplied with 119cc combustion chambers, chamber volume can be reduced to about 100cc's with some creative angle milling.

Companions to the bolt-on castings are part numbers 6000 and 6001 which respectively incorporate 320cc and 360cc intake ports. Originally designed for Pro Stock drag racing, these heads are cast

with combustion chambers measuring 140cc's, which makes life easier if you're building a turbocharged or supercharged engine. However, there is sufficient deck thickness to allow removal of .200-in. of material, in which case chamber volume will be 90+ cc's. Both the 6000 and 6001 castings require .250" longer-than-stock intake valves.

Although the name "bolt-on" often implies direct replacement of an original equipment component, that isn't exactly the case with Dart "bolt-on" heads. The only difference between the bolt-on and standard Dart big-block heads is the deck; bolt-on heads have fully machined deck surfaces, so no machining is required prior to installation. The standard Dart head is supplied with a deck surface that must be machined to bring chamber volume down to useable levels.

Big Chief—Dart's "Big Chief" cylinder heads were designed in response to the growing sophistication of Pro Stock-type engines. As opposed to part numbers 6000-6003, which are conceptually similar to stock Chevrolet heads, Big Chief castings are unique. They feature spread intake ports, revised valve angles, huge raised ports and tiny combustion chambers. The rocker bosses in these heads accept only shaft-type rocker arms.

The standard Big Chief head, part no. 9000 features 18-degree intake and 9-degree exhaust valve angles. Part number 9001 was subsequently released after Dart worked with a number of Pro Stock teams; it features 14-degree intake and 7-degree exhaust angles. Part number 9002 pertains to castings with 16-degree intake and 7-degree exhaust valve angles.

The shallow valve angles combined with a unique combustion chamber shape result in a chamber volume of 85cc's with 18-degree castings and 74cc's with 16- and 14-degree castings. All Big Chief heads also boast 395cc intake ports and raised exhaust ports. Big Chief heads are typically assembled with 2.375-in. or

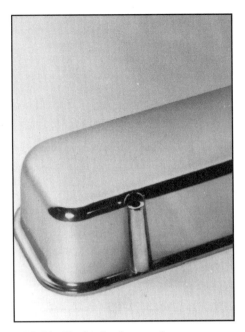

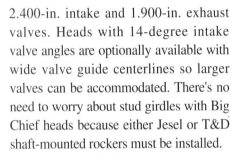

B&B big block aluminum valve covers are attractive, durable and tough. They help keep oil seepage to a minimum so the heads beneath them stay clean.

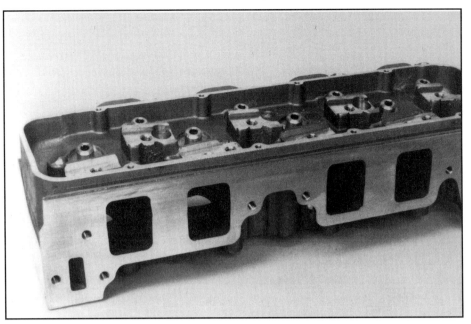

Dart's top-of-the-line big block race head is the "Big Chief" casting. It features spread intake ports and can be ordered with a variety of intake valve angles.

2.400-in. intake and 1.900-in. exhaust valves. Heads with 14-degree intake valve angles are optionally available with wide valve guide centerlines so larger valves can be accommodated. There's no need to worry about stud girdles with Big Chief heads because either Jesel or T&D shaft-mounted rockers must be installed.

The latest addition to the Dart big-block cylinder head catalog is an oval port casting designed for street, bracket and marine applications. Dart's oval port head is identical to the bolt-on head (including raised exhaust ports) except for the intake port, which has a volume of 265 cc's. These heads will accept 2.19-in. intake and 1.88-in. exhaust valves, but like their rectangular port counterparts, they're normally assembled with 2.250-in. intake valves. The port shape is compatible with all standard oval port intake manifolds.

With respect to Dart's cylinder heads, Kevin Feeney advises, "Both our rectangular and oval port heads can be used on standard and tall deck blocks because we offer intake manifolds for both configurations. Most people think that the rectangular port heads are the

way to go, but we've found that's usually not true. There's no question that the rectangular ports will make more horsepower, but the oval port heads make more torque and generally result in quicker 60-foot and quarter-mile times. Our general recommendation is that any engine smaller than about 500 cubic inches installed in a full-bodied car should use oval port heads. Obviously, street cars and most boats will also be better off with oval port heads.

"Something else that we've found is that on smaller engines, (under about 520 cid) the hot tip is *not* to use an intake manifold with a Dominator flange. A manifold with a standard flange and a 2-in. adapter will make more mid-range torque and horsepower will be about the same. We've also found that when an engine is mounted in a heavy vehicle and is equipped with rectangular port heads, you're better off using our oval port intake manifold with the runner openings enlarged to rectangular port dimensions. You get better mid-range power and that generally improves performance."

Feeney also notes that with all Dart heads, rocker studs with extra-long bottom threads should be installed in all

exhaust positions. The extra threads engage more of the casting for greater rigidity—and fewer broken studs.

World Products

The only company offering cast-iron, big-block heads other than Chevrolet, World Products offers both oval- and rectangular-port configurations. Called "Merlin" heads (supposedly because of their magical horsepower-producing capability), these castings include several unique features, including raised webs between rocker stud bosses for increased top deck strength, raised head bolt bosses adjacent to the exhaust ports for improved air flow capacity, hardened steel exhaust valve seats, integral valve guides and a three-angle valve job.

Both oval port and rectangular port castings feature 119cc open combustion chambers and seats for 2.19-in. intake and 1.88-in. exhaust valves; intake port volumes are 262cc for oval ports and 315cc for rectangular ports. The deck surfaces are .400-in. thick, so there's sufficient material to allow extensive milling without compromising strength. Angle milling up to .175-in. reduces combustion chamber volume to 100 cc's.■

INSTALLING SYMMETRICAL PORT HEADS

One of the big block's most significant power production assets is also its worst liability. Cylinder heads. Although standard configuration big-block heads offer excellent air flow potential, the siamesed intake ports do not have equal air flow potential. This isn't significant in engines designed for less than maximum power output. But when an engine's horsepower curve pushes into four digits, the penalty imposed by ports of measurably diffrent dimensions becomes unacceptable. Chevrolet engineering addressed the problem several years ago and developed symmetrical-port heads as a solution. Available as either a raw casting (part no. 10051129), or a fully machined casting with no valve seats or valve guides (part no. 10051128), symmetrical port big block heads are not simple bolt-on replacements for their conventional counterparts.

Ken Sperry, an engineer for GM Powertrain Division and race engine builder has put together several killer big blocks using symmetrical port heads. His formula for installing these heads proves once again that the quest for maximum performance is never easy. Precision machining capabilities are a definite requirement.

As a means of achieving optimum head gasket sealing, Sperry installs two additional head bolts on each side, providing six bolts around each cylinder. Before the additional bolts can be installed, two unmachined bosses in each head must be drilled to accept a 3/8-16 bolt. Since each hole passes right through an intake port, the floor of each port must be counter bored to accept an Allen-head bolt. The access hole that was drilled in the boss above the port must then be tapped to accept a plug. Holes must also be drilled and tapped in Mark IV blocks (the holes are included in Gen V Bow Tie blocks), and head gaskets may also need to be modified to accept the additional head bolts.

Tight clearance around several of the bolts doesn't leave sufficient room for a socket, so Sperry installs Allen-head bolts in all locations and recommends the following fasteners:

Description	Quantity
3/8-16 x 1.5" Allen head bolt	4
7/16-14 x 1.5" Allen head bolt	4
7/16-14 x 2" Allen head bolt	8
7/16-14 x 4.25" Allen head bolt	2
7/16-14 x 4.5" Allen head bolt	10
7/16-14 x 5.5" Allen head bolt	8
Washer- 7/16 x .75" OD (GM part no. 10051155)	28
Washer- 7/16 x .625" OD (GM part no. 14011093)	4
Washer- 3/8" AN	4
O-ring plug– Parker 8HP50N-5	4

Other special parts requirements include longer-than-stock valves and pushrods, shaft-type rocker arms and 5/8 hex, 7.08-in. reach tapered seat spark plugs. Intake and exhaust valve lengths for symmetrical-port heads are 5.85-in and 6.00-in. respectively, making them .060-in. longer than the valves typically installed in 862 Bow Tie heads. To achieve proper valvetrain geometry pushrods used in conjunction with symmetrical-port heads should have nominal lengths of 9.100-in. and 10.00-in. respectively for intake and exhaust. Just in case you don't have a flare for the obvious, a special intake manifold is also required.

5

CYLINDER HEAD MODIFICATIONS

Now that your head is swimming with casting numbers and combustion chamber and port volumes, you can turn your attention to the modification and preparation of big-block cylinder heads for maximum performance.

PORTING

Modification of intake and exhaust ports has been done since the dawn of high performance engines. While much has been written on porting techniques and their effect on airflow capabilities, misinformation still abounds. This is largely because most people fall victim to BIBS—"Bigger Is Better Syndrome." Huge, gaping ports may be the answer for full-on race engines that operate in the 7500+ rpm range, but for street, race and marine engines that operate in lower and middle rpm ranges, porting should be done with the discretion of a politician lining his pockets with money intended to finance his election campaign.

Mild Porting

Rather than picking up a die grinder and attacking a port like Rambo going after a group of terrorists, porting of heads for street, recreational boating and mild race engines should consist of smoothing and blending. The key is to not rock n' roll through a port, but to waltz through it. Pay particular attention to the valve bowl area because it's the most critical part.

A fully modified cylinder head involves countless hours of grinding and polishing. However, it's the shape, not the shine, that makes for outstanding performance.

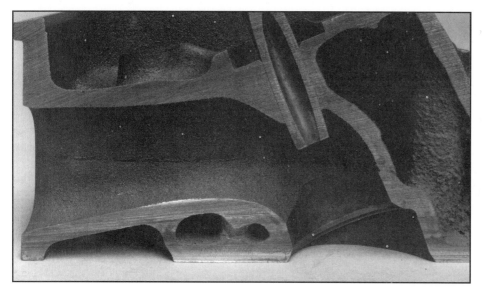

Sliced in half, it's easy to see where a standard head needs improvement. Note the sharp edge just above the valve seat where the machined surface meets the raw casting. This is the "pocket" or "bowl" area that's reworked when a head is ported for mild performance applications. A little work in this area pays handsome power dividends.

Head porting can be a potentially dangerous job because small pieces of iron or aluminum go flying everywhere, and air grinder noise tends to get tiresome after a while. If you plan to do any porting, be sure to wear eye and ear protection.

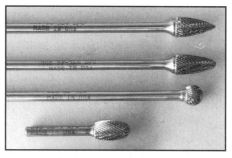

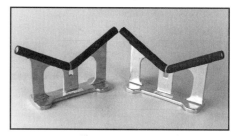

To port your own heads, you'll need a complete selection of abrasives. Porting kits are available from a variety of suppliers, or cartridge rolls and grinding stones can be purchased separately.

For extensive port rework, high speed steel or carbide cutters are required. These cutters are available in a variety of shapes and lengths, each one designed for a particular purpose.

It's difficult to port heads properly if they're flopping around all over a workbench. Special stands such as these can be used with all types of heads and provide a stable work surface.

As supplied, most cylinder heads (except for some aftermarket types) have rough edges where factory machining ends and as-cast surfaces begin. These junctions are primarily adjacent to the bowl area just beneath the valves. Typically, the factory uses a 70-deg. cutter to machine the port throat and to provide a transition from the raw, cast port surface to the machined valve seat. There is almost always a sharp edge down in the port left by the cutter. Some sharp edges may also be evident adjacent to the valve seat. Porting of heads for engines that won't receive a double shot of testosterone should be concentrated in this bowl or pocket area. Blending for a

smooth transition from machined to the raw cast surface is the first priority. Some porters also slightly enlarge the bowl area, primarily by blending the bowl into the port wall and narrowing the portion of the valve guide that protrudes into the port.

In instances where class rules prohibit porting, additional flow capacity can be achieved by either machining deeper (than the factory did) with a 70-deg. cutter, or by machining the throat with a 75-deg. cutter. Larger angle cutters, such as 80 deg., should be avoided because they can actually hurt flow. Tech inspectors rarely, if ever, measure the angle or depth of the cut below the valve

seat. Rather, they look for evidence that a die grinder has paid a visit to the ports.

Chemical milling is another technique used to remove material from port walls that are supposed to be unmodified. As the acid eats away the metal, the original as-cast surface contour is maintained, so without measuring port volume, it's virtually impossible to detect the modifications. Glass beading a set of heads further obscures evidence of modification, however, some sanctioning bodies prohibit glass beading or similar procedures. Big-block Chevy engines are rarely built for competition classes that have cylinder head modification restrictions, so use of sleight-of-hand porting techniques is rarely required.

Short-Turn Radius—Another section of the port that is deserving of special attention is the short-turn radius—the section of the port that transitions from the valve seat to the port floor. Opinions vary as to what constitutes the ideal short-turn radius, but in an intake port, what's desirable is at least a .090 in. straight, vertical drop between the bottom cut below the valve seat and the curve that leads to the port floor. Many times this profile is difficult to achieve unless oversized valves are installed. In fact, although the increase in power that results from installation of larger valves is usually attributed strictly to the difference in diameter, the improvement in short-turn radius contour is just as responsible—if not more so.

Consequently, it's common practice to replace a 2.06"/1.72" valve combination with a 2.19" intake/1.88" exhaust arrangement. In heads already equipped with valves of these diameters, 2.25" intake and 1.90" or 1.94" exhaust valves can be substituted. In a head that has had its valves sunk, oversized valves are especially useful in re-establishing the proper distance between the valve seat and short-turn radius. Contrary to popular belief, the exhaust ports also need to have their short-turn radii carefully massaged, so don't overlook them.

Gasket Matching—Additionally, it is beneficial to gasket-match the openings of both intake and exhaust ports. Fel-Pro gaskets with the proper port dimensions are available for both oval and rectangular port heads; they can be used as a template so you can open all the intake ports and manifold runner openings to the same dimensions.

Port Size—Having the intake port opening slightly larger than the manifold runner opening won't hurt and may help control reversion if a long duration camshaft is used. However, having a port mouth that is smaller than the manifold runner will impose a serious performance

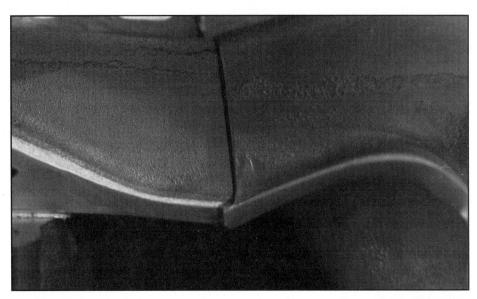

Whether being modified for street or race, intake ports are typically matched to the intake manifold runners so the transition is a smooth one. An intake manifold gasket is typically used as a template. If the entire port isn't modified, the revised opening is usually blended about an inch into the port.

When a head is fully ported, the boss around the valve guide is usually narrowed. Both the intake and exhaust guides in the center chamber have been modified. The exhaust guide in this photo has been narrowed and tapered to improve flow and reduce turbulence.

handicap as the incoming air/fuel mixture will be disrupted as it strikes the sharp ledge created by the undersized port opening.

On the exhaust side, the opposite is true. If the port mouth is larger than the header tube, the exhaust gasses will strike a sharp ledge as they exit. On the other hand, if the header tube is larger than the exhaust port opening, no serious ill effects will result and the resulting ledge may serve to control reversion.

Race Heads

Porting of race heads is considerably more involved than the procedure for heads to be installed on street or recreational marine engines. However, the proper way to port race heads isn't something that can be learned by reading

Winston Drag Racing

OLD BRIDGE TWP. RACEWAY PARK

Porting and polishing are not permitted in Stock Eliminator, yet racers like Steve Ficacci still manage some pretty impressive quarter-mile times. Careful selection of castings is the key.

a book—no matter how good the writer. Cylinder head specialists spend countless hours testing on the flow bench and engine dyno and have developed highly specialized port configurations, many of which they keep secret.

If you're convinced that you want to do your own competition-style porting, proceed cautiously. It's a lot easier to remove metal than to put it back. The problem with getting carried away with a grinder is that ports that are too large for an engine's requirements do not support good port velocities. Slow-moving intake charges don't fill the cylinder very well and aren't conducive to the development of maximum horsepower. An exhaust port that's too large doesn't hurt quite as much because the exhaust gasses move at

high velocities as a result of the heat and pressure that accompany them. However, oversized exhaust ports are difficult to achieve because in a big-block head, they rarely match the flow capacity of intake ports. If you can't create a port configuration that's optimized for a particular application, you're better off with a port that's too small than one that's too large.

It's also true that air flow doesn't always respond as expected. As an example, Mike Hedgecock of Eagle Racing Engines in Knoxville, TN, was porting a set of 077 castings for use on a 468 cubic-inch bracket engine and figured he'd remove the dimple for the head bolt that protrudes into the exhaust port. When he did, he found that it

actually reduced air flow, so he wound up welding the area back up. The best advice for head porting novices (aside from letting a professional do the job), is to start by cleaning up the bowl area and gasket-matching the port mouths. Narrow the OD of the valve guide as much as possible and STOP. If you truly need a set of fully ported heads, you need maximum air flow capability and that can only be achieved through years of experience and flow bench testing.

Combustion Chamber

Just as porting and a good valve job are essential for top performance, so is a properly shaped and sized combustion chamber. To ensure that compression ratio is consistent from one cylinder to

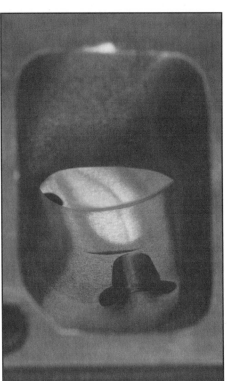

The Reher-Morrison-Shepherd Pro Stock team made quite a name for itself in the early 1980s. Although the late Lee Shepherd was known primarily as the team's driver, he was also in charge of cylinder heads. His expertise on the flow bench and with a grinder was a major factor in the team's ability to produce engines capable of churning out exceptionally high levels of power. Shepard was tragically killed while testing.

This modified rectangular intake port has been extensively recontoured, but notice that the walls have a light texture to them. That's the preferred finish for an intake port because it helps keep fuel in suspension. It's shape, not shine, that makes horsepower.

another, combustion chamber volume must be checked and equalized. Since adding material to a chamber is neither easy nor desirable, the most common approach taken to equalizing volume is to find the largest chamber in a head, and then grind all the other chambers to match. If the final desired volume is less than that of the largest chamber, the head can be milled after all individual chamber work is completed. As an example, if the smallest chamber in a head measures 118cc's, and the largest is 120cc's, all the chambers should be massaged to at least 120cc's. In fact, if the chamber wall around the intake valve is ground back, to unshroud the valve, all chambers may wind up at 121-123 cc's by the time volume and flow potential are equalized. Once this has been done, the head can be milled as required to bring all chambers to 118cc's or less, as required.

Sinking Valves—Some people advocate sinking the valves to enlarge

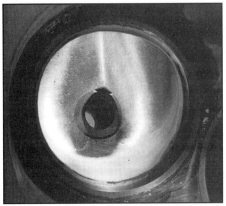

The bronze guide in this intake port has been narrowed and shortened and blended into the foil shape in the port. The position and shape of the foil helps direct incoming air and fuel into the combustion chamber for more efficient burning.

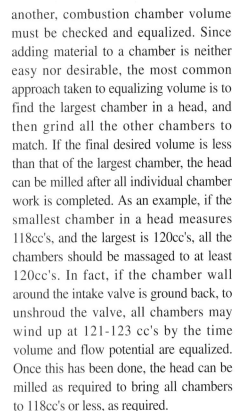

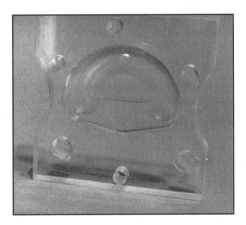

Checking combustion chamber cc's also requires that the chamber be sealed. Sealing plates can be fabricated, or purchased. The commercially available versions are usually manufactured of special plastic that's impervious to solvents.

chamber volume. This should *never* be done. Although it may deliver the chamber volume you want, it will reduce air flow. Sinking the valves was once a common technique applied to race engines built for classes with rules prohibiting grinding or polishing in the

combustion chamber. Those types of rules are pretty much a thing of the past, and where they still exist, most racers have developed new interpretations (sometimes called cheating) that allow chamber volume to be increased without sinking the valves.

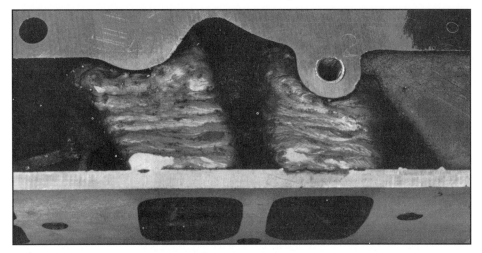

Back in the days before special race-type aftermarket heads were available, racers increased port size by heli-arc welding additional material on the port floor and roof because the original casting was either ground too thin, or completely ground through.

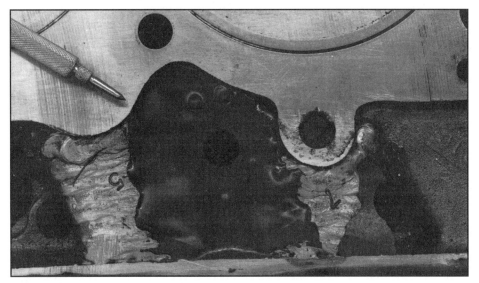

After all the port welding was completed, epoxy was used to seal the areas between the port walls. This time-consuming type of modification helped increase power, but didn't do much for reliability.

Exhaust port exteriors were also built up by welding, prior to final porting. The scribed lines near the top indicate the position of the original casting prior to welding and the round circle indicates the header tube size.

CC'ing—CC'ing the chambers is a measuring operation that requires nothing more than a clear plastic plate to seal the chamber, a burette to hold the fluid used for the measurements and some means of holding the cylinder head level from end-to-end and at a slight angle side-to-side. Once the head is properly anchored, place the plastic plate (which must have a small hole in it to admit fluid) over the chamber. The plate should be positioned so that the hole is at the chamber's highest point. Your measurement won't be accurate if any of the fluid leaks out, so keep an eye on the seal between the plate and the head, and around the valves and spark plug. Use grease to effect a liquid-tight seal between the plate and the head. If the valve job hasn't been completed, you may also have to smear grease around the valve seat to seal the valves. Obviously, you'll also need to install a spark plug to prevent leakage through the plug hole.

Once everything is in place, position the burette over the hole in the plastic plate and open the petcock so the fluid flows slowly into the combustion chamber. Be careful not to overfill the chamber and make sure no air bubbles are trapped beneath the plastic plate. After you measure and record the volume of one chamber, repeat the process on the next one and continue until all four have been completed. Then set up the other head and measure all of its chambers.

VALVE JOB

A good multi-angle valve job (three angles are most commonly used) includes a bottom cut ranging from 50 to 70 deg., depending upon the casting. A 70-deg. cutter is typically used on stock-type heads to smooth the area below the valve. In a stock port, the 70-deg. cut meets the 45-deg. cut of the valve seat. But when a 3-angle valve job is done, a 60-deg. cut is added to smooth the transition from the valve seat and narrow the valve seat. The

55

Cutters like the one on the right are used to machine the valve guide outside diameter spring seats in a single operation. Most kits include three arbors--5/16", 11/32" and 3/8" diameter--one to fit each of the most commonly used guide sizes.

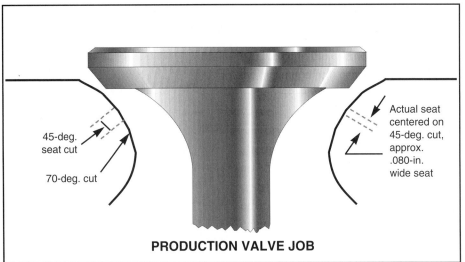

PRODUCTION VALVE JOB

45-deg. seat cut

70-deg. cut

Actual seat centered on 45-deg. cut, approx. .080-in. wide seat

A production type valve job has a single cut on the valve and on the seat. The resulting sharp edges aren't the hot lick for maximum air flow, which is the reason that high performance engines are typically treated to a multi-angle valve job.

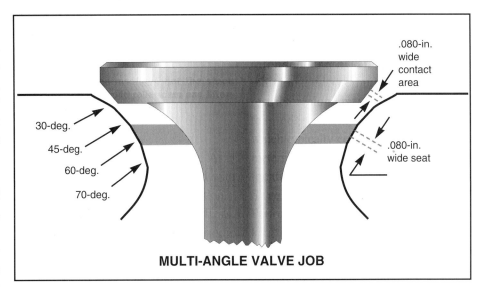

30-deg.
45-deg.
60-deg.
70-deg.

.080-in. wide contact area

.080-in. wide seat

MULTI-ANGLE VALVE JOB

The infamous three-angle valve job exposed. The valve itself has a 45-degree face which contacts the actual valve seat which is also cut at 45 degrees. The contact area on the valve should be centered on the 45-degree face. Below the 45-degree seat face is a 60 degree cut and then a 70-degree cut. On the top side, a 30-degree cut blends the seat into the combustion chamber. Depending on how you look at it, a three-angle valve job may actually involve four different angles (30, 45, 60 and 70 degrees).

seat itself is cut with a 45-deg. cutter and a 30-degree cutter machines the transition from the top of the valve seat to the combustion chamber surface. The accuracy of the valve job exerts a significant influence over performance because it affects the quality of the seal between the valve face and seat, and air flow. Compared to an inexpensive stock valve job, a high performance 3-angle valve job can be worth a solid 10-15 horsepower. If you consider the 30-deg. cut on the combustion chamber side of the valve, a 3-angle valve job is actually a 4-angle valve job.

Although some engine builders vary intake valve seat width according to application, Chad Hedgecock, the cylinder head specialist at Eagle Racing Engines, relies on a .060-in. wide intake valve seat for street, marine and race engines. However, he prefers exhaust seats .080-in. wide for street, some oval track and marine applications but holds them to .060-in. for drag and some oval track race engines. Hedgecock's reasoning for this is that the narrower seat provides a slight flow improvement and the heads on a race engine are removed for service frequently enough that the seats will be recut before they get beat up too badly. With a street or marine engine, the slightly wider seat is required for longevity.

While these dimensions have been used

successfully in thousands of high performance and race engines, they are by no means written in stone. Hedgecock feels it's important to note that some cylinder head specialists may have other ideas or have developed other combinations that they prefer. If you're paying someone to do a valve job, don't try to tell him or her how to do it. If you feel you have to, find another shop.

Gary Grimes, of Grimes Automotive Machine in Alpharetta, GA, also notes

that in many cases, the trade-off with a valve job is between flow and heat dissipation. He states:

"A wider seat provides more area for the valve to transfer heat into the head. That's why you can't use the same valve seat dimensions on heads built for the street, oval track or marine engine that you can on drag race heads. Every engine builder has his or her own technique, but there are still certain

things that are either right or wrong for a particular application. You can get by with narrow seats that are out near the edge of the seat surface in a drag engine because it's going to come apart before any damage is done. But on street, oval track, marine or bracket engines, where you're trying to get long-term durability, you have to give up a little flow to get reasonable valve life. And regardless of the application, the valves should be lapped. We can cut the prettiest-looking seats, with every angle just what it's supposed to be, and there's still no assurance that you'll get the best possible seal. When you lap the valves, you know for sure."

One of the best ways to determine final valve seat position and thickness is to coat the seat with machinist's blue solution and lap the valve. The bluing will be removed wherever the valve and seat touch, leaving no doubt as to the surface's location and integrity.

Valve Seats

Another aspect of the valve job to be leery of is the positioning of the valve head with respect to the combustion chamber roof. This is especially true with used heads. Each time a valve job is done, some material is removed from the valve seat. If a head has been the victim of numerous valve jobs, or was used for on-the-job training, the seating surface may have been ground so much that the valves have sunk like the Titanic. As previously noted, sinking the valves should be avoided because it hurts airflow and consequently power output. Sinking the valves shortens the distance between the seat and the short-turn radius which is exactly opposite of the desired condition.

If a pair of heads has a lot of redeeming features, but has seats that have been sunk excessively, either new valve seats should be installed or larger diameter valves substituted for the original ones. As previously noted, one of the reasons that castings with small valves (2.06/1.72-in.) respond so well when 2.19/1.88-in. valves are installed, is because the valve seats are raised, which increases the distance from the seat to the short turn. Remember, larger valves improve airflow two ways—with

increased diameter and better seat positioning.

Replacing Seats—Ever since leaded fuel all but vanished from the pumps, valve seat life has been a big question. Numerous tests have shown that without lead to provide a cushion between the valves and their seats, rapid seat erosion results. Consequently, all factory-installed big-block heads manufactured after 1971 have induction-hardened exhaust seats. While they're certainly advantageous, they're not always necessary. Valve seat erosion is typically only a problem when an engine is run continuously under a heavy load. While valve seat wear is unquestionably greater with unleaded fuels, it generally won't be severe enough to cause problems under most normal operating conditions. Marine engines, which operate under a heavy load most of the time, are the notable exception. If you're uncomfortable with unleaded fuel, use a lead or lead substitute additive—it's a lot cheaper than having hardened seats installed. You'll also find that it may be cheaper to buy a new head than to have hardened seats installed.

Installation of hardened seats (made of stellite material) is justified if a pair of heads is particularly valuable or

impossible to replace (such as an out-of-production casting). In such an instance, only the exhaust seats need to be replaced. However, this isn't a job for a shade-tree mechanic; extremely accurate equipment run by an experienced machinist is required for proper installation.

Rocker Studs

All Mark IV cylinder heads are factory equipped with 7/16" diameter rocker studs. As such, no changes are required for high performance engines and only the substitution of high quality studs, and the addition of a stud girdle, is required for full-tilt race engines.

Unfortunately, the situation isn't quite so simple with Gen V cylinder heads which employ a 3/8"-diameter bolt to hold the rockers in place. As previously noted, the Gen V rocker system is a double liability— not only are the 3/8" bolts weak, the spacer tube that surrounds them has such a large O.D. that it requires an extremely large slot in the rocker. Consequently, there isn't much surface area at the rocker ball/rocker interface and stress loads are extremely high.

The anemic Gen V rocker bolts should be replaced in any big block that will be

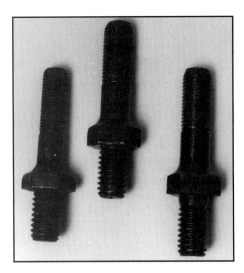

All Mark IV heads include screw-in 7/16" studs. They're adequate for most engines, but when cams with obscene amounts of lift are installed, the amount of valve spring pressure required rises dramatically. High quality replacement studs are often installed to prevent failures.

encouraged to flex its muscles. Although the machining operation is relatively simple, it requires a multi-axis mill or similar machine to assure that the holes are drilled at the proper compound angles. (Big block heads have intake valves angled 26 degrees and exhaust valves angled 17 degrees from the cylinder centerline. The valves are also canted 4 degrees in the opposing plane.)

It isn't necessary to mill the rocker bosses when installing studs in place of

Mini valve spring testers aren't as inherently accurate as professional models, but allow valve spring pressure to be checked in a vise. It's an inexpensive setup that's useful in finding valve springs that have lost tension.

the bolts. The modification entails only drilling the bolt holes with a .375" diameter bit and then cutting threads with a 7/16-14 (coarse) tap.

Spring Seats

Even if you're planning to use a camshaft that will rattle the fenders and the nerves of mothers, fathers and pillars of society, it may not be necessary to machine the spring seats in a big block head. Dual springs with a nominal 1.460" OD will slip onto any big block passenger car head without so much as a whisper of interference. Larger diameter springs are rarely necessary with just about any hydraulic or mechanical lifter cam, and some mild rollers (including those with over .650" lift).

With "take-no-prisoners" race roller cams, which raise the valves more than .675", either 1.550"- or 1.630"- diameter valve springs are usually required for adequate valve control. In such instances, spring seat machining on the ID and OD may be required. (As valve spring diameter increases, typically so does wire diameter. Consequently, ID decreases and OD increases.)

In addition to machining the seat area itself, it's also necessary to reduce the OD of the valve guide to provide adequate spring clearance. Cutters that machine valve guide outside diameter to .530" are readily available.

Also note that some valve springs won't precisely match categorical outside diameter dimensions. As an example, manufacturer specifications for 1.460-in. OD springs can range from 1.437-in. to 1.465-in. The same dimensional variations apply to all diameters of valve springs used on big-block Chevy heads —1.460, 1.550 and 1.630 in. Larger-than-stock diameters are needed to achieve the higher pressures required by high performance hydraulic, mechanical and roller camshafts. For specific valve spring pressure and installation information, see Chapter 6.

Valve Seal Machining

Machining for special valve seals is another routine operation when a head is prepared for use on a high performance engine. Most high performance valve seals clamp on the outside diameter of the valve guide. In a stock-type cylinder head, valve sealing is accomplished through one of, or a combination of, the following: an O-ring that fits over the valve stem, an oil splash shield that fits between the retainer and spring, and an umbrella seal that simply slides over the outside of the valve guide. High performance seals clamp on both the OD of the valve guide and the valve stem. These seals are considerably thicker than stock umbrella seals and consequently won't clear the inner spring of a dual valve spring assembly. It is therefore necessary to machine the OD of the valve guide to .530-in. or .500-in. to accept most high performance seals. Appropriate machining tools and arbors are available from major high performance camshaft manufacturers. Some companies offer combination tools which machine the valve guide OD and spring seat in one operation. Most high performance cylinder head specialists prefer rubber seals with Teflon inserts and specifically do not recommend all-Teflon valve seals. Irrespective of the type of seal used, retainer-to-seal clearance (or retainer-to-guide clearance if stock type seals are used) should be at least .100-in. at maximum valve lift. This amount of clearance is impossible to achieve with some stock late-model heads, when a high performance cam is installed. In such instances, the heads must be removed from the engine and machined as required.

Valve Guides

Of course, it doesn't make much sense to install high performance valve seals and ignore the valve guides. Stock valve guides in cast-iron heads are an integral part of the head casting. In aluminum

The outer diameters of bronze guides installed in aluminum heads are usually knurled to keep them in place. In spite of the fact that bronze guides are press-fit into place, they have been known to fall out, so OD knurling is usually required.

Solid bronze valve guides are found in aluminum cylinder heads and some cast iron heads destined for high performance applications. Bronze is also advantageous in marine applications because it won't rust.

heads, the guides are essentially thick-wall silicon bronze or cast iron guides that are pressed into place.

The latest versions of Chevrolet aluminum heads (such as the 077 castings) include iron valve guides with a knurled OD. Knurling was added because guides with a smooth outer surface developed a penchant for falling out. If you own an engine with Chevy aluminum heads, it's advisable to inspect the heads to determine whether the guide ODs have been knurled. If they haven't, seriously consider replacing the valve guides—before they demand that you do so.

Clearances—Clearance between the valve guide and valve stem is critical to both oil control and durability. Several valve guide preparation options are available. New heads shouldn't require extensive valve guide work, but guide-to-stem clearance should always be checked. Cast-iron heads being groomed for a high performance or race engine are frequently treated to a set of bronze guide liners. Cast-iron liners are also used on occasion. Both types are installed by drilling the stock guide oversized and then pressing the liner of choice into place. Once in position, the liners should be honed, not reamed, for a more consistent finish. Reaming tends to

fracture and distort the material and does not provide a consistent finish. With honing, clearances and concentricity are much more accurately controlled.

Knurling—Stock cast-iron valve guides can also be knurled if valve guide ID is too large, but this is a stock rebuild rather than a high performance technique. It should be avoided because knurling fractures the guide material, which isn't exactly the hot tip for longevity. Knurling essentially cuts a thread on the ID of the guide. Although the deep part of the "thread" is larger than the original ID, the material displaced by the cut "humps" up into a ridge which has a smaller ID. After knurling, the guide must be honed to a finished dimension.

Replacement Liners

Rather than knurling worn guides, replacement liners should be installed. For performance applications, bronze liners are preferred—especially with stainless steel valves. Bronze is more compatible with stainless steel than cast iron. For marine engines or powerplants that run only occasionally, bronze liners also eliminate the possibility of rust and corrosion seizing the valve in the guide.

Bronze Liners—Several methods of bronze liner installation are used by high performance cylinder head specialists.

Solid liners are pressed into place, then either knurled or broached to lock them against the original cast-iron guide. With knurling, the knurled "thread" offers a small reservoir of oil to keep the stem lubricated. On the other hand, knurling bronze fractures the material just as it does with iron, which is a detriment to longevity and makes the ID less consistent. However, acceptable results can be achieved if the liners are knurled strictly to lock them in place, and the ID is honed to the required size.

Many engine builders prefer to use a ball broach to lock solid bronze guide liners into place because heat dissipation is enhanced. A ball broach locks the liner against the guide without fracturing the surface material and cuts the guide to the required ID at the same time. For the best possible finish and consistency, an undersized broach can be used and the liners honed to final size.

Bronze liners are more expensive than iron but offer the option of running much tighter clearances and almost eliminate the possibility of the valve stem sticking in the guide. Typically, intake stem-to-guide clearances with bronze guides (and 3/8-in. valve stems) can be as tight as .0008-in. for drag race applications. Generally though, stem-to-guide clearance is .001-in. for intake and .0015-

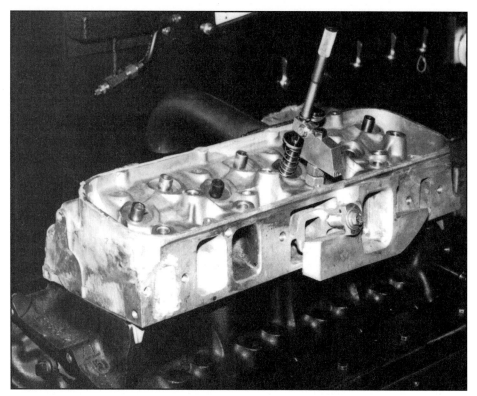

Air flow testing involves measuring air flow through a port at various valve openings. Special fixtures are often used to improve repeatability. Another common practice is to add a radius at the port inlet to minimize turbulence.

in. for exhaust valves. Engines pulling a high amount of manifold vacuum may frequently require tighter than stock clearances to avoid pulling oil through the guide.

Cast-Iron Liners—Cast-iron liners are occasionally recommended for street engines because they're claimed to offer longer life. Iron liners require less effort to install because they generally require no ID machining once they're pressed into place. After an iron liner is cut to length, it need only be relieved at top and bottom (where it's been cut) to ensure that these areas aren't undersized as a result of the cutting operation. However, the quality of cast-iron guides varies tremendously, and if you get the cheap kind, they're only liable to last for 20-30,000 miles. For all high performance engines, it's money well spent to go with premium guides.

Winona Guides—Rather than solid bronze liners, some engine builders prefer Winona-type threaded inserts. With this method, the guide is threaded with a coarse tap or roller and a strand of thin bronze wire is threaded and wedged into place. The ID of the guide is then honed to the desired diameter. In addition to providing a bronze surface for the valve stem, Winona-style inserts allow a small reservoir of oil to be maintained between the bronze threads, providing a bit of lubrication insurance and a path for heat transfer.

Guide Height—Although the size and condition of the valve guide ID is of vital importance, it isn't the only part of the guide that demands attention. You also have to consider valve guide height, especially if you've installed a high performance cam. Specifically, if the valve guide is too tall, it may cause the keeper or retainer to crash against the seal. See Chapter 6 for specific details.

HEAD MILLING

Like any other piece of equipment, cylinder heads are subject to warping as a result of repeated heating and cooling cycles. The thick deck surfaces of older original equipment castings and many aftermarket heads minimize or eliminate warpage, except under extreme operating conditions. However, it is advisable to check the flatness of any used cylinder head.

Warped head surfaces are milled a minimal amount to return them to their original perfectly flat condition. Milling is also occasionally done as a means of improving head gasket sealing; the comparatively rough surface left by the cutter grips the head gasket better than a smooth surface.

Head milling also serves as a means of reducing combustion chamber volume. Many aftermarket heads have extra thick deck surfaces because the manufacturers have anticipated extensive milling (to reduce combustion chamber volume) prior to installation. As an example, Dart aluminum "bolt-on" heads are supplied with 140cc chambers because the deck surface is .200" thicker than on a standard head. This relatively large combustion chamber increases the number of piston options when a supercharged engine is to be built.

By milling the head, the higher compression ratios demanded by naturally aspirated engines can be accommodated. And while the Dart head may appear to have exceptionally large combustion chambers, in reality the opposite is true— for any given deck dimension, the chambers in a Dart head will be 15cc's smaller than those in an equivalent Chevrolet head.

Each .001-in. cut from a cylinder head's deck surface reduces combustion chamber volume a given amount which is determined by the chamber's shape. Obviously, only so much material can be removed before the mill will be cutting into the valve seats. One means of getting around this is *angle milling*. By tilting the head so that more material is removed from the spark plug side of the head, the chamber volume can be reduced significantly more than from standard milling.

Milling the deck surface alters geometry at the head/intake manifold interface, necessitating removal of material from the manifold mating surface. As a general guideline, whenever a head's deck surface is milled, the same amount of material should be cut from its intake manifold surface to re-establish original gasket space and port alignment. Thus if .010 in. is cut from a head's deck, .010 in. should also be cut from the intake port face. It is usually necessary to alter the bottom of the intake manifold as well. When a head is milled, the intake manifold mating surface moves closer to the block. That reduces the clearance between the bottom of the intake manifold and top of the block along the front and rear rails. In fact, if a head is milled excessively, the front and rear rails may keep the manifold so high that the intake gaskets won't be thick enough to seal.

Manifold gasket thickness compatibility problems can be avoided by cutting approximately 50% more from the bottom of the manifold than has been cut from the head. Thus if a head is milled .010 in., the bottom of the intake manifold should be cut .015 in. In many cases, it's best to trial-fit the intake manifold before making any cuts. If a block has been decked, its manifold rails may have also been cut so machining the manifold's rails may lead to severe gaps. Heads that have been angle milled require machining of the intake face at a complimentary angle to make sure the manifold and head mating surfaces are parallel.

The easiest way to seal the manifold/block end rail interface is to follow the procedure used by most race engine builders who do not use manifold end rail gaskets—they opt for silicone sealer (RTV, which stands for Room Temperature Vulcanizing) instead. Standard end rail gaskets may keep the intake manifold from seating firmly against the heads, especially if block-to-manifold end rail clearance isn't sufficient. Silicone is much more conformable and will seal any reasonably sized gap without interfering with manifold/head seal.

VALVES

High performance engines deserve high performance valves. Although Chevrolet offers several swirl-polished valves, aftermarket suppliers such as Sealed Power/Speed-Pro, TRW, Rev, Ferrea and Manley offer equivalent or superior valves that can usually be purchased at lower cost. Aftermarket valves are used by virtually all high performance and racing cylinder head specialists because of their lower price and wider selection.

Manley Performance Products of Lakewood, NJ, Rev Inc., of Ft. Lauderdale, FL, Ferrea Racing Components of Fort Lauderdale, FL, and Flaming River Industries of Cleveland, OH, offer a very wide selection of high performance and racing valves for big blocks; be sure to leaf through their respective catalogs before making a selection. In addition to standard size valves with 3/8" stems, these companies also offer larger valves with longer-than-stock stems. Undercut stems for increased flow and valves with 11/32-in. and 5/16-in. stems are also available.

Note that nearly all factory replacement type valves have a .001-in. taper from one end of the valve stem to the other. The taper doesn't mean the valves are poorly machined; the stem diameters are smaller near the head to accommodate heat induced expansion which would otherwise cause galling.

The standard big block valve has a 3/8-in. (.375 in.) diameter stem which couples up with a 5.220-in. (intake) and 5.350-in. (exhaust) nominal overall length. Reducing stem diameter to 11/32 in. (.34375-in.) may not seem like much of a change, but it's enough to knock off a few grams of weight, and also bring

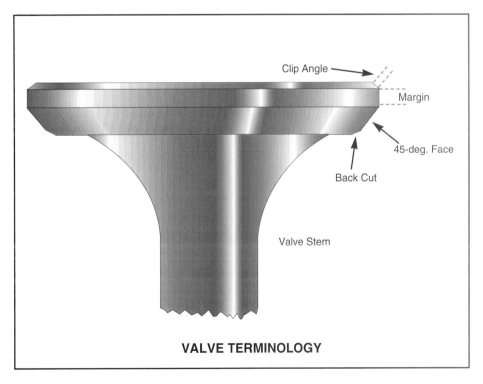

VALVE TERMINOLOGY

Valves vary considerably depending upon supplier and application. Some valves are supplied with a back cut and a clip angle or top cut may not be included. Generally, a margin of .050" to .080" is desirable. Except in unusual circumstances, if a valve has a margin of less than .030", it should be discarded.

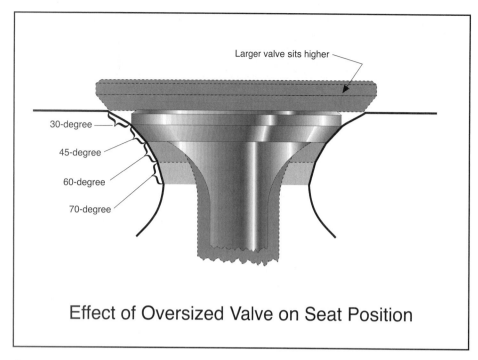

Larger valve sits higher

30-degree
45-degree
60-degree
70-degree

Effect of Oversized Valve on Seat Position

One reason that an oversized valve increases air flow (in addition to its larger diameter) is that it "unsinks" the seating position—with the valve sitting higher (in the combustion chamber), the distance from the seat to the short turn radius is increased, and that improves flow.

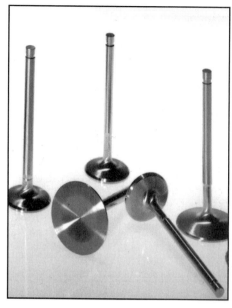

Manufacturers like Manley offer valves with undercut stems. The bulk of the stem has an 11/32" diameter, but the section adjacent to the head is reduced to a 5/16" diameter. Flow increases of up to 10% are possible with this design.

Most engine builders advise grinding valves before they're installed. Due to generous production line tolerances, many brand new valves are imperfect in both finish and concentricity. Both valves and seats should be ground to precise dimensions.

about a measurable increase in airflow—especially at lower valve lifts. Several companies also offer valves with 5/16-in. stems, but before any valve with an undersized stem can be installed in a set of heads, the valve guides have to be

modified so the stems don't rattle around like a coconut in a boxcar. That obviously adds quite a bit of expense to cylinder head preparation and that's difficult to justify in many cases. However, there is a way to take advantage of increased

airflow potential without breaking the bank.

A number of years ago, Manley introduced a series of high performance stainless steel valves with the stem undercut adjacent to the valve head. That portion of the stem that fits into the valve guide has a standard 3/8-in. diameter, but the portion of the stem that extends into the port measures only 11/32-in. If your valves need to be replaced, or if you're assembling a new set of heads and have to purchase valves, installing a set of valves with undercut stems will bring you some extra horsepower at no extra cost.

Titanium is the material of choice for valves used in "damn the expense, let the sponsor pay for it" classes of racing. Owing to their light weight and high strength, titanium valves allow for more radical cam profiles and higher power potential. However, at seven to eight times the cost of a top quality stainless steel valve, the expense can't be justified in anything less than a professional class of competition.

The difference between a swirl polished (left) and stock valve (right) is evident here. The polished valve has less of a lip and smoother head/stem transition area which contributes to increased air flow.

HEAD GASKETS

To ensure proper sealing with any cylinder head, you need high quality gaskets such as this one from Fel-Pro. The company offers several big block head gaskets including a few models designed for big bore engines.

It wasn't too many years ago that head gaskets were viewed as safety valves; they would burn or blow out before abnormally high pressures could cause any internal damage. But like every other component found in a big-block Chevy, head gaskets have enjoyed the benefits of technology. Current gaskets are so good that the pistons or valves may well be damaged before the head gaskets let go.

Composition Gaskets

One of the reasons that head gasket sealing has improved so dramatically over the years is the improvement made in composition gaskets. The stock steel-shim head gasket, with raised beads around the cylinders and water holes, is adequate for a stock engine, but it is marginal in many performance applications. Chevrolet lists a steel shim "LS-6" head gasket (part number 14015351) with a compressed thickness of .022 in. and a composition "LS-7" gasket (part no. 3969865) with a compressed thickness of .039-in. These gaskets are designed for use on 4.250-in. bore blocks; the steel shim gasket is intended for cast-iron heads, while the composition gaskets can be used with either iron or aluminum heads. For optimum sealing, the steel shim gasket should be coated with a sealer or aluminum paint; the composition gasket

should be installed with no sealer. Also available is a composition gasket (part no. 3976081) for blocks with 4.440-in. cylinders

When selecting head gaskets, match them to the bore size of your engine—and cylinder head material. As an example, Fel-Pro offers a wide variety of race quality composition head gaskets and lists part number 1017-1 for all big blocks with cast iron heads and a bore diameter of 4.340-in. or less. Fel-Pro part number 1027 is designed for use with aluminum heads; it contains a pre-flattened copper wire ring around each cylinder. The copper is relatively soft and prevents the gaskets from "brinelling" or indenting the heads. Gaskets designed for use with iron heads incorporate steel wires around the cylinders. However, the pre-flattened steel wire now used in all Fel-Pro performance head gaskets has eliminated brinelling problems. Note that the 1027 gasket has a bore of only 4.370-in. so it cannot be used with large bore engines.

Big blocks with monster bores should be equipped with appropriate head gaskets such as Fel-Pro's part number 1057 which has a 4.630-in. gasket bore, or part number 1093 which has a 4.620-in. gasket bore. The latter gasket is designed for 500-cu. in. Pro Stock

engines and features round gasket bores with no valve pockets. Special gaskets are also available for Pontiac and Oldsmobile derivatives of the big block Chevy engine.

Fel-Pro also offers two head gaskets with a stainless core for salt water marine use; part number 1037 (also available as marine part number 17046) has a 4.370" gasket bore and part number 1047 (also available as marine part no. 17048) has a 4.540-in. gasket bore. Both gaskets contain pre-flattened steel wire rings around the bores and both may be used with either Mark IV truck or Bow Tie blocks and Mark IV heads, or with Gen V blocks and heads. Fel-Pro specifically recommends that they not be used to adapt Mark IV heads to Gen V blocks.

Gasket Thickness

Head gasket thickness is often overlooked, but it is an important part of any engine build up. Keep in mind that a minimum of .035 in. piston-to-head clearance should be maintained if an engine is equipped with steel connecting rods. This dimension should be increased if aluminum rods are used. Since a "zero deck" condition (that is, no deck clearance—the top of the piston deck flush with the top of the block when the piston is at Top Dead Center) is desired for maximum power and reduced octane sensitivity, a gasket of appropriate thickness must be installed. Some amount of deck clearance must obviously be built into engines equipped with steel shim head gaskets. On the other hand, maximum power can't be achieved if a deck clearance of .020-.030 in. or more is combined with a composition head gasket.

Mark IV Meets Gen V

One look at the deck surfaces of Mark IV and Gen V production blocks is all that's required to determine that something more than a standard head gasket is needed if Mark IV heads are to be installed on a Gen V block (or vice versa). The incompatibility between Gen V and Mark IV blocks and heads results from changes in size, shape and location of the cored holes in the deck surfaces.

In some cases, mixing Mark IV and Gen V heads and blocks can be accomplished with no problems. Production tolerances being what they are, the cored holes in the heads and block can line up so that nothing more than a standard head gasket is required to achieve a proper seal. However, if alignment isn't right, a coolant leak will result. Adapter bushings which fit in the head gasket holes are available from Apple Chevrolet in York, PA, but many engineers and engine builders are of the opinion that if the bushings are required, that particular head/block combination should be scrapped. Jerry Rosenquist, Fel-Pro's performance gasket engineering manager, has researched the subject thoroughly and feels that the potential for problems is extremely high. He states, "With some special adapters, you can bolt Mark IV heads on a Gen V production block and the engine will usually run and not leak. But for how long? There are just too many areas where there just isn't enough sealing area between the block, gasket and head. What you've got is a leak just waiting to happen."

Gen V Bow Tie—When dealing with Gen V Bow Tie blocks, life is a bit easier. Whereas the Bow Tie Gen V block has round waterjacket coring holes in its deck surface, the production block has irregularly shaped ones. The round cored holes in Gen V blocks line up relatively well with the holes in Mark IV heads, so a marriage of the two isn't terribly difficult to arrange. However, if you do plan to install Mark IV heads on a Gen V Bow Tie block, check the alignment of the holes in the head, block and gasket. Also make sure there's enough gasket material at the inner and outer edges (beneath the intake and exhaust ports) to achieve a proper seal.

Gen V blocks have a relatively large cored hole in each deck surface, near the front dowel tubes. These holes are included to allow gasses to escape when the block is cast. Gen V head gaskets block these holes purposely to force coolant towards the rear of the block.

Mark IV gaskets have a large hole in the same location as the cored holes in the Gen V Bow Tie block. Consequently, if the two are combined, coolant will be short circuited across the front of the engine, causing overheating toward the rear. So anytime Mark IV gaskets are installed on a Gen V Bow Tie block, a plug should be installed in each of the cored holes.

Clamp Load

While temperature certainly plays a role in gasket life, the most influential factor is the clamp load exerted by the head bolts or studs. According to the engineers at Fel-Pro, the key to sufficient clamp load is to have adequately stretched bolts or studs. This can't be achieved if thread friction is too high, because when the desired torque reading is reached, the bolts or studs won't be adequately stretched. Also note that clamp load can decrease significantly if an engine is overheated or subjected to detonation.

When assembling a cylinder head, valve spring installed height must be accurately established according to camshaft requirements. "Hite Mikes" are specially designed for this purpose and are relatively inexpensive.

Abrasive flow machining is a process that has recently been applied to cylinder heads. However, it's not anything like porting. The putty that's forced through the ports leaves a smooth finish as shown here, but without special tooling, it does not dramatically change the port contour. For maximum air flow, a grinder or CNC machining is required.

Some form of lubricant, usually racing oil, anti-seize or a non-hardening sealer is required to assure the proper amount of

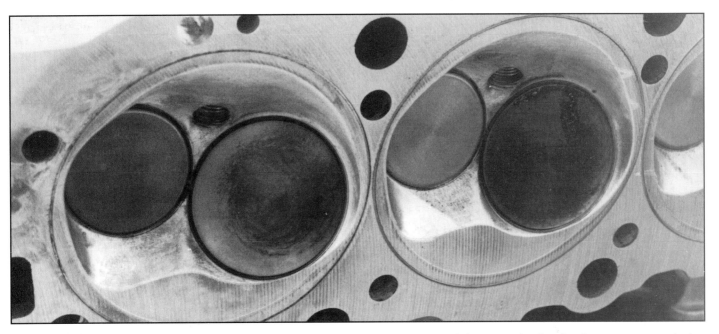

For super high output engines, such as those that are supercharged or fed a healthy dose of nitrous, combustion chamber pressures may be too much for conventional head gaskets to contain. Heads for this type of engines are cut for O-rings and filled with wire. This wire then embeds in the head gasket, providing an almost bulletproof seal.

stretch. Sealer must be used on all the bolts that enter the waterjackets. Note that none of the head bolt holes in Gen V Bow Tie blocks penetrate the waterjacket. Consequently, no sealant is required on the head bolts. Irrespective of cylinder block type, a worthwhile addition is a hardened washer under the head of each head bolt or nut, to prevent galling and reduce friction.

O-Ringing

As cylinder pressures increase, so does the load on the head gaskets. Although current composition gaskets have been used successfully in virtually every type of racing engine imaginable, the pressures encountered in some supercharged, turbocharged or nitrous assisted powerplants may require that the block be machined to accept O-rings around each cylinder.

The most commonly used system employs stainless steel O-rings and a solid copper gasket. While this does an excellent job of sealing the cylinders, coolant leakage is a common problem. About the only way to prevent coolant leakage with copper head gaskets is to apply a small bead of silicone around each coolant hole in the block and head.

An alternative solution is to O-ring the block as shown in the accompanying diagram and use a composition gasket installed upside down (standard composition gaskets can't be used on blocks with a separate O-ring groove around each cylinder). O-ring grooves should be cut so that the .041-in. stainless steel wire sticks up .010- in. above the block deck surface.

TORQUING HEAD BOLTS

When tightening the head bolts, follow the proper sequence and pull smoothly on the torque wrench—you want to sneak up on each setting because a sudden or jerky motion will give false torque wrench readings. Following are some tips for torquing head bolts from Jerry Rosenquist of Fel-Pro:

• Necked-down short bolts and studs are a good idea. Bolts with a full shank stretch only .002 to .005 in. If the gasket and/or casting relax .002 in., over 50% of the clamp load is lost. The necked-down bolts can increase stretch 100% over full shank bolts. "Short" bolts refers to the four 7/16-14 by 2.1-in. long bolts used in the outer row of holes on each head; 12 "long" bolts, with a 7/16-14 thread and a length of 4-in., are also used to hold each cylinder head in place. (These bolt lengths are applicable only to production-type cylinder heads. Bow Tie heads and some aftermarket castings with raised exhaust ports require the use of 5-1/4" long bolts in the five holes adjacent to the ports. Obviously, when studs are used in place of bolts, longer studs must also be installed in these locations.)

• With new bolts or studs, the clamp load won't be at its best; it takes two or three tightenings for the threads to burnish in.

• Bolts can be reused several times as long as they don't feel spongy when they're tightened. Discard washers when they become cupped or scored.

• It's difficult or impossible to get a proper seal if the head castings are too thin in the deck area. Weak castings bend, causing the bolts to lose clamp load. ■

6

CAMSHAFTS

ike all overhead valve engines, the big-block Chevy uses a camshaft to open and close its valves. If that's news to you, you're reading the wrong book. But if you don't have much experience with big blocks, it may be "news" that they have a reputation for chewing up new camshafts. Even with proper break-in procedures, experienced professional engine builders have camshaft failures. The block's oiling system and the angle at which the lifters are situated are the primary causes, and roller lifters appear to be the only foolproof solution.

Another caveat regarding big-block camshafts is that 1965 and 1966 engines require a cam with a .1875-in. wide, .109375-in. deep (3/16-in. wide, 7/64-in. deep) groove in the center of the rear cam journal to assure proper engine oiling. Installing a cam without a grooved journal in a '65 or '66 block is an invitation to engine failure because the groove is required to assure proper engine lubrication. In 1967, the oiling system design was changed, so a grooved rear camshaft journal is not required. Although rumors to the contrary have been around for years, use of an early-type camshaft in a 1967 and later block should not cause any problems. In fact, Chevrolet camshaft number 3883986 (originally an LS-5 camshaft) is offered for big blocks of all years and has a grooved rear journal.

A GMC blower, 526 cubic inches and 25 years of experience helped put Jim Oddy's Corvette in the Pro Mod record books. But even with enough boost to blow the crank out of the bottom of the block, it still takes the right cam to produce usable power.

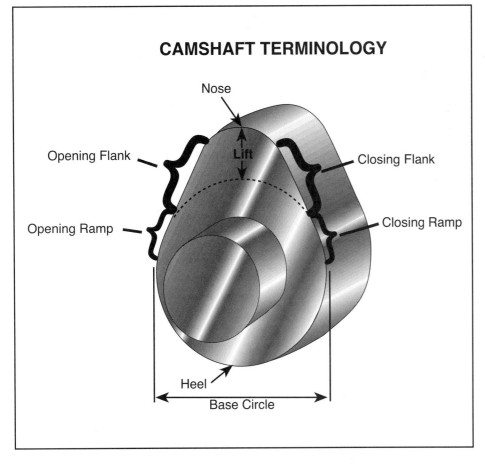

CAMSHAFT TERMINOLOGY

Nose

Lift

Opening Flank

Closing Flank

Opening Ramp

Closing Ramp

Heel

Base Circle

Now that your confidence is shaken, you can contemplate cam specifications. Big-block Chevys like to breathe, and a healthy camshaft is essential to accomplishing that goal. That doesn't imply that 320 degrees of duration and .700-in. lift are required in all cases, but most big blocks will respond favorably to slightly more aggressive valve timing than is used with some other types of engines.

Choosing a camshaft for a specific application requires a thorough understanding of camshaft basics. As luck would have it, the next few paragraphs are devoted to just that.

The valvetrain in an overhead valve engine like the big-block Chevy is a knee bone connected to the shin bone affair, so the lifters (also called followers or tappets), move the pushrods, which move the rockers which move the valves. By opening and closing the valves, the camshaft controls the timing of the flow of intake mixture and the exhausting of

burnt gases into and out of the cylinders. In terms of a functional definition, the previous paragraph is adequate. But it goes beyond mere definitions; camshaft technology has progressed to the point that a thorough knowledge of lobe terminology is helpful in selecting the correct camshaft for optimum performance.

CAMSHAFT TERMINOLOGY

As with any rotating shaft, a camshaft must be supported by a number of bearings spaced over its length. The portion of the camshaft that contacts each bearing is called a journal and is obviously round. Camshafts for big-block Chevy and other V8 engines have five journals. Although each cam lobe is egg-shaped, a portion of it, called the base circle, is concentric with the journal. In effect, the base circle, also called the heel, is that portion of the lobe where no lift is

generated. Directly opposite the base circle is the nose or toe of the lobe. The sections leading up to and away from the nose are called the opening and closing flanks, or ramps, respectively.

Lift

Maximum lift, which is the height to which a cam follower or lifter is ultimately raised off the base circle, results when the lobe is rotated so that the tip of the nose is directly beneath the lifter. Ideally, the transition from no lift to maximum lift would be instantaneous, but the laws of physics make such motion impossible to achieve. Therefore, the areas of the lobe between the nose and base circle must be engineered to raise the lifter quickly, but at a very smooth, specified rate. The precision with which the transition is made is often overlooked, but it plays a major role in determining camshaft performance—which is one of the reasons that two cams with "identical" specifications can offer significantly different operational characteristics.

Ramps

Coming off the base circle, the first segment of the lobe that contacts the lifter is the opening clearance ramp. While many people associate ramps with mechanical lifter cams, they are also essential to hydraulic lifters. Ramps were originally put on cam lobes for one purpose only—to make the valves quiet at the operating lash specified. Typically, early engines had .010-in. lash and the ramps were put on to take that .010-in. slack out gradually so that when a valve started to move off its seat and come back on to it, it did not make any appreciable noise. In fact, they were called "quieting ramps" and they were patented back in the Twenties.

Theoretically, a hydraulic cam runs at zero lash all the time. So why do you need a ramp? You have to look at a hydraulic lifter and see how it functions. The only reason that a hydraulic lifter

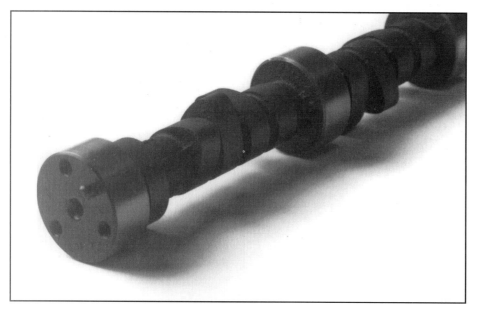

To either the naked or partially clothed eye, any cam designed for standard (non-roller) hydraulic or mechanical tappets looks pretty much the same. The black finish on the lobes is parkerizing. Most hydraulic and mechanical tappet cams are machined from cast-iron billets.

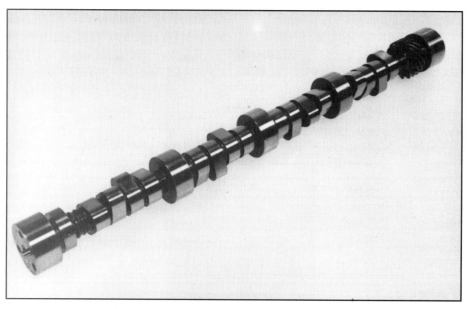

Roller tappet cams are characterized by shiny lobes which have a relatively broad nose. Roller cams are machined from 8620 steel billet cores.

works is because as you lift the valve, spring pressure increases and causes the hydraulic tappet to get shorter. It actually collapses a small amount by pushing the plunger deeper into the lifter body. Therefore you must have opening and closing ramps to allow for this loss of length during the opening and closing cycle. Very few high performance cam manufacturers have thought about that carefully and many are not putting the correct closing ramp on their cams.

Typically, the ramp area of the lobe brings the lifter off the base circle by raising it at relatively low velocity, so that shock loads are kept to a minimum. Once the tappet is riding on the flank, it is lifted at continuously increasing velocity until it has traveled approximately half the distance to the nose. At that point, lift velocity begins to decrease in preparation for reaching the maximum lift point where velocity is zero. As the lifter rides over the nose, it reaches the closing side

of the lobe where it is lowered back down towards the base circle. While descending on the closing flank, velocity increases until it becomes necessary to slow things down in preparation for transition to the low velocity of the closing ramp. This is the part of the lobe that sets the valve back on its seat so it must be properly designed both for quiet operation and long valve life.

On either side of the maximum lift point, which occurs in the center of the lobe, the tappet is moved at relatively high velocities. But at the opening and closing ramps, lifter velocity is slowed so that the transition onto and off of the base circle is smooth and gentle. So even with no clearance to take up, hydraulic lifter cams require opening and closing ramps to effect a smooth transition from the base circle to the flank and back again.

Duration

While lift at the cam and at the valve (valve lift equals cam lift multiplied by rocker arm ratio) are straightforward, duration is not. To be meaningful, duration must be referenced to a given amount of lift. Obviously, the lower the lift point at which duration is rated, the greater that duration will be.

According to the Society of Automotive Engineers (SAE), duration of hydraulic lifter cams should be rated by establishing the timing point baseline at .004-in. cam lift, assuming a 1.5:1 rocker arm ratio. However, it is common practice for cam grinders to juggle numbers for any number of reasons, so while some cams have advertised durations computed at .004-in. cam lift, others are referenced to a different cam lift figure, like .006 in.

Duration-at-Fifty—Because of the various rating data points, it is often difficult to compare two different cams. However, the industry standard for evaluating camshaft performance potential is the duration-at-.050-in. cam lift. Duration-at-.050-in. lift, also called net duration, is simply the number of degrees during which a lifter is raised .050 in. or more off the base circle. This figure was chosen because it usually requires this amount of lift to open the valve sufficiently to initiate a significant amount of airflow. It's also true that at .050-in. lift, the tappet is well off the ramps so duration at this reference point pertains to the lobe itself and is not influenced by ramp design. Many lobes with widely varying advertised durations look almost identical when profiled at .050-in. lift.

But duration at .050-in. lift doesn't tell the whole story. Advertised duration provides a key as to the idle quality that will be delivered by a particular camshaft. However, before cam comparisons can be made, you must know the lift at which the advertised duration is computed. To get an accurate comparison, the advertised durations must be computed at the same lift. Some hydraulic cam durations may be computed at a lift other than the SAE .004-in. lift standard. This can make cam comparisons downright confusing. However, when duration-at-.050-in. lift, lobe separation and intensity are used in the assessment of a cam's performance potential, you can be fairly sure of making the right selection.

Valve Lash—Whatever is said about hydraulic lifter cams also holds true for mechanical lifter versions—except valve lash must be considered and that alters the lift at which advertised duration is computed. According to SAE specifications, the timing point baseline for a mechanical lifter cam is .006 in. plus the specified valve lash. Therefore, if the manufacturer specifies a lash of .030 in., advertised duration is computed at a valve lift of .036 in. which computes to a cam lift of .021 in. assuming a 1.7:1 rocker arm ratio. This computation method does little besides make a confusing situation even more confusing. Valve lash figures chosen by original equipment manufacturers are largely

When you install a new cam, you also have to install new lifters, so it makes sense to purchase a cam and lifter kit because it will be cheaper than purchasing the individual components separately. Some companies also offer kits with springs, retainers, locks and valve seals.

arbitrary numbers that are easy for the mechanic to use when the engine is in the shop. It's almost always a number that applies when the engine is cold. But lash changes when things get hot so there's no point in relating timing points to lash. Most high performance cam manufacturers compute the advertised duration of mechanical lifter camshafts at .020-in. cam lift.

Although lash is necessary with mechanical lifters, it's also a liability—lash reduces valve lift. A cam with .650-in. valve lift specification actually raises the valve only .620-in if lash is set at .030 in. It's for precisely this reason that many mechanical lifter cams (intended for both flat and roller tappets) are now of the tight lash (.012-in to .020-in) persuasion.

Lobe Separation

Another term that is useful in describing a camshaft's performance characteristics is lobe separation (also

It doesn't take long for a camshaft to develop a normal wear pattern like this. Due to the crowned shape of the lifter bottom, most of the contact area is offset to one side. This offset causes the lifter to spin as the cam rotates, resulting in the pattern shown.

called lobe centerline). Lobe separation is the displacement angle between the center (maximum lift point) of the intake lobe and the center of the exhaust lobe. Typically, lobe separation runs between 102 and 114 camshaft (not crankshaft) degrees and is established through design and manufacturing—it cannot be changed.

Intake Centerline—Now for the confusion factor. Intake centerline, which is often referred to simply as "centerline," pertains to the position at which the cam is installed in the engine with respect to the crankshaft. This figure relates to the angle (in crankshaft degrees) at which maximum intake lift occurs relative to Top Dead Center. An intake centerline of 108 deg. means that the intake valve reaches maximum lift at 108 deg. after Top Dead Center. As Murphy's Law would have it, intake centerline will frequently be between 102 and 110 deg., so it and lobe separation are often confused simply because the numbers are in the same ballpark.

But there is a reason to all this rhyme. Lobe centerline is not adjustable by the engine builder; it is ground into the camshaft. Seeking to eliminate some of the terminology confusion, some people refer to intake centerline as the intake maximum lift point (expressed in crankshaft degrees after Top Dead Center). Its counterpart is exhaust maximum lift (expressed in crankshaft degrees before Top Dead Center) and both figures are frequently noted on camshaft specification cards.

Varying Degrees—For many years, virtually every high performance camshaft, whether intended for street use, drag racing, circle track racing or any other form of automotive competition, was ground with 108 deg. of lobe separation. Then, someone figured out that if the lobe separation was changed to 106 deg., an engine made more mid-range torque (at a slightly higher rpm).

In the real world, tighter lobe

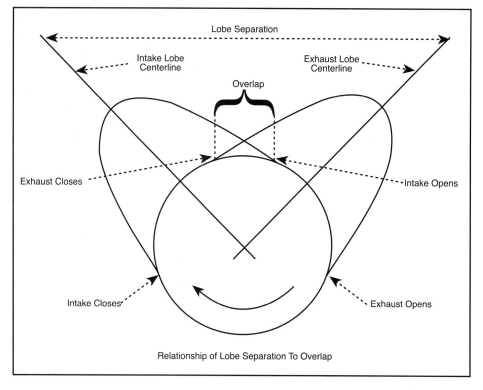

Lobe separation, also called lobe centerline, refers to the number of degrees separating the centerline of the intake lobe from the centerline of the exhaust lobe. As lobe separation is increased (spread further apart), overlap is decreased and vice versa.

separation closes the intake valve earlier, resulting in higher cylinder pressure which in turn produces more torque. So although lobe separation receives the credit for either increasing or decreasing torque, it is actually the intake closing point that is the controlling factor. The same effect can be achieved by altering cam phasing; advancing closes the intake valve sooner, resulting in more torque, while retarding a cam has the opposite effect.

Street Cams—Most high performance street cams are ground with a lobe separation of 108 to 114 deg. Opinions vary as to what constitutes the ideal amount of lobe separation, particularly for high performance street engines. Wider lobe separation—112 to 114 deg.—allows for a smoother idle and higher idle manifold vacuum, but it also reduces mid-range torque, while increasing top-end horsepower. Closer lobe separation—106 to 110 deg.—has the opposite effect.

Although the degree of change varies

according to the specific camshaft and the engine in which it's installed, if two cams are identical except for lobe separation, the cam with less separation will almost always produce a rougher idle, but more mid-range torque. That being the case, most street cams are ground with at least 110 deg. of lobe separation to minimize problems with idle quality.

Marine Camshafts—Marine engines are somewhat unique, but much of what applies to land-based big blocks should be considered when a Mark IV or Gen V engine is to be installed in a boat. Although boats don't operate in stop-and-go traffic, a clean idle is still important if docking isn't going to be a bump and grind affair. In general, for engines installed in pleasure and recreational ski boats, duration-at-.050" lift should be limited to about 234 deg. with hydraulic cams and about 245 deg. with cams designed for mechanical tappets. A lobe separation of 110-112 deg. is also suitable.

Those specifications should provide

Whether it's a race or recreational boat, it will fly with big block power–as long as the right cam is installed. Boats operate under different conditions than cars, so it takes a slightly different cam profile for optimum performance.

acceptable low-speed performance and strong mid-range torque. Most recreational boat engines rarely rev above 6000 rpm, so it doesn't make much sense to choose a cam designed for a 7500 rpm power peak.

Drag Racing—Drag race cars obviously have their own unique requirements, which translates into specific lobe separation specifications. Depending upon vehicle weight, engine size and transmission type, lobe separation typically ranges from 104 to 118 deg. Generally, drag cars with automatic transmissions respond best to camshafts with 104 to 108 deg. Powerglide transmissions, with only two gears (Low and Drive), rely heavily on the torque converter for torque multiplication. Powerglide-equipped engines therefore operate over a relatively narrow and low rpm band. In essence, during acceleration in Low gear, the engine remains at a constant rpm while the rest of the driveline tries to catch up.

Shortly after the torque converter's input and output speeds equalize (that is when converter lock-up speed is reached) the transmission is shifted into Drive and the output stage of the torque converter plays "catch-up" again. Consequently, an engine linked to a Powerglide will typically run a cam with tighter lobe centers than a powerplant connected to a three- or four-speed automatic, where dependency on the torque converter is much less. Similarly, when a clutch and a four- or five-speed manual transmission (or clutch-assisted automatic) is employed, lobe separation is wider yet, as the engine's operating speed range tends to be higher. Most Pro Stock engines run cams with a lobe separation of 114 deg. or more, which is the reason they idle surprisingly well, even though duration-at-.050-in. lift may approach 300 deg.

Oval Track—As might be expected, builders of oval track engines also have specific lobe separation preferences. Most engine builders prefer 106 deg. for

engines installed in cars that will only turn left. For this application, torque coming off a corner is the most important consideration and 106-deg. lobe separation appears to put the torque peak at the proper rpm for this type of racing. However, it's interesting to note that virtually all oval track engine builders install cams with the intake maximum lift point at 102 deg. Some cam designers feel that it would be more advantageous to use 108- or 110- deg. lobe separation for a broader torque curve—and advance the cam to build more mid-range torque. Engine builders seem reluctant to alter their thinking, so either no one knows the validity of the wider lobe separation theory, or no one is talking.

Intensity

Camshaft lobe intensity is computed by subtracting net duration (computed at .050-in. lift) from gross or advertised duration, which is computed at .004-in. lift in the case of a hydraulic and

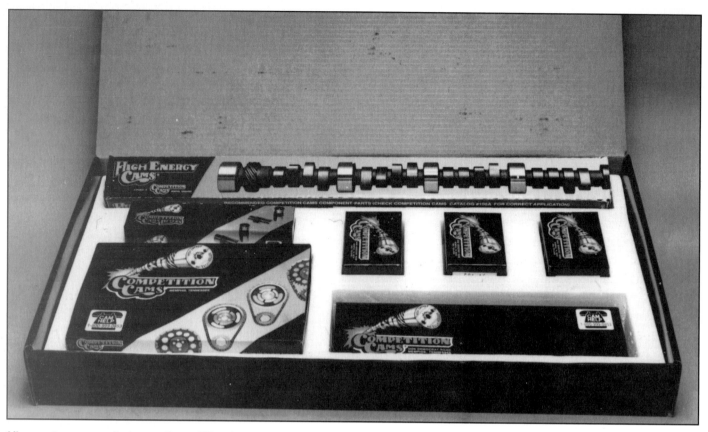

Like most cam manufacturers, Competition Cams offers several types of cam kits. The most extensive kits include cam, lifters, springs, retainers, locks, valve seals, timing chain and sprocket set and most importantly– instructions.

Used camshafts are to be found at most swap meets, and that's where they should remain. It's virtually impossible to detect some types of lobe damage, so the low price of a used cam can wind up being very expensive--when the cam, lifters and who knows what else needs to be replaced.

hydraulic roller cams, and a .020-in. lift for mechanical flat-tappet and roller cams. A hydraulic cam with a gross 284 deg. and a net duration of 228 deg. has a hydraulic intensity of 56 deg. When it comes to performance, less is unquestionably more—and for very logical reasons.

The ideal cam profile would raise the valves to full lift instantly, hold them open for a specified duration and then close them instantly. The laws of physics make it impossible to achieve instantaneous valve opening and closing, but recent advancements in design technology have made it possible to open and close the valves at higher maximum velocities. By so doing, engine efficiency is improved, because the valves spend less time at very low lift where they bleed off cylinder pressure, but do not permit any appreciable air flow.

In practical terms, if two cams with similar lobe designs have the same net duration, same lobe separation and same

lift, maximum torque and horsepower will be almost identical. But the cam with the smaller intensity figure will have a smoother idle, better off-idle response, superior low-speed driveability and a broader power curve. Viewed from another perspective, a lower lobe intensity number translates to more low-end power without any loss of top-end power. It also means that with a highly modified engine, it may be practical to install a cam with longer duration-at-.050-in. lift than might otherwise be possible. This is possible because problems with poor idle quality and compatibility with torque converter stall speed are minimized. State-of-the-art lobe designs therefore deliver "more cam" per dollar because they produce more power over a wider rpm band.

Overlap

Overlap is another commonly used camshaft term. It describes the period of time when a cylinder's intake and exhaust valves are both open. Valve overlap occurs as a piston approaches and leaves Top Dead Center, extending from the exhaust stroke of one cycle to the intake stroke of the next.

Although the term overlap is still used, it has been largely replaced by lobe separation as a means of evaluating a camshaft's performance characteristics, and for good reason; lobe separation can remain constant when duration is altered, overlap typically does not. So comparing the overlap of Cam "A" to that of Cam "B" may or may not indicate a significant change in performance potential, depending upon the difference in durations.

Another consideration is that from the design standpoint, lobe separation is a cause, overlap is an effect. When a cam designer wishes to fine tune the power curve produced by a cam, he will frequently alter lobe separation while leaving lift and duration unchanged. In some cases, two cams will have identical specifications except for lobe separation, which has been altered to shift the torque curve to better accommodate specific applications. Overlap understandably changes when lobe separation is altered, but aside from being an outdated reference specification, overlap has little meaning in defining a camshaft's performance potential. Therefore, you shouldn't use it as a basis for cam selection.

CAMSHAFT SELECTION

Swapping a stock cast-iron intake manifold for an aluminum high-rise model and scrapping the stock carburetor in favor of a performance-oriented four-barrel will perk up any engine. Installing a set of headers isn't a bad idea either. Of course, a tune-up never hurts. But without question, the best means of significantly increasing the performance of a stock engine is to replace the original camshaft with a high performance profile cam.

With a race engine, a cam swap won't usually provide the dramatic power gains realized with stock powerplants (unless the original selection was way off the mark—a common occurrence), but the right camshaft will make a significant power difference.

But where this power is gained is an area few people take the time to think through. It is a characteristic of older cam design technology that whenever a camshaft is responsible for a dramatic horsepower increase, the engine speed at which maximum torque occurs is pushed quite a distance up the rpm scale. In some instances, installation of a high performance cam can even result in a decrease in peak torque. But with horsepower being a function of torque and rpm, simply shifting the torque band to a higher engine speed will result in greater maximum horsepower—often at the expense of mid-range torque. While high horsepower numbers are impressive, trading off torque for a few extra horsepower is not a wise decision unless an engine is operated only within a narrow rpm band at the top of the scale, such as with a manually shifted drag race car. The best results, both on and off the track, seem to be achieved by engines with a broad, flat torque curve.

And that's just the type of torque curve state-of-the-art camshafts are designed to produce. Working with the latest engineering techniques, top cam designers have been able to develop street cams that boost horsepower considerably without moving an engine's torque peak above its stock rpm level—and race cams that greatly extend an engine's usable power range. Consequently, the road to higher horsepower no longer means that a detour must be made around mid-range torque.

The key to raising horsepower, without bringing low-speed and mid-range torque to its knees, lies in selecting the "right" high performance cam. That means more than playing the numbers game—it

Although properly torqued cam bolts rarely back out, it's best to "buy" a bit of insurance. Before installing the cam bolts for the final time, coat the threads with Loctite.

Roller lifters don't preload the camshaft towards the rear of the block, so roller cams have a tendency to "walk" forward. Cam buttons, which fit between the front of the cam and the timing cover, are used to ensure that camshafts don't take an unauthorized stroll. Although not usually necessary with a flat-tappet cam, cam buttons are occasionally used as insurance.

If you've always wondered why you shouldn't put used lifters on a new camshaft, or should use assembly lube and follow all the other standard installation recommendations, take a look at the lobes in this photo. Notice that the base circle area is still black (showing minimal contact with the lifter) while the flank and nose are excessively worn. By the way, in case you haven't guessed, this isn't a Chevrolet cam.

This camshaft started life like most others, with properly shaped lobes. However, lack of adequate lubrication during initial start-up and run in wiped the lobes. So to avoid premature lobe failure, eat your spinach, use assembly lube and prelube the engine before initial start-up.

Horsepower vs. Torque

Engine dynamometers measure torque. Horsepower, on the other hand, is computed based on an engine's torque output at a specific rpm. A look at typical torque and horsepower curves demonstrates that even though torque may be falling within a particular rpm band, horsepower can be increasing (as rpm is raised) because of the influence of engine speed in the equation (HP=torque x rpm/5252). As an engine's torque peak moves up the rpm scale, peak horsepower increases, even if the maximum torque reading remains the same, or even drops somewhat.

Most people think a high performance camshaft improves engine performance because it increases horsepower. Actually, such a cam raises the rpm level at which maximum torque is produced and broadens the torque curve. It may also deliver a slight increase in torque, but even if it causes the opposite, horsepower will increase because of the

means matching the cam to the speed range in which an engine operates. Many people mistakenly believe bigger is better; however it is often true that less duration translates into more usable power.

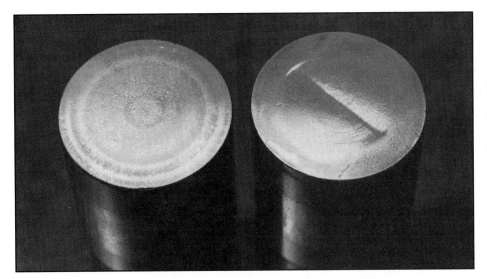

For every damaged cam lobe, there's usually a matching lifter. The lifter on the right was obviously not spinning as the cam rotated, and the lobe wore a groove in the bottom. The lifter on the left was broken in properly and shows a normal wear pattern.

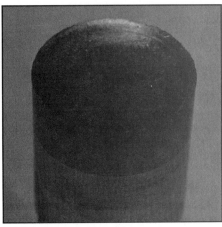

If a non-rotating lifter isn't discovered, and the engine continues to run, this is what you'll find. The fact that the lifter bottom is badly cupped will have an adverse effect on performance, but just think about where all the metal that was rubbed away went.

movement of the torque peak to a higher rpm. Certainly, the net result is a higher horsepower figure, but that increase is a byproduct of changes in the torque curve. More often than not, whenever peak horsepower is significantly increased, low-speed torque is reduced.

Although the latest camshaft technology has the potential to minimize loss of torque at very low engine speeds, losses can't be eliminated altogether. That being the case, you're better off with a current camshaft design than an older one. But irrespective of the profile or the application, the key to unlocking maximum performance is to cam an engine so that the torque and horsepower peaks are within the rpm range that an engine sees in normal operation—on the street or at the track.

High Performance Camshafts

Traditionally, high performance camshafts have not brought major increases in torque when installed in place of their stock counterparts. However, new technology developed during the Eighties has changed that to some degree. Cams designed using the latest concepts have relatively long durations-at-.050-in. lift compared to

their advertised durations. As a result, with properly selected duration specifications, a state-of-the-art high performance camshaft can produce a measurable torque increase compared to a stock cam. However, except for highly unusual cases, this increase will usually not exceed 5% and there will be some loss of torque at extremely low engine speeds. By comparison, the same cam that boosts torque only 5% can easily result in a horsepower increase of over 20% due to the rpm multiplying effect.

Compression Ratio—Compression ratio must also be considered when selecting a high performance camshaft. Significant increases in torque are almost always the result of raising compression. One way to achieve this is through bumping static compression ratio; another is through valve timing—specifically intake valve closing point—which affects cranking compression (also known as cylinder pressure). Obviously, static compression ratio must be taken into account when altering valve timing and valve timing must be considered when altering static compression ratio, or else cylinder pressure will be either too high or too low for optimum performance.

Even with the mildest of cams, the

intake valve doesn't close until after the piston passes Bottom Dead Center. Consequently, with the piston rising and the intake valve open, some of the air/fuel mixture that was just drawn in is pumped back out of the cylinder. With a later intake valve closing, there is less air and fuel to compress, so cylinder pressure is reduced. It is for this reason that cam duration and static compression must be carefully matched—a change in one very often requires modification of the other. Excessively long duration reduces cylinder pressure, which translates to less torque. Conversely, if duration is too short with respect to static compression ratio, cylinder pressure will be too high and detonation will result. This is the reason that many camshaft application notes include static compression ratio requirements.

However, some high performance camshafts are designed to function with stock compression ratios. This being the case, it would seem that performance increases would be slight because duration cannot be lengthened to a great degree if adequate cylinder pressure is to be maintained. But there's more to the story than duration. By definition, a high performance cam has more lift and faster opening and closing rates than an original

Improper break-in technique can also cause the cam nose to become pitted as metal is ripped from it. This is the first stage of damage and will ultimately lead to more extensive damage.

equipment (OE) cam. So with nothing more than factory duration specs, an aftermarket performance cam will deliver increased power.

Irrespective of cam type, duration should be matched to static compression ratio to provide a cranking compression of no more than 175 psi if an engine is to operate on pump gas. Engines that will be fed a diet of racing gas can survive with considerably higher cylinder pressures, with 225 to 235 psi being fairly typical.

Dual-Pattern Cams

In addition to providing acceptable durability, a street cam must also offer low-speed driveability. A high performance cam should make a vehicle fun to drive, not a chore. One method used by cam designers to generate profiles that have both a broad torque curve and strong top-end power is to use profiles of different durations and lifts on the intake and exhaust lobes. Known as dual-pattern cams, they typically produce more power than their single-pattern counterparts.

The need for a dual-pattern cam arises from the fact that the breathing capacity of most engines is limited by the exhaust port. With an original equipment type engine, restricted exhaust flow is fine because engine operating speeds aren't high enough to cause problems.

But with high performance and race engines, that isn't the case. The restriction imposed by the exhaust valve, port, manifold and pipe limits horsepower. One way to compensate for this is to lift the exhaust valve higher, and keep it open longer than the intake valve. Within a family, most cam manufacturers offer profiles that vary by 2 or 4 deg. of duration. Consequently, when two profiles are selected for a camshaft, exhaust duration is typically 6 to 12 deg. longer than that of the intake lobe.

Higher lift usually goes along with longer duration, but in the case of big-block Chevy cams, exhaust lift is sometimes held in check. It's not at all unusual to find big-block cams with more exhaust than intake duration but less exhaust lift. Reduction of exhaust lift is a

means of extending valve spring life.

If an engine has a highly modified set of cylinder heads, and the exhaust port has flow capacity sufficient to generate an extraction effect, it's possible to use the same lobe for both the intake and exhaust. At the other end of the spectrum, current Pro Stock technology makes use of cams with intake and exhaust durations that vary as much as 22 deg.; there are cases where Pro Stock engines have been equipped with cams having 290 deg. of intake duration and 312 deg. of duration on the exhaust side (at .050-in. lift).

In a sense, the most highly modified race engines respond best to the type of intake/exhaust duration patterning used to maximize the power of high performance street engines. The big split in durations of a Pro Stock camshaft are necessitated by the huge dimensions of the intake valves, ports and intake manifold which generate excellent cylinder filling. Like a stock engine, the exhaust ports, no matter how extensively modified, cannot dump the waste gases as efficiently as the intake

This cam also suffers from the effects of inadequate lubrication during break-in. Note the severe pitting on the middle lobe.

system brings in fresh air/fuel mixture. But if a Pro Stock engine were topped off by a single, rather than dual, four-barrel carburetor, and a conventional, rather than ram-type intake manifold, less exhaust duration would be warranted. Pro Stock-style, single four-barrel, small-block engines commonly have exhaust duration that is 4, 8 or 12 deg. longer than intake (8 deg. is the most common).

How Much is Enough?—With each engine being unique, the obvious question is, how do you select intake and exhaust durations for maximum performance? One method is to order a number of camshafts with different intake/exhaust duration combinations and test them. That's extremely expensive and time consuming, but with hydraulic lifter grinds, it's the only option. For street applications, the performance improvement to be gained from lengthening or shortening exhaust duration (compared to intake duration) isn't sufficient to justify the expense. Most cam manufacturers have learned which combinations are effective for popular engines so it's hard to improve

significantly on cataloged grinds. Cam grinders have been designing cams for this engine for well over 30 years, so there's very little that hasn't been tried in terms of intake and exhaust duration combinations.

Lash Loops—With mechanical lifter cams, it's a little easier to determine what an engine likes. It's possible to run a "lash loop" as a means of determining the optimum intake and exhaust durations. In most cases, if cam duration is in the ballpark, running a lash loop will not pay off with major performance improvements. But it will produce measurable power increases that just may spell the difference between a win and a loss at the race track.

Running a lash loop involves adjusting the intake lash to what appears to be the optimum setting, then altering the exhaust lash in .004 in. increments. Results are gauged by on-track or dyno testing. If the engine has more torque or mid-range power with the lash loosened .004 in., chances are the cam has too much exhaust duration; the exhaust lobe should be shortened by about 4 deg. The reverse

is also true. If tightening exhaust lash .004 in. causes the engine to run better, more exhaust duration is called for.

Once the exhaust lash loop has been run, use the same procedure on the intake side. If the engine runs better with more lash, intake duration should be shortened; if tighter lash brings about improved performance, intake duration should be lengthened. Whenever working with intake lash, do not alter exhaust lash at the same time, and vice versa.

There are a few things to beware of when running lash loops. A single test at each setting will not provide conclusive results; a series of tests should be run and the results averaged after throwing out the high and low times—kind of the Olympic scoring method. It's also essential to be very careful when running lash loops with any cam which has specified lash settings of about .012 in. When widening the lash, be very careful that the engine doesn't get into valve float as parts breakage will very likely result. Some reduced lash cam designs, which call for .012 in. lash, should be run at settings of no more than .014 in.

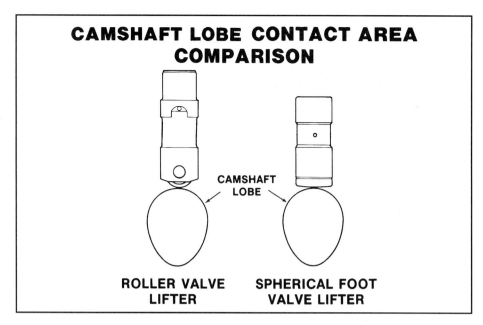

CAMSHAFT LOBE CONTACT AREA COMPARISON

CAMSHAFT LOBE

ROLLER VALVE LIFTER

SPHERICAL FOOT VALVE LIFTER

A roller lifter offers a number of advantages compared to a flat-tappet type. Aside from the obvious reduction in friction, a roller tappet can tolerate much faster opening and closing rates because the possibility of edge riding (where the cam lobe contacts the edge of the lifter rather than the bottom) is eliminated.

However, lash can be reduced all the way down to .001 in. or .002 in. The only requirement is that some clearance must exist so that the valve firmly contacts the seat.

Another point to keep in mind is that any changes in the intake or exhaust systems will invalidate previous test data. For optimum performance, it's necessary to run a lash loop any time a change is made to the cylinder heads, intake manifold, carburetor or headers. And of course, internal engine modifications also call for a rerunning of the lash loop. Obviously, lash loops are warranted only for serious racing efforts.

Valve Lash—Close or Wide?

Close lash is a relatively recent development in camshaft design which was pioneered by Harvey Crane, of Crane CamDesign, a business that designs and analyzes camshafts for other cam manufacturers. Although he has not been associated with Crane Cams since 1989 (and therefore his opinions expressed here do not necessarily reflect or apply to camshafts produced by Crane

Cams), he is considered to be a leading authority on camshaft technology. On the subject of valve lash, he states:

"Valve lash is a function of the ramp design. Why put all that ramp on a cam lobe, which is intended to take up the 'shock' of opening and closing the valves, if less ramp and less lash will accomplish the same thing? This philosophy comes from hydraulic lifter cam design. Theoretically, you don't need a ramp on a hydraulic cam because there's no clearance to take up. But you better have some ramp there, especially on the closing side, because the lifter is shorter at certain points. But with a hydraulic cam, it is possible to design the ramps so that they appear to be somewhere between very short and non-existent. Now if the average person looks at some of my hydraulic lobe designs, it will look like they have no ramps. But there are very carefully designed ramps in place. The success of these cams made me wonder why I couldn't apply the same technology to mechanical lifter cams. The problem was that I couldn't design the lobe with the existing computer software. So we

developed some new mathematics and wrote some new software and that enabled us to design mechanical cams with tight lash specifications. At first, a lot of engine builders looked at the .012 in. lash and said it wouldn't work, but we've proven otherwise. The thing you've got to keep in mind is that the more lash you have, the less lift you get at the valve. If you've got .030 in. valve lash, you've lost .030 in. lift."

The original impetus for wide lash was to reduce maintenance problems on stock engines. With a lash of .030 in., if an engine is run for 30,000 or 40,000 miles, some of the valves will have lash of .010 in. and others will be at .045 in. That really won't hurt anything. But if the lash were tighter—.012 in. to .018 in., as with the original Duntov Corvette cams—it was possible, over a period of time, to wind up with zero lash, which inevitably causes engine problems. Designing cams with relatively wide lash settings simply provided more latitude for lash changes between settings. This resulted in fewer burnt valves and also reduced the frequency of valve adjustment. With a race engine, the valve covers are off as much as they're on. Valve lash is monitored very closely and frequently, so there's no need to design for long maintenance intervals.

As noted, it's critical that lash be set at no greater than .014 in. with cams specifying .012 in. lash. At wider settings, the valve is moved at extremely high velocities because the lifter is off the ramp and well up on the flank when the clearance is taken up, and when the valve is closed. These extreme velocities will result in parts breakage.

CAMSHAFT POSITIONING

Selecting the proper camshaft is only one of the steps along the road to maximum performance. Another is how the cam is installed. Anyone who has done much bench racing has heard the terms advanced, retarded, straight-up and split overlap used to describe the positioning, or indexing, of the camshaft relative to crankshaft position. But as is the case with most terms that are casually bandied about, these words are wrapped in a cloak of misunderstanding.

One reason is that both camshaft degrees and crankshaft degrees are used in referring to various cam timing events. Valve opening and closing points, camshaft advance or retard, intake centerline (or maximum lift point), exhaust centerline (or maximum lift point) and duration are always referenced in crankshaft degrees. Lobe separation is always referenced in camshaft degrees.

A crankshaft makes two revolutions for each single revolution of the camshaft. That means a crankshaft rotates 720 deg. while a camshaft rotates 360 deg.; that relationship explains the existence of camshafts with over 350 deg. of gross duration. If duration were measured in camshaft degrees, a cam with 350 deg. of duration would keep the valves open almost all the time. But within a 720-deg. cycle, 350 deg. represents slightly less than half the entire cycle.

Straight-Up—"Straight-up" is one of those terms that has been in use since the days of the flathead Ford. However, it is not universally applicable because it is meaningful only with reference to single-pattern cams which have identical intake and exhaust durations. When a single-pattern cam is installed "straight-up," the intake and exhaust maximum lift points (which are specified in crankshaft degrees) are the same as the lobe separation (which is specified in camshaft degrees). That is, if a camshaft is ground with 112 deg. of lobe separation, it is installed "straight-up" if the intake maximum lift point occurs at 112 deg. after TDC and the exhaust maximum lift point occurs at 112 deg. before TDC.

Split Overlap—It is also true that

when a single-pattern cam is installed "straight-up," a condition known as split overlap exists. At "split overlap," both the intake and exhaust tappets for any given cylinder are raised an equal amount when the corresponding piston is at Top Dead Center.

Indexing—One method of indexing a single-pattern camshaft is to rotate the crankshaft until number one piston is at Top Dead Center. Then the cam is positioned (by using offset bushings or keyways) so that the lifters for number one cylinder are at equal heights. But this method will do nothing but cause trouble when used with dual-pattern camshafts. The correct method of indexing or degreeing-in a dual-pattern cam is described throughout the rest of this chapter.

Advancing the Cause

Many cams are ground "advanced" from "straight-up." Crankshaft degrees are always used when referencing camshaft advance; offset bushings and keyways are always marked in crankshaft degrees. This means that the intake maximum lift point and lobe separation figures will not be equal. Most high performance cams with lobe separations of 108 deg. or more are ground 3 to 5 crankshaft degrees advanced from "straight-up." That is, with a 108-deg. lobe separation, the intake maximum lift point occurs at 103 deg. after TDC and exhaust maximum lift occurs at 113 deg. before TDC. With dual-pattern cams, intake maximum lift point and lobe separation figures determine the amount of advance ground into the cam.

Camshaft advance is a bit confusing because there are two reference points. One is the amount of advance (from split overlap) ground into the camshaft by the manufacturer; the other is the amount of advance or retard that may be added during installation. When a cam is degreed-in, valve timing can be advanced or retarded—from the specifications

To accurately degree-in a camshaft, you need a large diameter degree wheel and a dial indicator. Both are available from most cam suppliers, but some degree wheels are too small to make accurate reading easy. Make sure the wheel is at least 11" in diameter.

listed on the spec card—through the use of offset bushings or keyways. So it would be correct to say that a cam was advanced 4 deg. because a 4 deg. bushing was installed in the cam sprocket. If the cam was already ground 5 deg. advanced from "straight-up," it would then be advanced a total of 9 deg. (from "straight-up").

Similarly, if an offset bushing or keyway is employed to retard a cam 4 deg., it is being moved with respect to the opening and closing figures listed on the spec card. A cam ground with 5 deg. of advance, if retarded 4 deg., is then advanced only 1 deg. from "straight-up." So even though it has been retarded, it's still advanced.

The important point to keep in mind is that advance is relative, so whenever dealing with the subject, keep the reference point in mind—you're either referencing advance from "straight-up," or comparing it to the timing numbers listed on the specification card. Many engine builders make it a practice to "advance the cam two degrees" to compensate for timing chain stretch. In this case, "advanced two degrees" is in reference to the valve timing figures, not to "straight-up." So to avoid excess

A dial indicator isn't much good without a holding fixture. Most cam suppliers offer a fixture like this, which screws into a head bolt hole in the block. Other models that thread into a rocker cover bolt hole are also available for degreeing cams on engines with cylinder heads installed.

confusion, whenever discussing camshaft advance, ask, "Advanced from what?" There are pros and cons to installing a cam either with advance or retard, which we will discuss shortly.

Degreeing the Camshaft

When you install a high performance camshaft, you can do it one of two ways—just stick it in the engine and button everything back up, or you can do it the right way. Without exception, the right way means degreeing it in (also called phasing the camshaft) to assure that valve timing events occur at precisely the right time with respect to crankshaft position.

The degreeing-in operation is simply a matter of checking an engine's real life valve opening and closing timing against the figures on the specification card that accompanies each camshaft. It is accomplished by mounting a degree wheel on the front of the crankshaft and utilizing a dial indicator to check cam lobe lift. However, even though cam

timing is being checked, erroneous readings are usually not caused by the lobes themselves. Mismatches between specifications and actual measurements are usually the result of errors in crank sprocket keyway positioning, cam sprocket dowel pin hole placement or an excessively stretched timing chain. Additionally, the dowel pin in the camshaft may be improperly located.

Finding TDC—But before cam timing can be checked, Top Dead Center must first be accurately determined. In many cases, the mark scribed on the vibration damper is not accurate. If the cylinder heads haven't been installed, simply bolt a positive piston stop over cylinder number one and follow the pertinent steps that follow. With the cylinder heads in place, the search for TDC can be conducted as follows:

1. Remove all the spark plugs to make engine rotation easier and bring number one piston to approximately Top Dead Center—just to get in the ballpark.

2. Mount a degree wheel on the crankshaft snout and rotate it so that the TDC mark is aligned with the pointer. Don't turn the crankshaft with the same bolt used to attach the degree wheel as this can move the wheel and cause incorrect readings.

3. Turn the crankshaft so that the piston moves an inch or so down the bore. Install a positive piston stop in cylinder number one spark plug hole.

4. Rotate the crankshaft clockwise until the piston just contacts the stop. Don't use excessive force—you want a positive stop, not a hole in the piston. Note the reading on the degree wheel.

5. Spin the crankshaft in the opposite direction until the piston once again contacts the stop. Note the reading on the degree wheel.

6. Split the difference between these two readings to determine true TDC. As an example, assume that the readings obtained by rotating the crank clockwise and counterclockwise are 22 and 18 deg. respectively. These two figures total 40 deg., an indication that the piston is actually being stopped at 20 deg. (1/2 of 40) before and after TDC. Therefore, the degree wheel is 2 deg. off. With the piston still against the stop, rotate the degree wheel until it and the 20-deg. mark are aligned. Re-tighten the degree wheel and check again. Each time the piston comes up against the stop (after being rotated in both directions), the pointer should indicate the same reading, in this case 20 deg. If it doesn't, correct it and check again. If it does, TDC on the degree wheel will correspond to the true TDC of the engine.

Once TDC has been established, remove the piston stop, install a dial indicator so that it measures lift at the pushrod or cam and check the intake and exhaust lobes of number one cylinder. Make sure that the indicator reads zero when the lifter is on the heel of the lobe. All duration specifications are tied to a specific amount of lobe (not valve) lift, hence the need for a dial indicator—it records lift while the degree wheel is read to check duration. All the necessary information can usually be found on the specification card that accompanies each camshaft. To ensure accuracy, it's a good idea to spin the engine over completely to verify that the dial indicator returns to zero when the lifter is back on the base circle. Many times the indicator mount will move, making the reading inaccurate; an apparent problem with the cam may in fact be a problem with the indicator mounting.

Cam Lift—Before you actually start looking at cam phasing, check cam lift. If measured lift does not match up with the specs on the cam card, the dial indicator may not be positioned properly. Should that be the case, opening and closing points cannot be accurately related to a given amount of lift because lift is not being measured accurately. To avoid these problems, make sure that the dial indicator is mounted exactly in line with the tappet or pushrod.

Example—As an example of a degreeing-in operation, assume that you've installed a hydraulic cam and the accompanying specification card lists gross valve timing at .004-in. tappet lift as:

• Intake opens 38 deg. Before Top Dead Center (BTDC).

• Intake closes 76 deg. After Bottom Dead Center (ABDC).

• Exhaust opens 82 deg. Before Bottom Dead Center (BBDC).

• Exhaust closes 32 deg. After Top Dead Center (ATDC).

You could use these as checking dimensions, but at those points, the cam is moving the lifter at such a slow rate that it is easy to be off by a few degrees. However, by the time the lifter has been raised .050 in. off the base circle, lift rate is pretty rapid so it is easy to see precisely when the dial indicator needle reaches .050 in. In the case of the camshaft used in the above example, the net valve timing figures (at .050-in. lift) are:

• Intake opens 12 deg. BTDC.

• Intake closes 46 deg. ABDC.

• Exhaust opens 56 deg. BBDC.

• Exhaust closes at 2 deg. ATDC (that is, right at TDC).

The actual checking procedure entails mounting the dial indicator so that it measures the lift of either the intake or

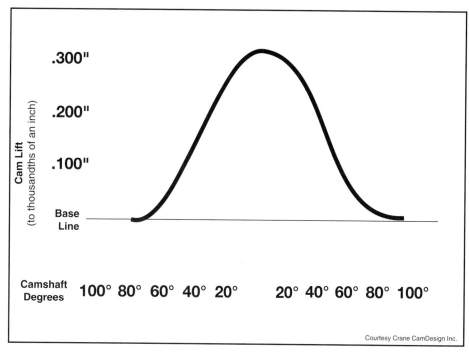

Camshaft Lift Curve
This lift curve is typical of one generated by a state-of-the-art high performance camshaft. Although difficult to see, it's not symmetrical– this cam opens the valves at one rate and closes them at another. The lift rate of the opening side is not the same as the closing rate.

exhaust lobe of cylinder number one. Then the crankshaft is rotated in the direction it normally spins, while the dial indicator is closely monitored. It's a good idea to rotate the crankshaft through a few complete revolutions to ensure that all critical dial indicator readings are repeatable.

Timing Check—When making the actual cam timing check, begin with the lifter on the cam's base circle and the dial indicator needle on zero. Rotate the crankshaft in its normal direction and as the needle swings by .040-in. lift, slow the rotation rate so that the needle sneaks up on the .050-in. figure. You should always arrive at .050-in. lift by spinning the crankshaft in its normal direction. Going past the desired point and then backing up until .050-in. lift is indicated will result in erroneous opening and closing point readings (due to lack of preload on the timing chain). Once .050-in. lift is achieved, note the reading on the degree wheel—it should correspond to the appropriate specification on the cam card.

With the opening point noted, crankshaft rotation continues in the normal direction of rotation, until the tappet begins descending. As already noted, reversal of direction will indicate erroneous opening and closing points. Once again, a slow turning rate is used to "sneak up" on .050-in. lift and when it is reached, the degree wheel reading is once again recorded. The entire procedure is then repeated to verify the results, then the other lobe of the pair working the valves of cylinder number one is checked.

Generally, if there is a disparity between listed and actual specifications, it is not that duration has been altered but that the entire opening/closing event is skewed a few degrees forward or back. With the cam referenced in the previous paragraphs, it wouldn't be at all unusual to come up with an intake opening of 10 deg. BTDC and closing at 48 deg. ABDC. This would indicate that the cam was two degrees retarded. And if, in the name of false economy, an old timing chain and sprocket set was reused, the

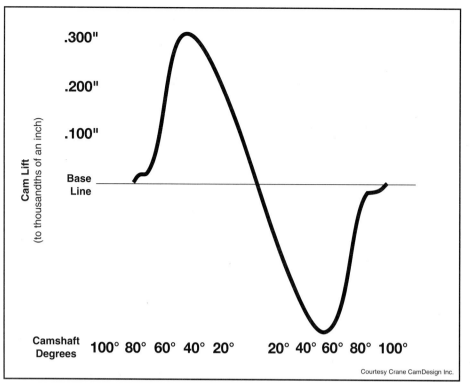

Velocity Curve
Velocity is the rate at which the lifter is raised and lowered; it's greatest just after the lifter is raised off, and just before it's lowered back onto, the base circle.

cam could easily be as much as 8 deg. or 10 deg. retarded. In the latter instance, a new timing set would probably cure the discrepancy and if it didn't, either an offset bushing in the cam sprocket, an offset key for the crankshaft, or a multi-keyway crank sprocket could be used.

Some racers insist on checking every lobe, but this is a very time consuming process and it usually isn't necessary. However, as a quick double-check, move the dial indicator to cylinder number six (this procedure works on almost all American V-8s because cylinders one and six reach TDC at the same time so it isn't necessary to move the degree wheel) and repeat the check. If there is a problem with camshaft quality, you're 95% certain of finding it here. A more thorough check can be made by checking three intake and three exhaust lobes. If the cam, rather than a single lobe, is out of specification, the timing of all six lobes should be off the same amount. In any event, a camshaft should not be advanced or retarded unless both opening and closing

points do not fall within specifications. If only the opening or only the closing point is off, there's a good chance that there's a mechanical problem with the cam rather than a phasing error.

Base Circle Runout—In the process of verifying opening and closing points, it's advisable to check base circle runout. Excessive runout is indicative of poor machining quality and will result in less than optimum performance. It will also make it difficult to check cam timing and establish proper lash or lifter preload. Most cam manufacturers strive to hold base circle runout to less than .001 in.; any cam with .002 in. or more runout should be returned to the manufacturer.

If the high spot is towards the opening flank, the valve will open prematurely and the engine will idle rough and have poor idle manifold vacuum. If the high spot is towards the closing flank, idle quality will be acceptable, but torque will be degraded because valve closing is delayed. These problems are especially noticeable with a hydraulic lifter cam. In

most instances, an engine never "sees" base circle runout with a mechanical lifter cam (except for extreme cases) because valve lash is usually greater than the amount of runout. Consequently, when a lifter is bumped by a high spot on the base circle, the only effect is that clearance is momentarily reduced, and that has no impact on performance.

However, before packaging up the cam, make sure that both the lobe and lifter surfaces are clean. In an effort to save time, runout and cam timing are often checked after moly assembly lube has been applied to the cam and lifters. This lubricant contains small flecks of moly which will "bump" the indicator needle when they pass between the lobe and lifter. These moly flecks may make it appear as though runout is excessive, and may also alter timing indications by one or two degrees.

Advance vs. Retard—Even if a camshaft checks right on the numbers, it may be desirable to advance or retard it to enhance certain performance characteristics. Advancing a camshaft increases low-speed and mid-range torque at the expense of top-end horsepower; retarding has the opposite effect. Translated into drag strip performance, advancing the cam tends to improve elapsed times while retarding cam timing tends to boost top speed. In an oval track engine, a cam is advanced to make a car come off the corners harder and it's retarded to produce higher straightaway speeds. However, before cam phasing is changed, baseline performance should be established with the cam installed "on the numbers."

Intake Centerline—Which brings up another point—checking cam phasing according to intake centerline. Intake centerline is defined as the point at which the intake lobe reaches maximum lift. Typically, high performance and racing camshafts reach intake maximum lift at 100 to 114 deg. ATDC. The shortcoming of using the centerline method is that actual opening and closing points are not checked, so machining inaccuracies go undetected. However, some engine builders use intake centerline as a reference point when altering camshaft phasing to shift an engine's power curve.

Oval Track Builders—By way of example, many oval track engine builders have found that an intake centerline of 102 deg. puts the torque curve where they want it. Consequently, whenever they install a new camshaft, they degree it in using opening and closing points at .050 in. lift, then they adjust phasing as necessary to establish a 102-deg. centerline. This way, performance can be accurately compared with that of existing camshafts. While intake centerline is useful for comparisons, it should never be used to establish camshaft position. Whenever the opening and closing points as listed on the cam spec card are not used for the degreeing-in operation, cam phasing probably will not be accurate. Many cams have asymmetric lobes, which means that actual centerline of the lobe is not at the point of maximum lift. While these two points may only be separated by a degree or two, that's enough to affect phasing.

With a symmetrical lobe, one side is the mirror image of the other. Intake centerline can be calculated by dividing intake duration in half and subtracting the intake opening figure. If a symmetrical intake lobe has a net duration of 236 deg., and the intake valve opens at 12 deg. BTDC, then its intake centerline is 106 deg. (236/2=118-12=106).

Suppose a cam's maximum lift point cannot be calculated and consequently can't be checked? Using the calculated intake centerline to determine camshaft phasing will most likely result in improper cam phasing.

In cases where it is useful to know the intake centerline, the cam should always be degreed-in using the opening and closing points at .050-in. lift. Then intake maximum lift point can be calculated

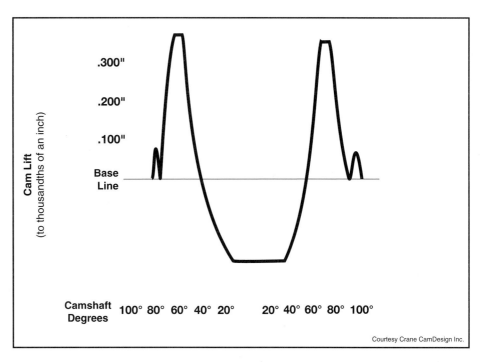

Courtesy Crane CamDesign Inc.

Acceleration Curve
Acceleration curves say a lot about a camshaft's reliability and maximum rpm potential. Ideally, an acceleration curve should be smooth with rounded peaks.

(intake duration/2 — intake opening), or the information can simply be read on the specification card that accompanies every cam.

A Word About Quality

The technology of both camshaft design and manufacturing has improved in quantum leaps over the past few decades. However, mistakes are still a part of life and shoddy workmanship can rear its ugly head at any time. It's for precisely these reasons that sharp engine builders check every component used in assembling an engine—even camshafts.

While absolute perfection isn't essential in a street camshaft, it's imperative in a race camshaft. The difference in acceptable quality latitude is due to operating environment. Junk parts don't belong in a street engine any more than they do in a race engine. But the latter operates primarily at maximum load and maximum rpm; the former loafs for most of its life and rarely reaches a camshaft's maximum rpm potential. Valvetrain stress is understandably much greater in a race engine hence the need for the absolute

highest quality.

The subject of camshaft quality is an interesting one because many people think it relates directly to power output, but it doesn't. Many times a poor quality camshaft will produce more horsepower than one that passes a much more stringent quality check. But while it's making horsepower, it's also destroying valvetrain parts. When a camshaft of substandard quality is installed in a race engine, the gamble is whether the engine will last long enough to finish the race. Over the years, engine builders have discovered that the old canard rings true, "You can't win if you don't finish."

With a street camshaft, quality translates to durability. Poor quality control results in camshafts that develop flat lobes, worn lifters and/or broken valve springs after just 10,000 to 20,000 miles of driving. Dealing with a reputable cam company is one way of minimizing the possibilities of being the victim of inferior camshaft quality. Degree-checking a cam, not only for lift and duration, but for base circle runout, is another. ■

7

VALVETRAIN

If you were standing on a solid floor, trying to hold a small piece of plywood firmly against the ceiling with a broom handle, you probably wouldn't have much trouble. Plywood isn't particularly heavy, so it doesn't take much strength to hold it in place for a few minutes. But suppose that instead of being solid, the floor was rolling like ocean waves. It would be almost impossible to hold the plywood firmly in place.

A valvetrain also needs stability if it is to allow the camshaft to produce maximum performance. Aside from performance considerations, an unstable valvetrain can cause any number of engine maladies, many of which are difficult to diagnose. The primary reason that camshaft manufacturers advise use of specific lifters, pushrods, valve springs and retainers is that they're attempting to

assure some degree of valvetrain stability. Parts from other manufacturers may work as well—or better—but they may also be inappropriate. If you do use all the suggested related components, troubleshooting is quite a bit easier when there is a problem, because the performance characteristics of those components is a known quantity to the cam manufacturer. On the other hand, if you've got a cam from one company,

Even though the cam gets most of the credit, the valvetrain plays an important role in establishing an engine's performance profile. As this old photo demonstrates, Reher-Morrison has known of the valvetrain's importance quite a few years.

lifters from another, springs from a third and retainers from a fourth, how is the cam manufacturer to know whether everything fits as it should and whether mating parts are compatible?

HYDRAULIC LIFTERS

Hydraulic lifters were originally designed in the Twenties as a means of eliminating the periodic valve lash adjustments that mechanical tappets require. With mechanical or "solid" lifters, some amount of clearance must exist in the valvetrain to accommodate the expansion and contraction that occurs as the engine heats and cools. This lash must be taken up gradually to avoid hammering the valvetrain, so even though only a few thousandths of an inch clearance are required to handle expansion and contraction, valve lash typically ranges from .014 to .030 in. depending on cam design.

Components

Hydraulic lifters eliminate the need for valvetrain clearance because they automatically take up any clearance introduced into the system. Inside the body of a hydraulic lifter is a plunger that rests on a reservoir of oil. Engine oil is continually pumped through this reservoir, which is contained in a space called a compression chamber. When the lifter is on the cam's base circle, a check valve at the plunger's bottom is open so oil can flow into or out of the compression chamber. When the cam lobe pushes the lifter up against the pushrod, the check valve closes, trapping oil in the compression chamber. Since oil is not compressible, upward movement of the lifter body is transmitted to the plunger, which raises the pushrod and rocker arm, thereby opening the valve (in the cylinder head). When the lifter returns to the cam's base circle, the check valve beneath the plunger opens again, allowing oil volume in the compression

chamber to adjust to compensate for any clearance or excessive plunger preload that may have been introduced into the valvetrain.

Lifter Preload

As a general rule, hydraulic lifter preload should be set so that the plunger is .020 to .045 in. below the snap ring. This will allow the lifter to compensate for normal valvetrain clearance and will not restrict rpm potential. The required amount of preload can be obtained by simply adjusting the rocker arm nuts 1/2 to 3/4 of a turn after all clearance has been taken up. This can be done most effectively by backing the rocker nuts off until there's measurable clearance between the rocker arm and valve stem. Then the nut should be slowly tightened while you twirl the pushrod between your fingers. Once all the clearance is taken up, the pushrod will become difficult to turn. At this point, an additional 1/2 to 3/4 of a turn of the rocker adjusting nut will set lifter preload correctly. Obviously, the lifters must be on the cam's base circle when this is done, so it's common practice to first warm the engine, then shut it off and spin the crankshaft until cylinder number one is at Top Dead Center on the power stroke. Lifter preload for cylinder one can then be adjusted, and the crankshaft rotated another 90 deg., so the rockers for the next cylinder in the firing order can be adjusted. Proceed through the 1-8-4-3-6-5-7-2 firing order, rotating the crank 90 deg. after each pair of rockers is adjusted, until all have been set.

On high performance and race engines equipped with hydraulic lifters, it is a common practice to set the rocker adjusting nuts 1/8th turn or less down from zero lash. This positions the hydraulic lifter plunger up against, or just a few thousandths of an inch below, the snap ring. With this setting, the hydraulic lifter is effectively functioning as a mechanical tappet because it can't take up

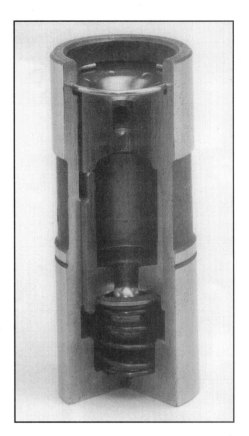

A hydraulic lifter is the most precisely fitted component in an engine. Plunger-to-shell clearance is critical because it affects leakdown rate. Several different types of check valves are used and each lifter manufacturer naturally claims that its mechanism is superior to others. In real life, performance is pretty much equal from one brand to another, provided the lifter is a quality part.

any clearance in the valvetrain. On the negative side, running the plunger up against the snap ring is risky because the snap ring may pop out and go flitting about the engine. If it does, serious engine damage is the typical result.

The practice of backing off the rocker nuts so that the plunger is up against the snap ring became popular in the Sixties when musclecar owners attempted to increase rpm potential with stock components. In some engines, valve spring pressure isn't sufficient to control the hydraulic pressure pushing against the plunger. At engine speeds above 5000 rpm, the hydraulic force is strong enough to overcome the valve spring pressure which normally prevents the plunger from moving upward to any great degree

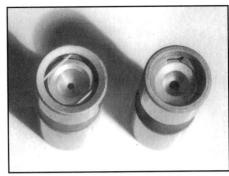

The biggest differences between a standard hydraulic lifter (on the left) and an "anti-pump-up" model (on the right) is the retaining ring and the depth of the ring groove in the lifter body. A stronger retaining ring is used in anti-pump-up lifters to keep the plunger from leaving when clearance exists in the valvetrain.

Big blocks have a tendency to wear-out cam lobes and lifters if proper break-in procedures aren't followed. These three lifters are from an engine that was obviously having problems. Note the excessive wear on the lifters shown at right and left. A normal contact pattern is visible in the center lifter.

(unless there's clearance to be taken up). With the plunger "pumped up" (raised) from its normal position, the valve cannot close fully and the engine appears to be in valve float. Backing the rockers off so that the plunger is close to or against the snap ring eliminates lifter pump up because the plunger can't move far enough to interfere with valve closure when hydraulic force overcomes valve spring pressure.

Lifter Pump Up—As noted, this is the hydraulic lifter equivalent of mechanical lifter valve float. When an engine goes into valve float, the hydraulic lifter, which is self-adjusting, tries to compensate. A hydraulic lifter "sees" the extra clearance caused by the lifter bouncing on the flank, so it attempts to take some clearance out of the system. When it does that, it never allows the valve to close fully because it takes up the clearance on the closing side of the cam lobe. Since the valves don't completely seat, the engine loses its compression (cylinder pressure) because pressure blows off through the open valve. Without compression, the engine

can't make any power, so it effectively shuts itself off. The same thing happens with a mechanical lifter cam when it goes into valve float, only instead of the hydraulic plunger preventing the valve from seating, the lifter itself, being up off the cam lobe, is the culprit.

Anti-Pump Up Lifters

What about anti-pump up lifters? Actually, there's no such thing. The one true anti-pump up design, which had a relief hole in the side of the lifter body to bleed off excess pressure, has never been available. The only difference between standard and anti-pump up lifters is retaining ring style and sometimes placement.

Some anti-pump up lifters are nothing more than standard lifters with a stronger retaining ring. In fact, one manufacturer made absolutely no changes in lifter design, but simply began calling its standard lifters "anti-pump up" as a means of increasing sales and price. The "anti-pump up" label is supposedly justified by the stronger clip which has a better chance of staying in place if the

lifters are adjusted so that the plunger rides up against the clip.

Other brands of anti-pump up lifters have the retaining ring groove machined lower in the lifter body so the plunger's up and down movement is restricted. It can still pump up, but the plunger just can't move as far as if the ring were in the standard location. This is all well and good, but what usually goes unnoticed is that the revised plunger position calls for a longer pushrod.

In anti-pump up lifters, the pushrod seat is .080 to .100-in. lower than in a standard lifter and that has a definite effect on valvetrain geometry if correct length pushrods are not used. If a standard to anti-pump up lifter change is made, and nothing else is changed, the rocker won't be in the right position and rapid valve guide wear and possibly parts breakage will result. Some people have even found that their engines don't run as well after anti-pump up lifters have been installed. That's because they didn't use pushrods of the correct length which resulted in less than ideal valvetrain geometry (which can reduce valve lift). But just sticking in a set of .100-in. longer-than-stock pushrods isn't the answer because that doesn't take things like block and head machining into account. Don't assume anything. Check for the exact pushrod length you need.

Variable duration lifters look just like standard lifters externally. However, they shorten cam duration at low speeds because their relatively high leakdown rate allows the plunger to collapse. At higher speeds, oil flow is sufficient to overcome the leakdown, so the plunger remains in its normal position. In theory, variable duration lifters are ideal for hot street engines; in practice, they're a band-aid for an improperly selected camshaft. Some brands appear to lead to premature valvetrain failure.

Selection

Surprisingly, all hydraulic lifters are manufactured by a handful of companies. While there are different styles of check valves, virtually all are widely available. So in spite of claims to the contrary, hydraulic lifter performance is pretty much the same regardless of design.

While it's hard to go wrong with brand-name lifters, some off-brands may be a teapot of trouble about to boil. Some companies purchase used lifters, remachine the bottoms and sell them as if they were new lifters. But if you buy brand-name lifters from a reputable supplier, it's hard to go wrong because hydraulic lifters are assembled to the highest precision standards of any engine component. To assure that leak-down rate (the rate at which oil bleeds out of the lifter between the plunger and shell) is within specification, the clearance between the plunger and lifter body is held to .0003 in. Both the lifter and plunger are machined to a tolerance of .001 in., then they are graded for size and separated into different categories. The plungers are also graded for size and then matched to an appropriate lifter body to obtain the nominal .0003 in. clearance. Tolerances are held to 200 millionths of an inch to assure that clearances are exact. If they aren't, the leak-down rate will be excessive and will result in valvetrain chatter.

Variable Duration Lifters

Leak-down is precisely what happens with so-called variable duration lifters. Either by virtue of increased plunger-to-lifter body clearance, or through a groove machined in the side of the plunger, variable duration lifters allow a higher volume of oil to leak out when the lifter is raised by the cam. As a result, the plunger doesn't rise with the lifter body (because the oil that would normally be trapped in the compression chamber is allowed to leak out). Ultimately, the bottom of the lifter contacts the plunger and that causes it to rise. This lost motion (when the lifter body is rising, but the plunger isn't) delays valve opening so cam duration is effectively shortened, but lift is also reduced. At higher engine speeds, there isn't enough time for the oil to bleed off, so valve duration returns to its normal specification.

The concept of a variable duration lifter is appealing because in theory it shortens duration at low engine speeds, which increases idle vacuum and low-speed torque, without compromising top-end horsepower. And true enough, depending on design, a variable duration lifter will add from one to two inches of manifold vacuum at idle, but not without exacting a toll on component life. According to Paul "Scooter" Brothers of Competition Cams:

"We sell two different types of variable duration lifters. They do have their place—like in a race engine that must have a certain amount of idle vacuum to meet the rules—but they make more noise than a standard lifter. That noise means that two parts in the valvetrain are banging together that shouldn't be. I don't know that it would ever create a problem, but it sure doesn't seem like the best situation. Variable duration lifters won't turn the wrong cam into the right one and they don't deliver big power gains. However, they do help in some situations, but you have to be aware of what causes them to make noise; it's because there's some slack in the system that shouldn't be there, and two pieces of metal are banging together and shouldn't be."

Irrespective of lifter type, the best way to control pump up is to switch to stiffer valve springs. This allows the establishment of proper lifter preload and minimizes the risk of engine damage caused by a snap ring that has been popped out of its groove and sent on a tour. Of course, if an engine is to regularly visit the other side of 7000 rpm, mechanical or roller lifters are the logical choice. The only real drawback to these types of lifters is the need for periodic adjustment.

Late-model big blocks offer excellent performance potential when modified, but the stock valvetrain is a definite handicap. Installing a high performance hydraulic roller cam and lifters will unleash a lot of power and may even improve fuel economy.

Hydraulic Roller Lifters

Hydraulic roller lifters are another option. Through the 1994 model year, Chevrolet had not offered a big block with hydraulic roller lifters (which is surprising because hydraulic rollers have been used in small blocks since the 1987 model year). However, most major high performance camshaft manufacturers offer hydraulic roller cams and matching lifters for big-block engines.

Hydraulic roller lifters offer several advantages compared to either flat-tappet hydraulics or mechanical rollers. Obviously, there's less friction when a roller, as opposed to a flat surface, contacts a cam lobe; that translates into improved fuel economy and a slight increase in usable horsepower. However, the principal advantage of a roller lifter is that it allows for significantly more aggressive cam profiles. With the same amount of gross duration, a roller cam can open and close the valves more quickly, raise them higher and keep them

at or near maximum lift longer. As a result, horsepower can be increased with little or no effect in low speed operation.

Unlike mechanical roller lifters, hydraulic rollers don't require periodic lash adjustment, so they're ideal for street and marine engines where low maintenance is an attractive option. On the negative side, hydraulic roller lifters are expensive compared to their flat-bottomed counterparts.

MECHANICAL TAPPETS

There isn't much to be said about mechanical tappets except that the standard caveats apply regarding the questionable quality of off-brand parts. However, it should be noted that oil flow to the rocker arms is affected by the lifter, and big-block Chevys turning high rpm have a tendency to flood the upper end with oil. One means of controlling the flow of oil up the pushrod is to install edge orifice lifters (available from some

camshaft manufacturers or Chevrolet part no. 5231585). With this style of lifter, oil is metered to the engine's top end through the clearance between the lifter body and its bore. Compared to a standard "piddle valve" lifter (carried by all high performance cam manufacturers and aftermarket suppliers, or Chevrolet part no. 5232695) the edge orifice lifter restricts oil flow by up to 20%. Edge orifice lifters are designed for use only on engines equipped with roller rocker arms; the restricted oil flow can cause galling when stock-type stamped-steel rockers are used.

Restrictor Plugs—While edge orifice lifters unquestionably restrict the flow of oil to the "attic" (the rocker arm area), they don't restrict it enough for some applications. Depending on the intended use of an engine and the individual engine builder's preference, restrictor plugs may be installed rather than edge orifice lifters. These plugs, which typically contain a .050 to .080 in. metering orifice, screw into the feed holes located in the rear cam bearing bore. Several companies, including B&B Performance and Moroso, offer restrictor kits with .080 in. metering holes. Obviously, restricting top-end oil flow is also a common practice when roller lifters are used. However, note that some roller lifters have built-in flow restrictions, so installing restrictors in the block may be redundant and may limit oil flow too much.

Cautions—The degree of oil restriction to the top end is a function of oiling system flow volume and engine speed. The high rpm at which race engines operate in normal operation assures that sufficient lubrication will reach the rocker arms. However, in a street engine, installing oil restrictors or edge orifice lifters is like planting a time bomb. A street engine spends too much time idling and running at low speed to provide adequate top-end lubrication.

Another caveat: When installing

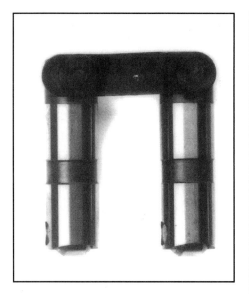

Roller lifters not only reduce friction, they allow for much more aggressive lift rates. Some type of link bar is required to prevent the lifters from rotating in their bores. The lifters shown are manufactured by Competition Cams.

LOW-FRICTION ROLLER HYDRAULIC VALVE LIFTER EXPLODED VIEW

LIFTER CAM ROLLER

18-NEEDLE ROLLER BEARINGS

A hydraulic roller lifter is nothing more than a standard hydraulic lifter with a roller on the bottom portion of the lifter body. The only real drawback is weight–they tend to be relatively heavy and limit maximum practical rpm potential to approximately 6500 rpm.

restrictors, check your silicone at the door. Some people think that an engine can't possibly be assembled correctly unless two or three tubes of silicone sealant are used. Then, when a gob of the stuff breaks off and closes up an oil passage, they wonder why they have an oiling system failure. It doesn't take much silicone to completely shut off an .080 in. oil metering restriction.

Mushroom Tappets

A unique type of mechanical lifter is known as the mushroom tappet, which has a standard sized (.842-in. dia.) body and a larger base or foot (.960 in. dia.). This type of lifter allows the use of specially designed race camshafts which move the valves at much higher opening and closing velocities (for increased horsepower) than would be possible with a standard .842-in. diameter lifter. Mushroom tappets are intended for use in racing categories that prohibit the use of roller tappets. Special block machining is required for mushroom tappet installation.

Mushroom tappets are designed to circumvent the limitations placed on cam lobe design by the stock .842-in. diameter tappet. Lobes with the extremely high opening velocities required for maximum horsepower border on a condition known as edge riding; sometimes they go over the border. When a lifter is edge riding, it contacts the cam lobe at its sharp edge, rather than on its base—a situation that accelerates cam and lifter wear and instigates instability in the valvetrain. In some racing categories, mushroom lifters are illegal, but the lifter bores in Chevrolet blocks can be modified to accept the same .875 in. diameter lifters found in Ford engines. Installation of .875 in. or mushroom lifters is advantageous only if a camshaft designed to take advantage of the increased lifter diameter is also installed.

Roller Tappets

Viewed from afar, all roller tappets are pretty much the same. However, each manufacturer will be quick to point out the superiority of its particular design. When examined up close, significant differences can be seen between various brands of lifters, but oddly enough, virtually all have been used successfully in a variety of race engines. Roller lifters differ primarily in their oil metering, link bar design and strength, needle bearing and axle diameter, overall weight and quality. Most of the larger high performance cam manufacturers produce their own roller lifters, so differences from one manufacturer to another can be significant. However, all of the better brands offer excellent strength and durability. As previously noted, some brands of roller lifters have built-in oil restrictions, so check with the manufacturer to see if restrictor plugs will create problems.

ROCKER ARMS

Stock

By the time Chevrolet introduced the big-block V-8 engine, stud-mounted rocker arms on the small block had been in production for 10 years. And in spite of original doubts as to their durability, they had proven themselves entirely adequate, so it was only natural that the big block would also have stud-mounted rockers. (Actually, there wasn't much of a choice because the big block's canted valves eliminated the possibility of using shaft-mounted rockers.)

Stock Pivot Balls—One of the liabilities of stock stamped-steel rockers is their tendency to gall or split in the vicinity of the pivot ball when subjected to high rpm operation and extreme valve spring pressure loads. When an engine is built for a class that requires use of stock-type rocker arms, component selection is critical. Obviously, the rockers themselves must be checked for ratio accuracy, but perhaps of even greater importance is the selection of pivot balls. The most commonly found type of pivot ball has several grooves machined into the surface that contacts the rocker. In theory, these grooves are supposed to increase the flow of oil between the ball and rocker. However, in virtually all grooved pivot balls, the grooves do not extend up to the top, so oil has just as much trouble getting between the ball and rocker as it would had no grooves been cut. Although the grooves can act as small oil reservoirs, any advantage this might offer is more than negated by the reduction in surface area. Consequently, for maximum effort race applications, a non-grooved rocker ball is preferable. Note that grooved rocker balls have

In endurance applications, rockers such as this Hi-Tech stainless steel model from Competition Cams are frequently used rather than those with aluminum bodies. Stainless steel or chrome/moly are advantageous because they're stronger than aluminum and don't fatigue or work harden.

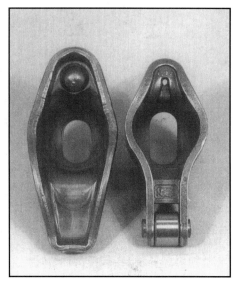

One benefit offered by high performance rockers is accurate rocker ratio. Magnum roller rockers are designed to be a relatively low cost alternative to stock rockers on high performance street and mild race engines. They feature a roller tip, long slot and will clear large diameter valve springs.

proven to be a problem only when extremely high valve spring pressures are used.

Stock rockers are most commonly (and erroneously) faulted for their non-rolling tip. While the plain surface would appear to create high friction with the valve tip, it really doesn't. The radius of the contact pad is so large, the area is so well lubricated and the amount of sliding movement is so small that friction between the rocker and valve tip is really insignificant. It's far greater between the rocker and the pivot ball.

Roller Rocker Arms

Aluminum and steel roller rocker arms, with needle bearings on the pivot trunnions and at the tips, unquestionably reduce friction, but their primary advantages are strength and stability. Roller rockers for big blocks are typically available in the stock 1.7:1 ratio as well as 1.6, 1.73 and 1.8:1 ratios. All are designed to be compatible with stock 7/16" diameter rocker studs.

Although 7/16" studs are quite beefy, on race engines, a stud girdle is usually added to reduce stud flex to an absolute minimum. Several stud girdle designs exist and all do the same thing. Specifically, they reduce stud deflection by tying all the rocker studs on a cylinder head together. The primary differences in the various designs have to do with installation and ease of use. The latter consideration is pretty much a matter of opinion.

About the only drawback to roller rockers is expense—they cost three to five times as much as stock-type rocker arms. That's a moot point with a race engine (and some killer street engines) because rocker cost has no bearing on choice; cam lift and valve spring load demand the use of roller rockers. Conversely, for most high-performance street and marine big blocks, roller lifters are not required. There's nothing wrong with installing them on non-racing engines, and contrary to some claims, durability is not a problem. However, some engine builders feel that aluminum's tendency to work-harden may lead to breakage, so they specify stainless steel rockers for all endurance-type engines. On the other hand, an aluminum rocker will typically wear out

ROCKER TIP-TO-STEM GEOMETRY

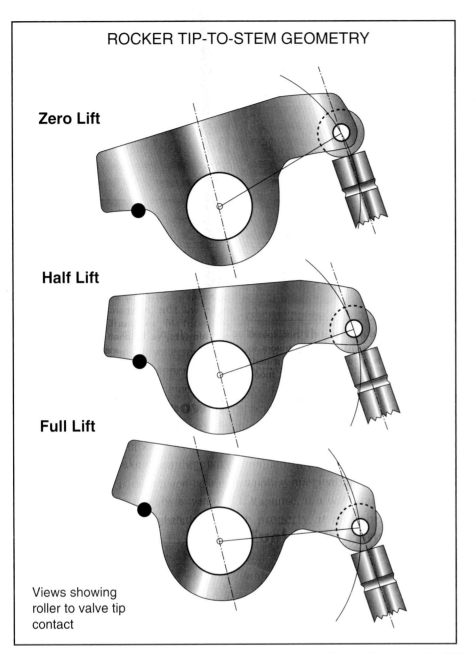

Zero Lift

Half Lift

Full Lift

Views showing roller to valve tip contact

Keeping the rocker tip centered on the valve stem is essential for good long-term durability. With proper valvetrain geometry, the rocker should contact the valve stem as shown throughout its range of travel.

Race-type valve springs place a tremendous load at the cam and lifter junction and this can prove fatal during break-in. Special "short ratio" rocker arms (shown at right) are available to make break-in easier. With a ratio of only 1.2:1 the valves aren't raised very high, so open pressures remain low. Once the cam and lifters are broken in, standard ratio rockers are installed.

Many camshaft manufacturers offer such rockers at surprisingly reasonable prices.

Rocker Arm Ratio

Rocker arm ratio is another factor that influences valvetrain stability; it's also another area of compromise. Increasing rocker arm ratio increases power potential, but it does so at the expense of valvetrain durability. In most applications, the trade-off in favor of power is a good one because the increased valvetrain stresses aren't large enough to make much of a difference in durability. However, for some types of endurance racing, the possibility of premature valve spring failure cannot be tolerated, so rocker arm ratios are sometimes on the conservative side. In fact, some engine builders use ratios lower than stock. It's quite common for the big-block Chevrolets found in off-shore race boats to be equipped with 1.6:1 rather than the stock 1.7:1 rocker arms. In such an instance, a bit of horsepower is traded for increased valve spring life.

On the other hand, most drag race and

its trunion bearings before the rocker body fails. There's no question that stainless steel is more durable, but it's also more expensive, so stainless rockers are typically used only in applications where spring loads and rpm are extreme.

Rocker Ratio

While stock-type rockers are only a fraction of the cost of exotic race pieces, you don't always get what you pay for; many stamped-steel rockers don't deliver the proper ratio. Rather than the specified

1.7:1 ratio, some of these rockers only muster something in the area of 1.6:1 ratio. The only way to tell is by individually testing each rocker arm, which is precisely what racers do when required to use stock-type rockers. This type of diligent checking isn't necessary for street engines, as the loss of a few horsepower due to reduced valve lift isn't critical. But for maximum performance, you need all the lift a cam can deliver, so the best procedure is to purchase name brand rockers from a reputable supplier.

ROCKER ARM RATIO

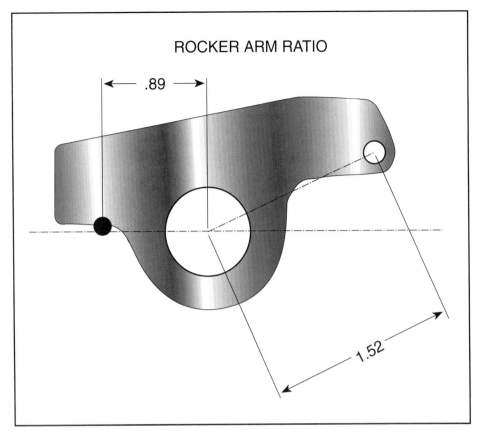

.89

1.52

Rocker arm ratio is determined by dividing the length from the trunion centerline to the tip by the length from the trunion to the pushrod seat. Computed ratio will usually be higher than actual ratio because compliance in the valvetrain reduces the rocker's effect.

All Mark IV engines are fitted with adjustable rockers. When setting hydraulic lifter preload, the adjusting nuts are snugged until all clearance is removed. Then the nuts are usually tightened an additional 1/2-turn. Other adjustment settings are also used, but the end result is to wind up with the plunger being pushed .020-in to .065" below the retaining ring.

oval track engine builders have developed their combinations around higher than stock rocker arm ratios and have experienced no problems. However, there's rarely a problem when an engine is assembled with higher-than-stock ratio rockers, because the valvetrain is thoroughly checked before the engine is ever fired. Trouble doesn't usually start brewing until an engine is already running and in a vehicle, and a switch is made to higher ratio rockers. The effect of rocker ratio on the valvetrain is the same as when one cam is swapped for another with greater lift. The valve spring stresses and the stresses coming back down the pushrods are raised.

Unfortunately, when rocker changes are made on a running engine, checks for coil bind, retainer-to-seal interference and piston-to-valve interference aren't done and that's what causes problems and failures.

Advantages—Significant horsepower gains—or losses—can be achieved through experimenting with the rocker arm ratio because a ratio change has an effect similar to that of a cam swap. Even people who flunked Auto Shop 101 can figure out that a rocker ratio change alters valve lift. But it may not be apparent that it also impacts effective duration—it makes the engine think the cam is more radical because the valve opens and closes more quickly (or less quickly if a change is made to a lower-than-stock ratio). But the ratio that's right for one engine won't necessarily be right for another. All you can do is give the engine what it wants, and that's done by trying different ratios and seeing which one works out best. It may be "trick" to run 1.8:1 ratio rockers on a big block, but the engine just may run best with a stock ratio. Much depends upon the aggressiveness of the camshaft. In a mild engine, high ratio rockers typically pay a better dividend when used in conjunction with a stock-type cam; most high performance cams move the valve fast

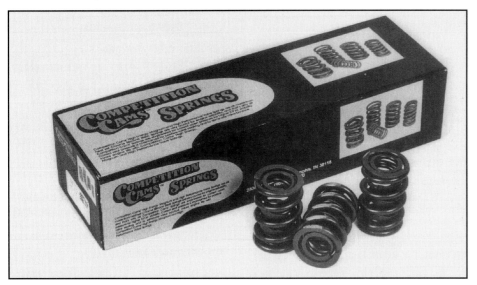

Valve springs play a critical role in determining horsepower, reliability and wear. Too much spring pressure and the cam and lifters wear out rapidly; too little pressure and rpm, and consequently horsepower, is limited. For best results, follow the camshaft manufacturer's recommendation for spring pressure and installed height.

At first glance, these two springs may look identical. But if you're Sherlock Holmes or an experienced engine builder, the difference is obvious. On the left is a single spring with a damper. On the right is a dual spring. For a race engine, the best arrangement is a dual spring with a flat wire damper. All three pieces should fit together snugly.

enough and lift it high enough that the increase in ratio doesn't have much of an effect on airflow because the ports and manifold runners are a limiting factor. On a race engine, high ratio rockers frequently bump up horsepower because the ports have enough airflow capacity to take advantage of the increased valve lift. Trial and error testing is the only way to be certain, but every time you change the engine combination, your trials and errors start all over again. While such experimentation is warranted in a race engine, the horsepower gains don't justify the expense for most street or recreational marine applications.

VALVE SPRINGS

Although the valve springs play the most significant role in maintaining stability at high engine speeds, coordination of all valvetrain components serves to reduce the potential for problems. To assure valvetrain stability, you have to begin with adequate spring pressure, a consideration that's frequently overlooked when a high performance camshaft is installed in a stock or slightly modified engine. Stock valve springs are designed to handle the loads imposed by

a mild camshaft rotating at relatively low engine speeds. Although some very mild high performance camshafts are compatible with stock valve springs, stiffer springs are generally required if the cam is to live up to its full potential. Not only does a performance cam open and close the valves more quickly, its power range is further up the rpm scale than its stock counterpart; higher engine speeds and higher opening and closing velocities require higher spring rates. But pressure isn't the only criteria that should be used when selecting valve springs.

Resonant Frequency

That point is well illustrated by a series of tests General Motors ran a number of years ago. A group of engineers testing a "Duntov 30-30" cam found that the engine's maximum rpm was lower than anticipated. To correct the situation, the engineers installed some "trick" valve springs from a Chevrolet "mystery" engine. But they still couldn't get the engine speed much over 7200 rpm. Then they installed a set of special aftermarket valve springs and very carefully set the open pressure exactly the same as it had been with the previous set of springs. The results were quite surprising—the engine

ran 1000 rpm faster. The reason? A change in the natural resonant frequency of the valve springs.

During engine operation, as speeds increase, the cam "excites" the valve springs as it spins through its opening/closing cycle. In turn, the springs begin to vibrate at a frequency determined by wire diameter and number of coils. When a spring's natural resonant frequency is reached, strange things begin to happen—most commonly, engine speed is abruptly limited because the vibrating springs can't control the valve.

Dual valve springs offer higher rpm potential because of their increased pressure, but that rpm potential is increased further if the inner and outer springs have vastly different natural resonant frequencies. On the other hand, if the inner and outer springs have a similar natural resonant frequency, much of the advantage is lost because both springs become "excited" and start to vibrate at approximately the same engine speed; the resulting spring surge will literally shut off the engine. That was precisely what happened with the Chevrolet valve springs—they reached their natural resonant frequency at approximately 7200 rpm.

Stud girdles are standard equipment on race-prepared big blocks, because individual studs tend to move when a high lift cam is working against stiff valve springs. Stud girdles also tend to keep valves in adjustment longer.

Most big-block stud girdles are manufactured of five individual pieces of aluminum, but Competition Cams offers a unique one-piece model that offers improved rigidity.

Aftermarket Springs—By comparison, the aftermarket springs were comprised of inner and outer coils with vastly different resonant frequencies; when one vibrated, the other was rock solid. Consequently, by specifically tailoring the resonant frequencies of the individual springs which comprise a dual or three-piece spring, vibration never becomes a built-in rpm limiter. Viewed from a different perspective, a single spring imposes a built-in terminal point for engine speed—once the spring's natural resonant frequency is reached, the engine will spin no faster. A damper helps the situation a bit, but dual springs

are a better solution; dual springs with a damper are better yet. Although three springs offer maximum rpm potential, most engine builders stick with dual springs with a damper because they feel a three-piece spring has too much coil-to-coil friction (which results in the generation of excessive heat).

You don't have to get up into race engine speeds to experience the effects of valve springs gone berserk. The typical passenger car engine will frequently run strongly to about 5000 rpm, but will run into trouble about 5200 rpm and absolutely cannot be coaxed up to 5300 rpm. The engine begins to miss because

the springs are surging and not controlling valve movement.

Valve Float—Another rpm-limiting factor is valve float, which occurs when spring pressure isn't sufficient to make the lifter follow the cam contour. What results is called separation—the lifter does not remain in continual contact with the cam lobe. Instead, it launches itself over the nose and bounces on the flank. Once valve float is reached, there is no way to further increase engine speed.

Rpm Upper Limits

Stories abound of Chevy big blocks equipped with hydraulic lifters turning 8000 rpm. In most cases, these tales should be taken with a grain of salt and about 2000 rpm. With an average high performance camshaft designed for 50,000 mile durability, and installed in conjunction with the valve springs recommended by the manufacturer, 5500 to 6000 rpm is a practical upper speed limit. Stiffer springs will increase the rpm ceiling, but to little purpose—the higher spring loads result in more rapid cam and lifter wear and most high performance hydraulic cams are designed to pump out peak horsepower at 6000 to 6500 rpm. Certainly, there are numerous grinds that will make peak power at 7000 to 7200 rpm, but typically, when an engine is built for operation in this speed range, a mechanical lifter cam is installed.

Consequently, for most applications where engine speed rarely exceeds 5000 rpm, single valve springs with seat pressures of 85-100 psi are sufficient. For more aggressive engines and driving styles, stiffer dual valve springs will raise practical engine speed maximums to the 6500-7000 range. Some race engines, when equipped with a lightweight valvetrain, can be reliably turned as high as 8000 rpm with hydraulic lifters. But this type of rpm requires more than just stiff springs. Valvetrain weight has an effect and is especially critical on the valve side (as opposed to the pushrod side) of the rocker arm because of the multiplying effect of the rocker arm ratio—that means titanium valves and retainers.

High engine speeds are one thing, high power output at high engine speeds is another. If an engine is going to produce meaningful power at elevated rpm levels, the camshaft must have sufficient duration and lift and the induction and exhaust systems must be suitably tailored. It serves no real purpose to turn an engine 7500 rpm if its power peak is at 6000 rpm.

Coil Bind

Just as valve springs should be checked for coil bind whenever a cam with greater lift (than the one currently in place) is installed, they should also be checked when switching to higher ratio rockers. As a general practice, when an engine is being assembled, notes should be taken about where coil bind occurs. When this is done, it's possible to compute potential problems rather than waiting to be surprised after a cam or rocker arm change is made.

Checking—A common method of checking for coil bind is to place a valve at maximum lift and attempt to insert a .060-in. diameter wire between the coils. That's an excellent means of getting into trouble. The fact that at least .060 in. of clearance exists between coils (with the valve at maximum lift) does not prove that the same amount of clearance exists between all coils in a spring. The coils near the top and bottom are closer together when the spring is in its extended state, and they're also closer together when a spring is compressed. So adequate clearance between center coils doesn't guarantee that the end coils aren't in a bind. And it doesn't necessarily follow that the coils that reach coil bind are the ones that will break. In fact, springs usually break one coil up from the point of hardest coil bind. When a spring breaks right in the middle, it's usually the result of a bad piece of wire or

The valve on the right is at maximum lift, and there's still plenty of open space between the coils of the valve spring. That's as it should be because coil bind kills valve springs and that can lead to engine failure.

extreme surging problems.

Avoiding—The best way to avoid coil bind is to follow the manufacturer's recommendations regarding installed height and valve spring part number to be used with a specific camshaft. As an example, a typical dual valve spring used on high performance big blocks with a flat tappet or hydraulic camshaft has a nominal seat pressure of 120 lbs. at an installed height of 1.875 in. Nominal open pressure is 395 lbs. at a compressed height of 1.175 in. That translates to .700-in. of valve lift (1.875-1.175 = .700 in.). This spring also has a nominal solid height of 1.080 in, which means that with an installed height of 1.875 in., the spring will be solidly in coil bind if valve lift is .795 in. or greater (1.875-1.080 = .795 in.).

Installed Height—If you've been thinking that coil bind will only be a problem if valve lift approaches .795 in., you have been lured into the same trap that catches a surprising number of knowledgeable engine builders. The amount of lift that a spring will tolerate without reaching coil bind is partially dependent upon installed height. The

Gen V big-block heads are not machined for 7/16-in rocker studs. Instead, they are drilled and tapped for 3/8" diameter shouldered bolts. This is definitely a marginal arrangement for anything other than a bone stock engine. (And even then, it's questionable.) The stud boss should be remachined to accept Mark IV-style studs.

spring described above is also suitable for roller cam applications, in which case the installed height is reduced to 1.750 in. as a means of increasing seat pressure to 165 lbs. With this setting, an open pressure of 426 lbs. is achieved at a height of 1.110 in. This translates into a valve lift of .640 in. (1.750-1.110 = .640 in.). The nominal solid height is still 1.080 in., which leaves only .030 in. between a maximum valve lift of .640 in.

and coil bind at .670 in. Consequently, to retain the appropriate safety margin, this valve spring is recommended only for roller camshafts providing a maximum valve lift of .625 in. or less.

But what happens when rocker arm ratio is bumped? If the .625 in. lift figure was achieved with a 1.7:1 rocker, a switch to 1.8:1 rockers will put lift at .662 in. and the springs in coil bind. Obviously, a change to 1.8:1 rockers necessitates installation of different valve springs which can tolerate higher valve lift.

Spring Options

Before venturing off into the land of high performance camshafts, it's advisable to take a long look at an engine's cylinder heads. Stock production big-block heads will accept valve springs with an outside diameter of up to approximately 1.460 in. Most high performance dual valve springs will fit stock spring pockets, but "killer" race springs have an OD of 1.550-in. to 1.625-in. Spring seat machining is therefore required before these types of springs can be installed.

In most instances, the OD of the valve guide must also be machined (to a smaller diameter) to accept the high performance valve seals that are required to clear the ID of the inner valve springs. These machining operations must be done with the heads disassembled and removed from the engine, so plan ahead.

Dampers—Some, but not all, dual valve springs contain a flat wire damper that fits between the inner and outer coil springs. This type of spring is definitely superior to dual springs with no damper. In all cases, it should require some amount of effort to pull the inner spring out. If you can set a dual spring on a bench, stick your finger into the inner spring, raise your hand and have only the inner spring come with it, the spring is either excessively worn, or wasn't properly assembled in the first place.

Interference between the inner spring, damper and outer spring is essential to maximum pressure retention.

Unfortunately, when inner and outer springs rub against the damper, small particles of metal chip off and go traveling throughout the engine. Generally, the particles are too small to do much damage, but if nothing else, the thought of metal shavings working their way between critical surfaces is unsettling. To eliminate the problem, many race engine builders have valve springs coated with a dry film lubricant.

Although the amount of material chipped from the valve springs isn't very much, it is a measurable amount. To demonstrate the point, one coating company tells its customers to weigh their uncoated springs before installation, and then again after the engine has run for a while. Each spring will actually lose a measurable amount of weight.

To date, most engine builders prefer dual springs with a damper to three-piece valve springs. The three-piece springs do not produce significantly more pressure than a top-of-the-line dual spring and seem to run hotter.

Spring Set-Up

Regardless of the type or brand of spring selected, the most important consideration is how well the springs are set-up. Springs must be matched to the proper retainers so that excessive shimming isn't required to achieve the proper installed height. It's also advisable to ensure that the spring pocket OD matches the spring OD to prevent the springs from "walking." Spring cups can be installed if spring pocket OD is too large.

Retainers—For a time, aluminum retainers were all the rage for high performance street and race engines. But aluminum has a nasty habit of work-hardening and cracking, so aluminum retainers have gone on to the great recycling bin in the sky. Steel retainers

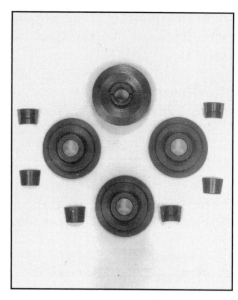

Retainers and locks (also called keepers and split keys) must be matched to each other with respect to angle. A seven-degree taper is used with stock and many high performance locks while a 10-degree taper is exclusively used in high performance and race engines. Either steel or titanium retainers and machined steel locks should be installed on a healthy big block. Avoid aluminum retainers at all costs.

are most commonly used, with titanium being the material of choice for killer drag race and oval track engines.

Except for some specially prepared race heads, big-block Chevy cylinder heads are machined to accept valves with 3/8 in. diameter stems. Consequently, the retainer/lock package must also be suited for an 3/8-in. stem. Most cam manufacturers offer several styles of retainers to allow for some latitude in installed height; a stepped retainer provides for more installed height than a flat version.

Another valve retainer variable is the lock angle. All stock-style retainers and many race types are machined for 7-deg. locks; some race retainers accept 10-deg. locks. Obviously, retainers must be installed with compatible locks to ensure that the valves stay in place.

Is a 10-deg. retainer/lock combination better than a 7-deg.? That depends upon who answers that question. Some engine builders swear by one style, others have the opposite opinion. For a street engine and most race engines, a 7-deg. assembly, which is most economically priced, is more than adequate. Typically, 10-deg. retainers and locks are used only in professional-caliber race engines.

Valve Locks—Also called split keys or keepers, valve locks fit between the retainer and valve stem and, as the name implies, lock the valves into place. The wedging action of the retainer clamps the lock against the valve stem; the small tang on the inside of the lock is for location purposes. While most locks utilize a standard tang location, some companies offer a selection with standard, .050 in. higher and .050 in. lower locations. This arrangement allows for relative quick and easy adjustment of installed height.

All top-quality valve locks are machined; the garden variety stock replacement types are stamped. Although failure of a stamped lock is rare, the cheapest insurance you can buy is to step up and buy machined locks. Most high performance engine builders make it a standard policy to use only machined

Pushrods are especially critical to successful valvetrain operation. For all-out racing engines, the main areas to consider when it comes to pushrods for your big-block are length, diameter, straightness, and whether or not they were heat-treated.

locks—even on a stock rebuild. They feel that for the relatively small difference in price, it just doesn't pay to gamble.

PUSHRODS

Stock big-block Chevy intake pushrods measure 8.250 in.; exhaust pushrods are 9.250-in. long and both have a 3/8-in. diameter. However, you'll find that some manufacturers cite a slightly different length. Many race engines are equipped with longer or shorter pushrods, so some people have come to the mistaken conclusion that non-standard lengths offer some type of performance benefit. Of course, some people also believe that the world is flat and that Democrats won't raise taxes. In all cases, nothing could be further from the truth. In fact, installing longer- or shorter-than-stock pushrods, when they are not required, can lead to serious engine problems.

Length

Legitimate use of special length pushrods is called for only when standard

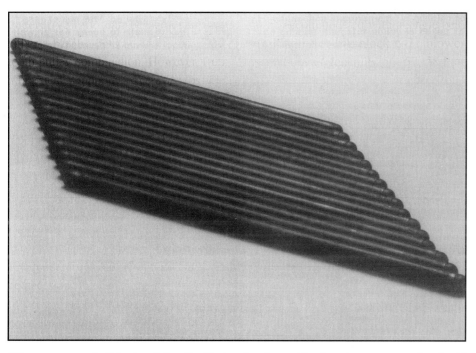

Whenever a camshaft is changed or the block or heads machined, rocker arm geometry should be checked. Ideally, the contact point between the valve stem and the rocker tip should be exactly in the center when the cam is at half maximum lift. Longer or shorter pushrods may be required to achieve proper geometry. Race quality pushrods are available from a variety of manufacturers in just about any length desired.

One of the most common problems with big-block valvetrains is improper pushrod alignment caused by guideplates being manufactured incorrectly. On this engine, the only way to properly align the pushrods was to split the guideplate.

Competition Cams released this guideplate a few years ago and it eliminates pushrod alignment problems. A sophisticated design technique known as stereo lithography was used to assure that the compound angles at which the pushrod slots are positioned are correct.

length parts don't allow for proper valvetrain geometry. If longer-than-stock valves are installed (to achieve a desired spring installed height), if the block or heads have been milled excessively, if aftermarket cylinder heads or special rocker arms are installed, then standard-length pushrods are usually required.

Proper pushrod length places the rocker arm precisely in the middle of the valve stem when the valve is at half its total lift. If a cam provides total valve lift of .550 in., the rocker tip should be perfectly centered when the valve has been raised .275 in. off its seat. This should occur with very little movement across the face of the valve tip. Ideally, the rocker/valve stem contact point should be slightly to the intake manifold side of center when the valve is closed. As the valve opens, the contact point should move towards the exhaust manifold side of the tip and then should move back towards the intake manifold side as the valve reaches maximum lift. In all, there should only be a few thousandths of an inch of lateral movement. Excessive motion places a heavy side load on the valve stem and leads to rapid guide wear.

The quickest and easiest way to determine proper pushrod length is through use of an adjustable pushrod. Once in place, an adjustable pushrod is lengthened or shortened as required to center the rocker arm on the valve stem at half lift. Then its overall length is measured, giving you the proper pushrod length for the engine.

Many custom-length pushrods consist of a piece of steel tubing with hardened ends pressed into place. However, some manufacturers offer one-piece pushrods with swedged (the word is swedged, not wedged) ends. These ends should be machined so that their radii match those of the pushrod seats in the lifter and rocker arm.

Diameter

Although most high performance pushrods are 3/8-in. in diameter, 7/16-in. pushrods are available. These are typically installed in large displacement full-tilt race engines with special cylinder heads. These engines are usually built around a high deck block, which in combination with the heads calls for pushrod lengths in excess of 11 inches. With pushrods that long, a 7/16-in. diameter is necessary to minimize flexing.

Heat Treating

The guideplates that keep pushrods properly aligned in big-block engines require the use of heat-treated pushrods. The heat treating process increases surface hardness and prevents pushrod wear. Use of non-heat-treated pushrods is hazardous to an engine's health, as the guideplates will slice through the pushrod

The quality of roller timing chain and sprocket sets varies dramatically depending upon the manufacturer. Many of the low cost sets that are manufactured "offshore" have crank sprockets with keyways seemingly cut by blind people. Name brand sets are usually machined accurately, but if you degree-in a cam during installation, there's no doubt about valve timing accuracy. Some timing sets are supplied with a thrust washer to protect the block.

tubing like a sharp knife through butter. Make sure to check that the pushrods have been heat-treated.

Timing Chain & Sprockets

Much ado has been made of the difference between a link- or silent-type and a roller timing chain. However, it has never been conclusively demonstrated that one type is clearly superior to the other. Since the beginning of time, Chevrolet has installed link chains in all passenger car engines and roller chains in most truck engines. Both types of chains stretch and some engineers claim that a roller chain actually stretches more than a link type. The big advantage of a roller is that it will not jump a tooth when it gets old and feeble whereas a link chain will.

The major objections to a stock chain and sprocket set are the aluminum gear/nylon tooth camshaft sprocket and 5/8-in.-wide chain that has been in general use since 1967. While this piece of bean-counter engineering doesn't do much to inspire confidence, it is used in a surprising number of race engines. Some

engine builders use a stock chain set because it's cheap and they simply replace it after every race or after a few races. Other people would rather pay a bit more and get a 3/4-in.-wide chain and sprocket set that will last longer. Whether that set is a high quality link type with iron gears or roller type is a matter of preference. There's even some controversy over whether a "true roller" is in fact superior to a plain roller.

Roller Chains

All roller chains for big-block Chevys have two rows of rollers, but with some designs, the rollers or the pins on which they're mounted don't actually spin; by virtue of their being round, they will roll over the sprocket teeth, but their position within the chain is fixed. With a "true roller" design, the individual rollers and pins are free to spin, so there's less friction. On the other hand, the pins in some standard roller timing chains are larger than those found in a "true roller," so they're also stronger. Another consideration is roller construction— some are seamless, others are seamed.

The seamless versions are kinder to the sprockets, which help longevity. On the other hand, being more expensive, they aren't as kind to your wallet.

Recommendations—All this background is informative, but you may not care. What you want to know is which timing chain to buy. The answer to that is—a good one. Keyway accuracy is of prime importance. Many off-brand (and some name-brand) chain sets are manufactured in countries that are known for low cost and equally low quality. Some of these sets have keyway locations that are off by up to 8 deg. So the best advice is to purchase a name-brand, top-quality chain set and to degree-in the camshaft in all cases.

Among high performance and race engine builders, the consensus of opinion is that the best type of chain for a particular engine depends upon the intended use of that engine. For a drag race engine that will be serviced regularly (the operative word here is regularly) a stock-type link chain—with aluminum/nylon cam sprocket—is often the "hot tip." This type of chain and sprocket minimize the transfer of torsional shock loads from the crankshaft to the camshaft, which results in more consistent valve and ignition timing. In dyno testing, these benefits have surfaced in the form of a more efficient fuel curve. However, with this set-up, the chain and sprockets are changed every time the engine is torn down—and it's usually torn down after every race.

For street, bracket, oval track, marine or any other use where regular and intense maintenance isn't planned, a roller chain should be used, because in general, it will provide superior long-term durability. Gary Grimes, of Grimes Automotive Machine, suggests that before you install the chain, put it in a pan of oil with a little moly lube mixed in. Then heat it up to about 200 deg. F for an hour or so. You'll be amazed at the difference that will make—it almost

When installing a crank sprocket with multiple keyways, be sure to match marks properly. With the appropriate keyway positioned at 1 o'clock, the matching mark by the tooth should be at 12 o'clock. The "0" marks on this set indicate a "straight-up" position.

totally eliminates chain stretch. It may sound strange, but it works.

Torrington Bearing—Some chain sets are supplied with cam sprockets that are machined to accept a Torrington bearing. Rear thrust of the camshaft is controlled by the cam sprocket riding against the front of the block. This arrangement is satisfactory with standard flat-tappet cams, but with roller and mushroom-tappet cams, thrust control is more critical, so use of a bearing is advantageous. Forward thrust must also be controlled and most cam manufacturers offer a needle-bearing "anti-walk" cam button that fits in the center hole of the cam sprocket, between the cam and front cover.

The crown shape machined on the bottom of a flat tappet, combined with a taper .001 in. across the cam lobe (both are difficult to detect with the naked eye), essentially eliminates the need for forward thrust control. However, that's not the case with a cam designed for roller or mushroom tappets, hence the need to prevent the cam from "walking" fore and aft.

Regardless of cam type, a thrust bearing reduces friction and block wear so it's always worth the investment. Competition Cams offers a one-piece thrust bearing (the bearing and thrust plates are "encapsulated" to form a single piece measuring .142-in. thick) which is listed as part number 3110 TB. In all instances, when a thrust bearing is installed, the back side of the cam sprocket must be machined to accommodate bearing width.

Gear Drives

Of course, the best way to eliminate chain stretch (which is really more a case of chain and sprocket wear) is to eliminate the chain—which is what a gear drive does. Like any other piece of automotive equipment, gear drives have their positive and negative aspects. On the positive side, gear drives eliminate valve timing variations caused by chain stretch and flex (on a big block, each .020 in. of stretch retards the cam approximately 1 deg.). Gears also last almost indefinitely.

On the negative side, gear drives are expensive, noisy and require exacting tolerances to keep the gear teeth meshing properly. Any time a block is align-honed, the camshaft-to-crankshaft distance changes so some compensation must be made. Some gear drives incorporate an adjustable idler that can be positioned as required. Also note that drives using only two gears spin the camshaft in the reverse direction (compared to a chain drive) so a special "gear drive" cam must be used. Drives with three gears incorporate an idler and rotate the camshaft in its normal direction.

The most significant disadvantage to a gear drive is its extreme rigidity, which is very efficient at transferring crankshaft torsional vibrations to the camshaft. Many engine builders feel that this leads to premature camshaft or valvetrain failure. Although this theory has never been conclusively proven, most top engine builders prefer a timing chain and sprocket. Or a Jesel belt drive.

Jesel Belt Drive

As the name implies, Jesel's system uses a rubber belt, rather than a chain or gears, to spin the camshaft. The belt-drive assembly needs no lubrication and mounts on the exposed side of a special timing cover. The cam sprocket is a two-piece affair that allows for quick and easy advancing and retarding of the cam. In addition to providing extremely accurate and consistent valve timing, the Jesel belt drive simplifies cam changes significantly because the timing cover doesn't have to be removed. ■

8

IGNITION SYSTEMS

Put air and fuel inside a cylinder, compress it, put some fire to it and you've got combustion. Sounds simple enough, but at engine speeds over 4000 rpm, ignition demands are such that the system isn't always able to supply enough electrical energy to light a fire inside the combustion chamber. With the advent of electronic ignition, shortfall of ignition energy joined wide whitewall tires as a thing of the past. This is largely due to prodding by the Federal government, whose invasion of the automobile industry during the last two decades has prompted an acceleration in automotive technology.

Federal mandates, in the form of Corporate Average Fuel Economy (CAFE) requirements, and Environmental Protection Agency clean air standards, pitched the automakers on a course of positive action with respect to reducing exhaust emissions while increasing fuel economy and engine efficiency. Concurrently, dramatic increases in fuel prices, along with the gas shortages of 1973-74 and 1979-80, made fuel economy an important priority of new car buyers. Ignition systems played an important role in the attainment of fuel economy and exhaust emissions goals. With those challenges having been met, Detroit engineers turned their attention to high performance, and by the mid-Eighties the big-block Chevrolet once again began to shine.

But the road to compliance with Federal standards was not an easy one to

Big-block-powered Camaros are a mainstay in bracket and "Super" class racing. With electronic ignitions handling the generation of spark energy, current big blocks are tough to beat—a lesson the driver of the Mopar in the far lane is about to learn.

Points are as out of date as the Flat Earth Society, but if you have to use a point-type distributor, or are too stubborn to change to electronics, invest in a good set of points. High performance points have higher spring pressures for improved high rpm stability, but lead to accelerated rubbing block wear. A little dab of lubricant extends rubbing block lift.

travel, and it took several years for the necessary technology to be developed and successfully applied. Consequently, all manner of ignition systems exist for the big block—some good, some not so good and some downright rotten. Fortunately, any big-block ignition system can be easily upgraded. However, before delving into the pertinent modifications, I'm duty-bound to lead you to the following disclaimer: Making any change whatsoever to an ignition system may be in violation of local, state or Federal regulations governing vehicles of certain model years. This is especially true in California, where the California Air Resources Board has made just about everything besides opening the hood illegal. Check local emissions regulations before performing any ignition modifications.

BREAKER POINT SYSTEMS

When Louis Chevrolet introduced the first vehicle to bear his name, it was the wizardry of Charles Kettering that caused the air to be filled with the melody of internal combustion. And for all the improvements wrought upon the automobile during the first seven decades of the Twentieth Century, the Kettering-designed ignition system survived largely unchanged. It wasn't until 1974 that Chrysler Corporation broke with tradition and began installing electronic ignition systems on all new vehicles. The following year Chevrolet, along with other GM divisions, followed suit with the High Energy Ignition (HEI) system.

One of the major advantages offered by an electronic system is the replacement of the breaker points with a non-mechanical triggering device (an electronic switch). This is desirable because point wear increases with mileage, resulting in a continual deterioration of ignition system operation. After 10,000 to 12,000 miles, a typical set of points is as worn as a 10-year-old pair of shoes and must be replaced.

How it Works

Breaker-point wear can best be understood through an examination of the system's operation. When the ignition key is turned to either the "On" or "Start" position, current flows through the primary circuit, which includes the battery, ballast resistor or resistance wiring, the primary side of the ignition coil and breaker points. A condenser is connected to the points, but does not come into play just yet. Current in the primary side of the ignition coil (up to four amperes) increases to a value determined by the primary resistance and ballast resistor and reaches its peak in approximately .006 seconds (6 milliseconds).

Primary Winding—The primary winding of a coil is composed of approximately 200 turns of relatively heavy gauge wire wound around an iron core. Between the core and the primary winding is the secondary winding which consists of about 20,000 turns of extremely fine wire. The relationship between primary and secondary windings is known as "turns ratio," which in this instance would be 100:1.

With 12 volts making the grand tour through the primary winding (at a rate of four amps), a strong magnetic field is

One way to avoid the limitations of a single set of points is with dual points. By overlapping the opening and closing cycles of each set, dwell time is extended and consequently so is coil saturation time. The payoff is improved high rpm spark quality, but the system still falls short when compared to an electronic set-up.

In both the older point-type and later HEI electronic distributors (as well as MSD distributors), centrifugal advance is controlled by a spring and weight assembly that is located just beneath the rotor. Generally, it's only necessary to change springs and limit total travel when building a custom calibrated advance curve. For regular maintenance, it's a good idea to periodically remove the cap and rotor and pull out on the advance weights to make sure they move smoothly and reach full advance.

developed, inducing a voltage in the secondary. Due to the turns ratio (100:1), voltage in the secondary is stepped up to about 1,200 volts—a sizable increase, but still not enough to fire a spark across the plug gap.

Once through the coil's primary winding, the current must be given some place to go. However, since there is no more work for it to do, it is simply dissipated to ground. Ground is nothing more than a return path to the battery. So long as current is flowing through the coil, the magnetic field is maintained. When the points open, the only path available to the current leads it into the condenser, which serves as a temporary energy storage device. Were a condenser not included in the circuit, the current would arc across the opening points, quickly burning the contacts and destroying them. But the condenser serves another purpose; once the points open it becomes charged with a high voltage and when it reaches its saturation point, current flow stops and the magnetic field collapses. The high voltage built up in the condenser is then discharged back into the primary side of

the coil which steps up the voltage, by virtue of its turns ratio, to approximately 30,000 volts. This aspect of the condenser's operation explains why an engine will run, but won't perform well, if a condenser is damaged or eliminated from the circuit. Without it the ignition system can't produce the level of voltage necessary to initiate combustion in an engine under heavy load.

Dwell Time—Interruption of primary current flow is accomplished by simply opening the breaker points, an action that is controlled by the cam on the distributor shaft. (The rubbing block attached to one arm of the points rides on this cam.) In effect, the points are a mechanically actuated switch used to turn current flow through the coil on and off. But there's a little more to it than that; increasing the time period during which the points dwell in the closed position lengthens the time available to build up the current in the coil. Not too surprisingly, "dwell time" is the term used to note the duration, in degrees of engine crankshaft rotation, that the points are closed.

By aligning the distributor rotor with a terminal in the cap, at precisely the time

that the points are opened, an escape path is provided; the current flows out of the coil, into the distributor cap, across the rotor to a terminal, out of the cap and through the plug wire to the spark plug. And, if in jumping across the plug gap the current (now termed a spark) encounters a fresh mixture of air and fuel, combustion occurs.

Limitations

In spite of an excellent record for reliable performance, point-type ignition systems contain a number of built-in limitations:

• The breaker points must carry a relatively high amount of current (2-3 amps), which leads to erosion of the contact surfaces.

• As engine speed increases, the time available (dwell time) to build high voltage in the coil decreases, dramatically reducing spark intensity.

• Breaker point opening and closing timing tends to be irregular. As the rubbing block wears and the contacts erode, dwell time, and consequently spark timing, is altered. Distributor shaft bushing wear also leads to timing irregularity.

• At high engine speeds, the rubbing block may not stay in contact with the distributor cam with the result being "point bounce," which leads to misfire.

• Since both the point contacts and the rubbing block are subject to wear, point sets must be replaced periodically.

These are the major shortcomings that prompted the automakers to universally convert to electronic ignition. And while that conversion didn't occur until 1975, electronic ignitions have actually been available since the early Sixties.

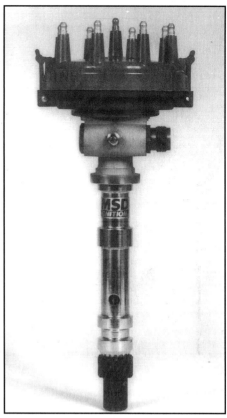

As a means of eliminating spark scatter and timing inaccuracies that come along with a distributor, many big-block race engines are fitted with a crank-triggered ignition. With this arrangement, timing is fixed at a particular setting unless a timing computer is included in the circuit.

Special low-profile distributors are often used in a crank trigger system. These distributors have no advance mechanism, they're only for starting the engine (and driving the oil pump). Once the engine is running, the driver throws a switch and the crank trigger takes over.

ELECTRONIC IGNITIONS

A number of years ago, when electronics were first applied to the point-type ignition system, manufacturers devised a variety of displays as a means of demonstrating the worth of their products. The one most commonly used (variations are still employed) simulated a spark plug with an adjustable gap. A standard ignition was fired up and the gap gradually opened until the spark no longer jumped across. Then the electronic ignition was connected and the spark flitted across an opening as wide as the Grand Canyon. While the demonstration is impressive, with sparks flying about as if a thunderstorm had invaded the display booth, it illustrates but a single aspect of the superiority of electronic ignition—increased voltage output. Unfortunately, many people are misled by these types of demonstrations and come away thinking that voltage is the only criterion of

ignition system performance. But there's a lot more to the story.

Transistor Ignitions

As previously noted, in a conventional system, the points are required to handle a relatively high amount of amperage which erodes the contacts. Early electronic devices, then called "transistor ignitions," altered the points' position in the circuit and in so doing, significantly reduced the amount of current flowing across the contacts. In essence, the points became a mechanical switch used to control the system's electronic circuitry. This arrangement boosted voltage output by increasing the current flow through the transistors to levels not possible with the breaker points alone. And since the electronic circuitry, not the point contacts, handled the lion's share of the current flow, point life was extended. But it still didn't address the problem of rubbing block and distributor cam wear, and the

resulting irregularity in spark timing. False firing of the system, caused by high rpm point bounce, is also a characteristic of any point-type ignition system.

Pointless Triggers

Clearly, the points had to go. When connected to electronic circuitry, breaker points become nothing more than a pulse generator that signals the control module when it's time to discharge the coil into the distributor. This being the case, there's no need to maintain a mechanical triggering device with all of its inherent problems. So magnetic, optic and Hall effect triggers have become the devices of choice in electronic ignition systems.

While each of these devices offers a unique advantage, they also have drawbacks. Light emitting diodes can burn out (although they rarely do) or get

For best performance, a custom calibrated spark curve, created on a distributor machine, is a necessity. Full centrifugal advance should occur at 2500 to 2750 crankshaft rpm.

For street applications, once the centrifugal curve is set, the vacuum advance should also be dialed in. The easiest way to optimize the vacuum advance curve is with an adjustable canister, usually identified by the hex-shaped area adjacent to the nipple. Turning the Allen wrench clockwise brings advance in quicker, turning it counterclockwise slows it down. Adjust it so that vacuum advance comes in as quickly as possible without causing the engine to ping.

Why Electronic?

In the late Sixties, the high compression, high rpm engines that were standard fare in performance cars created energy demands that conventional systems could no longer meet on a consistent basis. In an effort to solve this problem, Chevrolet offered optional Delcotronic Transistor Controlled Magnetic Pulse Type Ignition Systems on some high performance Corvette engines during the Sixties. Although this system is highly revered by Corvette restorers, it isn't a particularly good ignition system by current standards.

When the performance craze was throttled back by concerns over exhaust emissions, the need for high energy ignitions didn't evaporate. In fact, it became more critical. Igniting the exceptionally lean air/fuel mixtures necessary for reduced exhaust emissions requires at least as much spark energy (not just voltage) as demanded by a high performance powerplant.

One method of achieving this is to widen the plug gap so that more fuel is exposed to the heat of the spark. Another approach, and one that should be used in combination with the first, is to increase spark current and duration. That can be easily achieved with a GM HEI (High Energy Ignition) system, which was designed specifically to provide a "fat" spark.

When an air/fuel mixture is excessively lean, gasoline molecule density is low; the gap between the plug electrodes is therefore widened, and spark duration lengthened, to improve the chances of "zapping" a sufficient number of gas molecules. A conventional point-type ignition system could ignite the lean mixtures used in late-model engines, but its energy level would be so low that an inordinate number of misfires would result. Many of these would be barely detectable to the driver, but poor fuel economy would result and, under heavy load (as during full throttle acceleration

dirty enough to interfere with light transmission. Hall effect circuits can fail due to heat. Consequently Chevrolet, like other auto manufacturers, has relied on magnetic triggers in original equipment systems. Although the failure rate of aftermarket systems using LED and Hall effect triggers has been well within the margins of acceptability, the automakers feel that only a magnetic trigger, consisting of a reluctor and a magnetic pick-up, offers an acceptable level of reliability—magnets and steel reluctors are virtually failure proof.

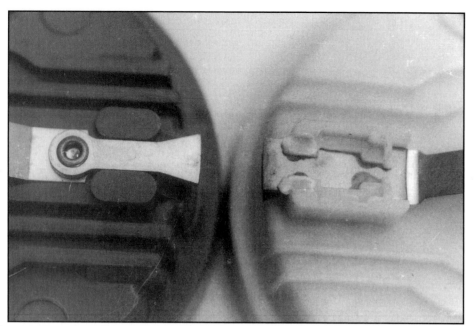

All rotors for big-block distributors may look pretty much the same, but there are big differences. The flimsy stock-type unit on the right doesn't inspire a lot of confidence. The high performance rotor on the left is made of better materials and more of them. The rotor tip is also longer and better reinforced for improved durability.

or when climbing a steep grade), the engine would stutter badly since all cylinders would not be "giving their fair share."

In addition to eliminating problems related to breaker points, HEI systems fire a considerably "hotter" (increased voltage) and "fatter" (higher amperage) spark across the spark plug electrodes. With these systems, voltage is sufficient to consistently ionize (jump across) gaps of .045 to .060 in.; amperage is high and burn time relatively long. Therefore, these systems produce considerably more spark energy than a conventional system.

This being the case, you could reasonably wonder about the need for other aftermarket ignition systems and whether they are of any advantage. But GM designed the HEI system primarily to meet the requirements of Federal new car emissions and fuel economy testing. Since unit cost is a major consideration in a mass production environment, these systems aren't as powerful as they could be. But more importantly, their energy output falls off dramatically at engine speeds of 4000 rpm and above.

Inductive vs. Capacitive Discharge

Once you cut through all the electronic technospeak, you find that there are two types of electronic ignition—inductive and capacitor discharge (CD). The problem with the inductive system (like an HEI) is that it's subject to the same limitations as a standard point-type system—specifically, current is induced in the coil and therefore spark output is dependent upon the amount of time between firings. At high rpm, there is insufficient time to build up current in the coil, therefore spark output is reduced.

Conversely, in a capacitive discharge system, capacitors are used to store electricity which is discharged at a later time. The primary advantage of this arrangement is that a capacitor can be charged to maximum in a fraction of the time (known as rise time) required to induce voltage in a coil. Therefore, in a properly designed CD system, output is virtually unaffected by engine speed as high as 12,000 rpm—even though current still flows through the coil. This is possible because the coil is used as a

simple transformer to step up the voltage fed to it by the CD unit. But instead of 12 volts, the coil will receive an input of 375-450 volts, which places output in the 35,000 to 55,000 volt range irrespective of engine speed.

On the other side of the coin, inductive systems, such as the GM HEI, produce 50,000-55,000 volts at low speeds, but drop to less than 15,000 as the engine approaches 5,000 rpm. The reason for this is quite understandable. As a means of determining whether a vehicle's exhaust emissions levels and fuel economy are acceptable, a variety of tests are conducted by the Environmental Protection Agency. Chevrolet, like other manufacturers, must therefore engineer their vehicles to pass these tests, which are administered in a laboratory, not on the highway. That is why EPA gas mileage figures seem as realistic as a science fiction fantasy. Since engine speed is kept quite low throughout the test series, and since the average driver rarely coaxes his or her engine to exceed 4000 rpm, there is no need for the ignition system to maintain its top energy output level at high rpm. Inductive ignitions appeal to auto manufacturers for another reason—they're cheaper to produce than capacitive discharge systems.

But when a vehicle is placed in the real world and subjected to the abuse of rpm-crazed racers and performance enthusiasts, it must be able to operate efficiently at relatively high engine speeds. This is where the original equipment systems come up short. However, basic capacitive discharge ignitions aren't the answer either. One of the most commonly heard criticisms of CD ignitions is that in spite of their ability to fire a plug under the most adverse conditions, spark duration is too short to reliably initiate complete combustion.

Ignition Energy

"If some is good, more is better and too

This classic big block–a 375-horsepower 396 installed in a 1965 Chevelle–has a built-in handicap. The stock point-triggered ignition system. But with high performance components, it can be upgraded, yet still retain its stock external appearance, which will bring a smile to the faces of Muscle Car purists.

much is just enough." Anyone who has spent much time at a race track (or reading this book) has undoubtedly heard that expression. Although it's usually said with tongue-in-cheek, it is quite appropriate when applied to an ignition system. Even with a fully charged battery and an ignition system in top condition, there may not be enough electrical power to fire the spark plugs under all conditions. In cases such as this, what's needed is simply more energy—the ignition system requires "supercharging."

Voltage

Traditionally, increased ignition output has been equated with greater voltage, but that concept is somewhat erroneous. Voltage is but one component of the spark which must ignite the mixture hanging around the combustion chamber; it is merely the pressure that pushes electrical energy through a wire, or enables it to arc across a gap. Irrespective of an ignition system's voltage generating potential, it will produce only the amount

required to bridge the gap that exists between the electrodes of a spark plug. Generally, between 4,000 and 20,000 volts is sufficient, with specific requirements being determined by the resistance created by gap width, compression ratio, engine speed and air/fuel ratio. Many of these factors are variable, so some reserve voltage should always be available; under some conditions, in excess of 30,000 volts may be required to fire a spark plug.

With an inductive system, installation of a high performance coil will generally cure most problems with voltage deficiency in the low and middle rpm ranges. But at engine speeds of 4500 rpm and above, any inductive system runs into the same problem—time, or rather lack of it. There simply may not be a long enough interval between firings for the coil to generate sufficient voltage to avoid misfire. Dual-point distributors were once a popular means of somewhat alleviating this condition. By having both sets of points closed for overlapping time

periods, point dwell time is lengthened, thereby giving the coil more time to build up current. Maximum dwell with a single set of points is 32 to 34 deg.; with dual points, dwell can be lengthened to 38 to 40 deg. Another approach to improving an inductive system's ability to operate at high rpm involves the use of a coil with an extremely high turns ratio—up to 360:1—and an electronic ignition module which feeds a 12-15 ampere current into the coil. This system works well, but it cannot rival long duration of multiple spark CD systems in terms of total spark energy output.

Voltage vs. Energy

Ignition system energy output levels are important because increasing voltage alone isn't sufficient to eliminate misfire. The fact that a spark has jumped across the plug gap does not guarantee that the air/fuel mixture in the combustion chamber was ignited. As noted previously, one of the shortcomings of a standard capacitive discharge system is that spark duration can be too short to reliably light off the mixture in the combustion chamber.

That's where energy enters the picture. Measured in millijoules or watt-seconds, electrical energy may be thought of as the amount of "fire" that jumps across the spark plug electrodes. The effect of that fire may be enhanced by creating a bigger, more intense flame, lengthening its burn time or both. Irrespective of the approach chosen, the goal is the same—increased energy at the plug increases the chance that the spark will hit a fuel molecule and start a roaring flame front traveling across the combustion chamber.

Since you can't see that energy, consider this analogy: a fat man and a skinny man both run through a crowd at the same speed—who's going to knock down more people? In an engine's combustion chamber, the "crowd" consists of fuel molecules which the spark must ignite. If the flame is so "thin"

Multi-spark discharge systems can be connected to virtually any type of distributor. These systems put a fat spark across the plug gaps which not only makes for excellent power output, it also is very effective at preventing plug fouling when an engine is run at lower speeds.

that it does not contact a sufficient number of molecules, a misfire will occur, resulting in a reduction in fuel economy and power output. Exhaust emissions levels will rise as well. Obviously a fatter spark has a better chance of "knocking down" a group of molecules, but irrespective of flame width, the longer a spark hangs around the plug gap, the better its chance of zapping a gas molecule. The ideal ignition system therefore produces not only a "fat" spark, but one with a long duration or burn time.

Fast Fire

Viewed from another perspective, you could reasonably ask, "Why does a fatter spark increase horsepower and fuel efficiency?" That, after all, is the bottom line. Simply stated, by increasing spark energy, you're getting the fire in the combustion chamber off to a roaring start, rather than allowing it to smolder before it ignites. A faster, more active flame-front assures complete combustion so every bit of power available from the fuel is used and no fuel is wasted.

Torch or Match?—You can visualize the effects of various levels of spark energy by picturing two different approaches to setting a piece of paper on

fire. Suppose you want to burn a piece of paper as quickly as possible and you have two "ignition devices" available—a match and a welding torch. If you take the match flame and move it quickly beneath the paper, there won't be any smoke—nor any fire. But hold the match still, and the paper will begin to smolder and eventually ignite. Now do the same thing with a gas-welding torch. It produces enough heat that even when moved rapidly across the paper, it will catch fire. Hold the torch still and it will not only ignite the paper, it will almost instantaneously start a large flame-front moving across it.

Since it's desirable to burn the paper as quickly as possible, there's no question which ignition device you'd choose—the torch. When you move inside an engine's combustion chamber, you're substituting an air/fuel mixture for the piece of paper and an ignition system for either the match or torch. But the task at hand is the same—you're still trying to get the combustible material to burn as quickly as possible. To accomplish that, you want to put as much heat—or spark energy—as you can across the plug gap. Once a good flame-front develops, the time it takes to burn the fuel is both predictable and consistent. It is smolder time—the time between the firing of the spark and development of a fast-moving flame-front—that tends to be erratic and cost horsepower. That's the advantage of a super high energy spark—smolder time is minimized.

Smolder Time

What does smolder time really have to do with the production of horsepower? Quite simply, it fights against it. In order to produce maximum power, maximum cylinder pressure must be present at the very start of the power stroke. The ideal situation would be one in which complete combustion occurred instantaneously with ignition firing. Were this possible, ignition timing would be set at Top Dead

Center—no advance would be required. However, this Utopian scenario won't play in the real world. Some amount of time, however short, is required to burn the fuel in a combustion chamber. This being the case, the spark must be fired before Top Dead Center so that the point of maximum pressure is reached as the piston begins descending on the power stroke. As rpm increases, the piston moves faster, requiring earlier plug firing (more spark advance) in order to achieve maximum cylinder pressure at the very beginning of the power stroke.

The only problem with this arrangement is that as the piston rises in the bore, approaching Top Dead Center, it must fight against the pressure that is building on top of it. That pressure is nothing more than another form of friction and the power required to overcome it reduces engine output. That is precisely the reason that a super high energy ignition system increases horsepower and overall engine efficiency—by lighting the intake charge with a nice fat spark, the time interval between ignition and maximum cylinder pressure is reduced. Therefore, spark lead can be retarded a bit but maximum cylinder pressure will still be reached at the desired time. And since the piston is now spending less time working against initial combustion pressures, more usable horsepower is produced.

The Multi-Spark Approach

Multi-Spark Discharge—In the early Seventies, Autotronic Controls developed multi-spark discharge (MSD) ignitions. In so doing, they married the advantages of the CD system's fast rise time and the inductive system's longer duration spark. Multi-spark systems have been extremely successful and are widely used on all types of race and high performance engines. Other manufacturers such as Accel and Mallory also offer high output ignitions that are suitable for high

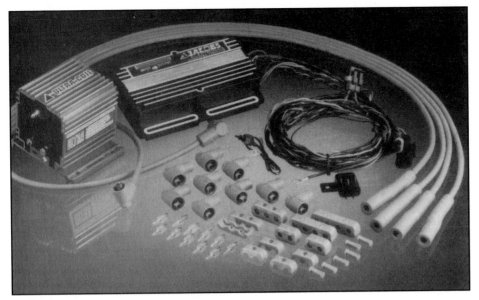

The Jacobs Ultra Team is a complete ignition system featuring high output coil, control module, plug wires and separators. Independent dyno testing has shown this system capable of increasing power output compared to other race type systems.

Jacobs Electronics offers a number of Energy Pak ignition systems for street, race and marine applications. These patented systems tailor spark intensity and duration according to engine requirements.

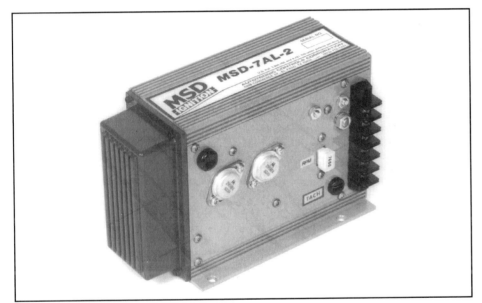

MSD's 7AL-2 is designed for drag racing and provides a tremendous amount of spark energy. The unit also includes a built-in rev limiter; maximum rpm is controlled by a plug-in chip.

performance use.

Rather than attempting to fire a single high-energy spark, multi-spark electronics produce several. Not only is the possibility of initiating combustion improved by multiple firings, but the secondary pulses can also reignite a fire that goes out. (At higher engine speeds, turbulence within the combustion chamber is quite severe and may be so great, it literally blows out the fire started by the ignition system.) However, due to the short time interval between firings of successive cylinders, at high rpm, there isn't sufficient time to fire more than one spark per cycle. Keep in mind that multi-sparking is actually the means, not the end. The end is a long duration spark.

Burn Time—In a multi-spark system, the overriding factor is burn time as measured in degrees of engine rotation. Regardless of engine speed, the spark will burn for 20 deg. of crankshaft rotation in an 8-cylinder engine; 30 deg. in a 6-cylinder and 40 deg. in a 4-cylinder. The electronics therefore generate the maximum number of sparks according to the time allowed. There simply comes a point where a second spark can't be generated within the time frame defined by 20, 30 or 40 deg. of crankshaft rotation. But since maximum spark energy is maintained irrespective of the number of firings, a single spark at high rpm produces the same ignition potential as multiple sparks at lower engine speeds.

SPARK ENERGY SELECTION

The question that has yet to be answered is, "How much spark energy is really required for optimum performance or fuel economy?" It may come as a shock, but it appears that short of burning the electrodes off the ends of the spark plugs, there is no such thing as "too much." Obviously, there comes a point of diminishing returns where a doubling or tripling of energy levels becomes extremely costly and results in a barely measurable increase in operating efficiency. However, to take full advantage of a high energy spark, the entire system must be configured

From a performance standpoint, the principal drawback to an HEI system is that output falls off sharply above 4500-5000 rpm. A high output coil helps that situation somewhat. Accel's HEI Super Coil is unique in that it fits on the distributor cap, in place of the stock coil.

In order to install an external coil on an HEI system, the stock coil and cover must be replaced. This MSD dust cover accepts an external coil lead and feeds the spark to the distributor cap.

The Ultra Coil from Jacobs is a "take-no-prisoners" unit that delivers up to 1950 watts of spark power. But not all coils are compatible with all ignition systems. Be sure to verify compatibility before installation--especially with electronic systems.

properly. The distributor cap and rotor and plug wires must have high dielectric strength to contain the spark energy and plug gap must be opened up to take full advantage of the system's fire power.

Recommendations

For anything less than a maximum output, professional race engine, a high output ignition system such as an MSD-6A, -6AL or -6T, Jacobs Energy Pak or Accel Laser II is more than adequate. More powerful systems might produce slightly more power, but considering the operating environment, the added expense isn't justified. Another point to be considered is that some super high output systems aren't designed to run for hours on end. They may prove to be unreliable when installed on a street, marine or oval track engine due to heat build-up.

As with most aspects of life around internal combustion engines, selecting the best ignition system for a particular application is a matter of making the best series of compromises. It's not so much a matter of right or wrong as it is a situation where some decisions are just more correct than others. As an example, most NASCAR Winston Cup engines come to

life with an MSD-6T (which is also marketed through GM Performance Parts as Heavy Duty Ignition Control part no. 10037378). These engines have a displacement of 358 cid, produce in excess of 675 horsepower and run at 7500+ rpm for hours on end. If the MSD-6 circuitry is adequate for these engines, it is certainly more than capable of firing the plugs in a 454, 502 or even a 600 cubic-inch big block designed for street, bracket race, marine, off-road or short track use.

The 6A, 6AL and 6T all have the same output specifications; the 6T is the professional race version of the 6A and includes added internal bracing, rubber shock mounts and a special coating to protect the electronic components from shock and vibration loads. MSD-6T modules also include provision for hooking up a rev control. MSD-6AL modules have the rev control built in.

On the other hand, the MSD-7AL2 has become the system of preference for Pro Stock and similar hard-core drag race vehicles. The MSD-7AL2 puts out 800 millijoules of energy, compared to 600 millijoules for the MSD-6. MSD-6 circuitry produces a maximum of 45,000 volts; MSD-7AL2 modules produce a

maximum of 50,000 volts.

Considering the differences in output specifications between these two ignitions, it's understandable that the MSD-7AL2 offers somewhat more horsepower potential than an MSD-6. If you're racing in a class where every last ounce of horsepower is essential, and can tune the engine to take advantage of a super high output ignition, there's no question which module to select. However, for most bracket categories, road racing, short track, marine and street engines, something less than a maximum output system is more than adequate. Such systems are also considerably cheaper than their super high output counterparts—and frequently, they're more reliable.

COILS

Aside from an electronic control module, the coil is largely responsible for ignition system energy output. As previously noted, most stock-type coils are capable of producing 25,000 to 30,000 volts; high performance coils generate 40,000 to 55,000 volts. While it may require only 10,000 to 15,000 volts to fire the plugs, the reserve capacity is

The HEI system, introduced in 1975, contains all ignition components in the distributor. The centrifugal advance weights are located in the same position, and function the same way as in a point-type GM distributor. However, the weights have a unique shape, as does the tang around which they pivot. This tang is connected to the distributor shaft and has a habit of breaking loose, especially in high mileage distributors. Whenever you have the cap off, pull the rotor and check to make sure that the tang is still properly attached to the shaft.

good insurance against misfire. Reserve spark voltage (reserve being the amount of voltage above actual system requirements) will be tapped as plug gaps erode and as the electrodes wear and accumulate deposits, all of which increase voltage requirements. Normal deterioration of plug wires, distributor cap and rotor also increases resistance, so after a time, voltage requirements may rise to 20,000 volts or more. This is still within the capability of a stock coil, so a stock ignition system can for some time continue to fire away when called upon.

However, at higher engine speeds, there won't always be enough time between plug firings to allow a stock-type inductive ignition system to build maximum voltage. Even if the voltage does jump the plug gap, there may not be enough energy to initiate combustion. That's the reason that a high output coil alone won't suffice on a high performance engine. Without an electronic system to

augment energy output, the best a typical inductive system will produce is 150 to 200 millijoules of energy. By comparison, an MSD-6 puts out 600 millijoules—three times the spark energy. By all means, don't overlook the coil when assembling a high output ignition system, but don't rely exclusively on the coil to deliver the firepower needed for maximum power.

DISTRIBUTORS

Prior to 1975, virtually all Chevrolet big blocks, like most other GM engines, were equipped with a conventional point-type distributor. The only exception to this was the Delcotronic transistor ignition system. The distributor used in this system appears identical to a standard point-type distributor externally—but there are no points inside. In their place is a magnet and an eight-toothed reluctor. These systems have always been

comparatively rare, and although they eliminated the points, they didn't do much else to increase ignition system performance.

Unless you're doing a Concours restoration that calls for a Delcotronic distributor, there's no sense searching for one. Both the cast-iron and aluminum distributors that have been used as original equipment in big-block Chevrolet engines are suitable for high performance use. The cast-iron models are stronger and more rigid, the aluminum ones are lighter. In actual use, there really isn't much operational difference and arguments can be made for the superiority of each type. It's not worth losing much sleep over the decision— either type will provide satisfactory performance. For engines operating at extremely high rpm, or under very heavy loads, the extra strength of a cast-iron or aftermarket aluminum distributor is advantageous.

Triggers—Of far greater importance than housing material is the triggering device used. Avoid points at all costs. Points, even dual points, are nothing more than a failure waiting to happen. The only people still advocating the use of points are also members of the Flat Earth Society. If you have any doubts, just take a look at the top running race cars—from Pro Stock drag racing to Winston Cup oval track to SCCA road racing, electronic ignitions are used exclusively. Assuming you have a point-type distributor, the most economical way to eliminate points is with a conversion kit. Stinger and Mallory are a few of the companies offering conversion kits.

HEI Distributors

Another option is to substitute an HEI (High Energy Ignition) distributor. HEI systems first came into play on engines installed in 1975 model year cars and since big blocks and small blocks take the same distributor, either new or used distributors are easy to find.

One of the best ways to improve the performance of a big-block equipped with an HEI ignition system is with a custom spark curve. The Super Curve Kit from American Speed Centers in York, PA, includes special weights, pivot piece, springs and vacuum advance canister.

Performance Distributors of Memphis, TN, offers a stock appearing HEI unit that's anything but. It contains a super high output coil and internal module that cranks out enough spark energy to light up a small town.

Although the HEI electronics aren't up to handling the demands of a high performance engine, there's nothing wrong with the trigger mechanism. An original style HEI distributor also features a large diameter cap which offers a greater distance between terminals and therefore less chance of a crossfire within the cap. MSD also offers a Cap-A-Dapt kit which includes a large diameter cap and matching rotor and an adapter to mate it to a standard point-style distributor.

HEI Modifiers—If you do use an HEI distributor, either an MSD Super HEI Kit or an Accel HEI Intensifier Kit should be added. The MSD kit eliminates all the HEI electronics and replaces them with a 6A module and Blaster-2 coil. A coil-to-distributor cable, dust cover (which fits the cap in place of the integral HEI coil) and coil bracket are also included. The Accel kit includes a Super Coil, dust cover, distributor-to-coil wire and advance weight springs. The MSD kit brings multi-fire capacitive discharge capability to the party whereas the Accel kit intensifies the original inductive system's output. Accel also offers a Super Coil that plugs into the original HEI cap as another alternative to spicing up the spark delivery of an HEI system.

Another option is to upgrade the HEI electronics with high output components such as those produced by Performance Distributors in Memphis, TN. Used extensively in oval track engines, Performance Distributors' Racing HEI unit incorporates a special control module to increase coil saturation, high output coil and heavy duty cap and rotor. It produces a strong spark up to 8000-8500 rpm and is a completely self-contained system.

Aftermarket Distributors

Aftermarket distributors are another option. They're available from a number of manufacturers, but MSD offers the widest variety. The basic MSD distributor (part no. 8461) has a cast aluminum housing, .500 in. steel shaft, reluctor and magnetic pick-up and centrifugal advance mechanism with extra springs for customizing the advance curve. Vacuum advance is not included, but can be added. A ready-to-run version of this distributor is also available. This unit (part no. 8460) includes an integrated high output inductive module, cap, rotor and vacuum advance canister. MSD also offers a race distributor with a housing

machined from aluminum billet and ball bearings (as opposed to bronze bushings which are used in other models).

Aftermarket electronic distributors, such as this MSD model, eliminate the nuisance of points, yet drop right in, in place of a stock distributor. This distributor contains an ignition module so the only other requirement to bring spark to the party is a coil. The same basic distributor is also available with no ignition module attached, and a tach drive version is also available.

Accel offers both dual point and electronic distributors for big blocks. Externally, the distributors look identical, but there are obvious differences once the cap is removed. A Super Coil can be used with either one.

What's a gear doing in among all this electrical equipment? Serving as a reminder. If you install a roller cam, which is machined from a steel billet rather than cast-iron core, chances are you'll have to equip the distributor with a bronze gear. Some roller cams are manufactured with a cast-iron distributor gear in which case no change is required. But for the most part, a bronze gear goes with a roller cam like double talk goes with a politician.

Other MSD distributors include a tach drive version and two low profile models—one with tach drive and one without—for use on race engines with Tunnel Ram-type manifolds (where distributor clearance is limited). Both low-profile distributors are designed to operate with crankshaft triggered ignitions.

Accel—Accel is another company offering an assortment of distributors for the big-block Chevy. In addition to electronic distributors, Accel offers dual-point models. If you absolutely have to use points, you can choose from a 37-Series racing distributor or a 34-Series "Super Stock" model which is available with or without vacuum advance. All Accel high performance distributors use a Chrysler-style cap and rotor and the electronic Unispark models incorporate an HEI control module. Accel also offers a line of blueprinted OEM replacement distributors. Besides being completely remanufactured, these distributors incorporate high quality cap and rotor and adjustable vacuum advance canister. Point-type distributors include points with 32-ounce arm tension (for higher

rpm potential) and electronic (HEI) distributors contain a new specially programmed control module.

Mallory—Mallory also offers both dual-point and electronic distributors. The Comp 9000 series includes a large diameter cap and special rotor to resist arcing and carbon tracking, heat-treated aluminum housing and a screw-mounted plug wire retainer. In addition to the dual-point model, both optic and magnetic trigger electronic models are available. In the oval track version (98 and 99 series), two magnetic pickups are mounted for use with two complete ignition systems. This provision allows the driver to substitute one ignition system for the other at the flick of a switch. Comp 9000 distributors do not have vacuum advance mechanisms. Mallory also manufactures lower cost Unilite and dual-point distributors with and without vacuum advance.

Distributor Gears

Regardless of the type of distributor you select, pay attention to the gear. Standard iron gears are acceptable if a conventional hydraulic or mechanical

camshaft is in charge of valve timing. However, roller cams are machined from SAE 8620 billet steel and the gear on the cam isn't compatible with a cast-iron distributor gear. Whenever a roller cam is in residence, the distributor should be fitted with a high quality bronze gear—with one exception. Steel roller cams with cast-iron gears were developed during the very late stages of the 1980s. These cams can be used with standard cast-iron distributor gears.

Durability—In a high performance or race engine, distributor gear life isn't always what it should be. While bronze is compatible with steel, it doesn't have the strength of iron, so it wears at a higher rate. The situation can be particularly bad in Chevrolet big blocks because the splash lubrication of the distributor gear is inadequate at low engine speeds.

Things are even worse when a high volume oil pump is installed in an engine that doesn't really need one. High volume

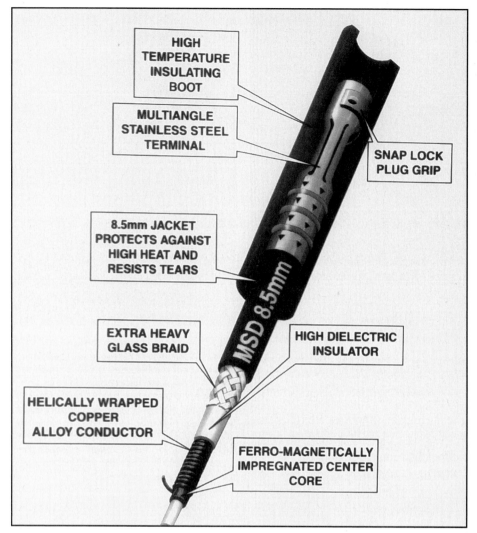

HIGH TEMPERATURE INSULATING BOOT

MULTIANGLE STAINLESS STEEL TERMINAL

SNAP LOCK PLUG GRIP

8.5mm JACKET PROTECTS AGAINST HIGH HEAT AND RESISTS TEARS

EXTRA HEAVY GLASS BRAID

HIGH DIELECTRIC INSULATOR

HELICALLY WRAPPED COPPER ALLOY CONDUCTOR

FERRO-MAGNETICALLY IMPREGNATED CENTER CORE

The best ignition system in the world will come up short if the plug wires give up. Exhaust heat is a plug wire's biggest enemy and use of heat resistant materials isn't always enough. Special sleeving is necessary to keep wires "alive" in some race applications.

Ceramic 2000 wires from Jacobs feature 8mm silicone jacketing, spiral wound suppression metal core and unique ceramic spark plug boots that are burn-proof at temperatures of over 2000 degrees. Just what you need for a hot big block.

SPARK PLUG WIRES

Listen to a bunch of old-time Chevy racers talking, and you'll probably hear about Packard 440 wire which had a silver-plated copper core. Solid, metallic core wires used to be the hot tip, but like many pieces of automotive legend, they've been replaced by something better. Back in the Sixties, resistance-type or radio suppression wiring was poorly designed and likely to fail when it was most needed to succeed. Some resistance wires actually had nothing approaching a wire beneath the insulation—carbon grains filled the core. As heat and vibration took their respective tolls, the grains settled, leaving a series of gaps in the wire core. Another type of suppression wire employed a graphite impregnated nylon core—which worked fine until the wire was bent sharply and the nylon cracked. As with the carbon grain core, the papooses in the core forced the spark traveling through the wire to jump an air gap. In turn, each time a spike of electrical energy jumped the gap in the core, it burned away a bit of insulation. It didn't take long for the insulation to be eaten away enough to let

pumps are designed for use in engines with wide bearing clearances. With normal production clearances, oil doesn't flow as freely through the engine, so the oil pump is working against considerable back pressure. Since the distributor shaft turns the oil pump shaft, the load on the distributor gear caused by a high-volume oil pump can be substantial. That leads to accelerated wear—even with a stock iron gear.

Increasing oil flow to the distributor gear significantly improves gear life, primarily because of its cooling effect. This can be most easily accomplished by using a 3-cornered file to cut a .030-in.-deep notch in the lower sealing flange on the distributor housing. For maximum effectiveness, the notch should be oriented so that it is aimed towards the camshaft when the distributor is installed in its normal position.

Distributor housings should be notched—irrespective of the type of distributor gear used—in all engines operating under high loads and/or at relatively low rpm, especially if a high-volume oil pump is in place. True race engines rarely experience a distributor gear wear problem because their higher operating rpm provides sufficient lubricant flow, and proper matching of oil pump volume and bearing clearance eliminate excessively high lubrication system back pressures.

Magnetos contain their own energy source–a self-contained generator. Although not considered a "high tech" system, magnetos are favored in certain applications where it may not be practical to run a battery. One advantage of a magneto is that the spark intensity increases as rpm rises.

Sprint cars and Super Modifieds typically don't have batteries because they spend a lot of time upside down. Consequently, magnetos are used since they generate their own spark energy.

the spark escape from the wire. This phenomenon still occurs with "el cheapo" plug wires; it doesn't do much for performance, but it is good for relieving boredom. Open the hood at night, and an engine fitted with low-quality plug wires will put on a fireworks display like the Fourth of July.

Resistance Wires

At one time, metallic core wiring was the only alternative, but it wasn't the proper solution. Dependable resistance-type wire is the answer. Such wire has been available for many years, but the poor reputation of the early resistance wire caused many people to stick with metallic plug wires. Then came electronics, and metallic-core wires became unviable because they interfered with the operation of on-board computers and high energy ignitions. Consequently race cars, as well as street cars, are now universally equipped with high quality radio suppression wires, with the helical-wound type being most prevalent.

Resistance wires are actually superior to their metallic core counterparts because most ignition systems are designed to operate with some amount of secondary resistance. Secondary refers to the part of the ignition system that transports the spark. The problem with cheap resistance-type plug wires is that after a short period of time, they offer too much resistance. On the other hand, solid-core wire allows current to flow after the spark has jumped the plug gap. It's this "follow-on" spark that creates radio frequency interference (RFI) which plays havoc with radios, televisions and onboard electronics. What you need is a low resistance, RFI-suppression wire that doesn't deteriorate. This type of wire is available from any number of companies, including Accel, MSD, Mallory, Moroso and Taylor. As a general rule, solid-core wires, like ignition points, should be avoided—there's absolutely no reason to use them.

MAGNETOS

Any discussion of ignition systems would be incomplete without mention of magnetos. Like many pieces of

equipment used on big-block Chevy engines, there are both good and bad aspects of a magneto. As an ignition device, a magneto is about the least sophisticated type available. In fact, the lowly lawn mower engine is sparked on to feats of grass-cutting prowess by a magneto system. That doesn't imply that a magneto is unsuitable for anything but mundane applications. Quite the opposite—everything from sprint cars to Top Fuelers to aircraft engines are magneto equipped. In fact, until the advent of electronic ignitions, magnetos were the only systems capable of providing acceptable spark output at engine speeds above 7500 rpm.

The beauty of a magneto is that it generates its own electricity, so it's completely self-contained. That means neither a battery, coil nor alternator are required. Another attractive characteristic of a magneto is that its voltage output increases linearly with rpm. The flip side of this is that at cranking speeds, voltage output is very low, so starting can be a problem. Mallory Super Mags utilize a separate coil so they're more suitable for street and low rpm operation.

Currently, automotive magnetos are

widely used only in certain types of race cars such as fuel and alcohol dragsters and Funny Cars, sprinters and the like. Vibration is severe enough in these types of cars to damage a battery, so being able to run without one is a definite advantage—not to mention the weight savings. And since sprint cars spend a good deal of time on their heads, elimination of the battery removes the potential hazard of battery acid dripping on the driver in the event of a flip or rollover.

Magnetos can be used in street engines, but they rarely are. Street cars have to be equipped with a battery for purposes other than operating the ignition, so a magneto offers no weight-savings benefit. And since a street engine spends most of its time operating at low rpm, it rarely spins a magneto fast enough to generate high spark voltage. A third drawback is that it takes a bit of horsepower to spin a magneto, and while it isn't a lot, it represents a power loss that electronic ignitions do not impose.

SPARK PLUGS

A spark plug performs a relatively simple function—it provides a gap, inside the combustion chamber, for electrical energy to spark across. The only way for this energy to jump the gap between a spark plug's center electrode and ground electrode is to arc across it. When it does that, a spark is created—hence the name spark plug. But as you might have guessed, it's not quite that simple.

Heat Range

Heat range refers to a spark plug's ability to transfer heat from the tip of the insulator into the cylinder head. In order for a spark plug to perform satisfactorily for more than a few miles, it must be of the proper heat range. If a plug is too hot, it will cause pre-ignition, but even if combustion is normal, excess heat can ultimately burn the center electrode

completely away. On the other hand, a plug with too cold a heat range will have a tendency to foul and misfire and can reduce horsepower. Heat transfer rate is largely controlled by the distance the heat must travel through the spark plug body before reaching the head. Plugs that are considered "cold" have insulators that contact the metal plug shell very close to the threaded base. The insulators in "hot" plugs contact the shell towards the top, which makes for a longer path to the head surface (see diagram). Keep in mind that the terms "hot" and "cold" are relative—a plug that's "hot" for one engine may be considered "cold" for another. That's because combustion chamber temperatures vary considerably depending upon an engine's state of tune and the conditions under which it is operated. When heat range is properly matched to requirements, insulator tip temperature will range between 700 and 1500 deg. (F) under all operating conditions. This will provide maximum power and maximum plug life.

Recommendations—With a stock engine, it's best to follow the plug manufacturer's recommendation unless there's a good reason to deviate—such as a modified spark advance curve, poor fuel quality, extreme operating conditions or experience with the recommended plug being inappropriate. With a modified engine, standard recommendations can be used as a basis for determining where in the heat chart to start. Raising compression ratio, leaning the fuel mixture, increasing initial spark advance or reworking the advance curve to come in quicker are all reasons to switch to a plug with a colder heat range.

Cam Duration—An often overlooked factor when selecting proper plug heat range is cam duration. If no other changes are made, swapping a short duration cam for one with longer duration decreases cylinder pressure, which has the same effect as lowering compression ratio. Shortening cam duration increases

If a spark plug has too cold a heat range, it will foul. If it's too hot, the plug may self-destruct. This warm-up plug was accidentally left in an engine during dyno testing and the center electrode was completely burned away.

cylinder pressure, which has the same effect as raising compression ratio.

So even though a long duration cam is designed to produce more horsepower at higher engine speeds, it will create a condition that calls for a hotter, rather than a colder spark plug under some circumstances. On the other hand, if a shorter duration cam is installed as a means of increasing low-speed torque and smoothing the idle, a colder plug may be required because of the increased heat which is generated by higher cylinder pressure.

Octane—Another factor that influences heat range is gasoline quality. Lower octane fuels burn more quickly and create higher combustion chamber temperatures. In years past, when premium leaded fuels were widely available, octane was sufficient to meet the demands of virtually all high-compression street engines. But with the advent of unleaded gas, octane ratings of all grades of fuel dropped. Consequently, pre-ignition, detonation and run-on became more prevalent problems. If you've been running the same heat range plugs for years, but have been plagued by detonation, pre-ignition or run-on for no apparent reason, it just may be that the

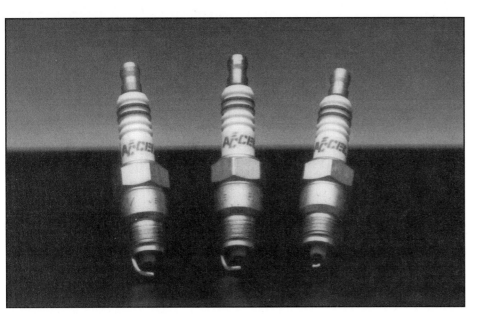

Several different heat ranges and tip configurations are available from spark plug manufacturers. A projected core is usually best for most applications, however, with large dome pistons, limited clearance may require installation of standard core plugs.

plugs you're using are too hot because of lower fuel octane. Many times, a switch to colder plugs will eliminate those ugly knock and ping noises.

Obviously, selection of spark plugs with a proper heat range isn't a cut and dried affair. So many factors enter into the equation, that some experimentation is usually necessary to optimize performance and plug life. As a general rule, if you're off on heat range, it's better to be too cold than too hot. Plugs that are too cold will foul more easily, build carbon deposits more quickly and slightly decrease power. Plugs that are too hot can cause preignition, detonation and run-on—all of which can cause your engine to eat its own pistons and valves.

Plug Size

When selecting spark plugs for a big-block Chevy, another point to be considered is plug size. Prior to the 1970 model year, all stock big-block heads were machined to accept 3/4-in. reach plugs with 14mm threads and a 13/16-in. hex. These plugs are identified by an "N" prefix in Champion Spark Plug's numbering system.

Beginning with the 1970 model year,

Chevrolet switched to "slimline" spark plugs with 14mm threads, .460-in. reach, a tapered seat (which eliminated the need for a washer) and a 5/8 in. rather than 13/16 in. hex in all cast-iron heads. (The change in plug styles does not pertain to aluminum heads.) The 5/8-hex plugs were formerly identified by a "BL" prefix in Champion's numbering system, but that has been changed to a "V" prefix.

Seat Style—While the hex size is the most obvious difference between these two types of plugs, the seat style is of most significance. Plugs with a 13/16 in. hex have a flat seat and require a gasket; plugs with a 5/8 in. hex have a tapered seat and no gasket is used.

Torquing—In cast-iron heads, 13/16 in. hex plugs should be tightened to 26-30 lbs-ft., which in educated wrench-hand terms translates to 1/4-turn past finger tight. In aluminum heads, tightening torque should be 18-22 lbs-ft., which is also approximately 1/4-turn past finger tight. Plugs with a 5/8-in. hex should be tightened to 7-15 lbs-ft. or 1/16-turn past finger tight (in either iron or aluminum heads). Some aftermarket heads require the use of .708-in. reach plugs. Tightening specifications are the same as

for equivalent 3/4-in. reach plugs.

Although it is physically possible to screw a J-, V- or BL-series plug into plug holes that were machined for larger N-series plugs, such a substitution should be done only in an emergency situation, when proper plugs can't be found.

Types of Plugs

Irrespective of size or heat range, two types of plugs are most commonly used in big-block Chevy engines—standard and projected tip. In a standard plug, the center electrode protrudes a minimum distance from the base of the plug. With a projected tip, the electrode extends considerably deeper. This is advantageous in most applications because it places the plug tip deeper in the combustion chamber and somewhat in the path of the incoming air/fuel charge. At higher engine speeds, the intake mixture has a cooling effect on the plug tip. Consequently, a projected tip plug has a wider operating heat range— it's designed to run slightly hotter at low speeds because it has less of a tendency to overheat at high speeds. However, in some endurance-type racing applications, where an engine runs wide open for hours on end, a standard plug is often preferable because heat build-up can exceed a projected tip plug's dissipation capabilities.

While projected tip plugs are clearly advantageous for most applications, there is one point to beware of: since they protrude further into the combustion chamber, piston-to-electrode interference is a distinct possibility when super high-compression pistons are used. If clearance is even a remote question, after installing projected tip plugs for the first time, spin the engine over by hand— slowly—and make sure everything clears. Your pistons and your bank account will thank you for taking the time to check.

Retracted Gap—In engines fitted with pistons having obscenely large

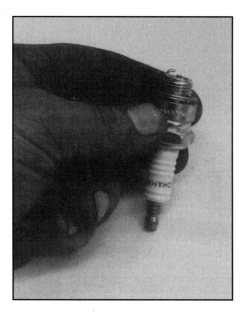

Want to pick up five horsepower free? Cut back the ground electrode so that it covers no more than 1/2 of the ground electrode. The plugs won't last as long, but dyno testing has shown definite power increases. (Photo by Myron Cottrell)

domes, it may be necessary to install retracted gap (R-gap) plugs. In a retracted gap plug, neither the center nor the ground electrode protrudes beyond the threaded shell. This type of plug is frequently used in supercharged engines because they are better able to withstand extreme heat and pressure. However, by tucking the gap up inside the shell, the electrodes are excessively shrouded and that imposes a power penalty. Need I say more?

Electrode Shapes—A relatively recent development in spark plug design is a series of unique electrode shapes. Champion manufactures fine wire and cut back electrodes; Accel offers a U-Groove plug; Bosch has a tapered electrode; and Split-Fire offers a Y-shaped ground electrode. All of these designs are intended to expose more of the spark by eliminating some of the shrouding that characterizes a traditional ground electrode. The question is, do they work?

At this point, the jury is still out. There's no question that unshrouding the ground electrode increases horsepower—

racers have been cutting back the ground electrode of conventional plugs for years. Myron Cottrell of TPI Specialties, in Chaska, MN, states that in back-to-back dyno tests, he's seen cut-back electrodes deliver a solid five to eight horsepower increase. Tests of more recently developed electrode designs have produced mixed results. These specialty spark plugs probably offer some advantage—the question is whether it's enough of an advantage to justify the added cost. Some people feel that special gap designs are worth the additional cost, others prefer to buy conventional plugs, file the ground electrode back and save two or three dollars a plug.

Resistance Movement

Spark plugs with internal resistors are factory installed in newer vehicles to improve control of radio frequency interference (RFI). Although resistor-type plugs are widely used in passenger vehicles, they are generally not part of a high performance or racing ignition system. There's nothing inherently wrong with resistor plugs and contrary to popular belief, they have only slightly higher voltage requirements compared to conventional plugs. But if the heat, vibration and voltage levels encountered in a passenger vehicle make life difficult for the resistor element, imagine what racing conditions do to it.

Even if RFI suppression wire is in place, resistor plugs may be required to optimize radio clarity. So if you like music with your horsepower, you may have to install resistor plugs. You'll also get another benefit—the resistor reduces electrode erosion, so plugs can run longer before being regapped or replaced. These characteristics are advantageous in a street-driven vehicle, but in a race car, the resistor simply becomes another element that can fail at the most inopportune time. For that reason, you'll have to search long and hard to find resistor plugs with a cold enough heat range to suit a race engine.

CROSSFIRE & OTHER MYSTERIES

Once the distributor, coil and ignition module are all properly introduced and working together harmoniously, the next task is to ensure that the spark energy leaving the distributor cap reaches the appropriate spark plug at precisely the correct time. But there are several detours that can be thrown into the path of unwitting bands of sparks. Crossfire—the firing of one plug by the spark intended for another—can be deadly, especially in a high performance or racing engine. It usually occurs when the high resistance found in a cylinder during the compression cycle causes the current leaving the rotor to jump to an adjacent terminal (where resistance is lower) and fire the plug to which it's connected. Since that is usually the next one in the firing order, the cylinder has already started filling with an intake charge when the misdirected spark occurs. This charge is ignited and combustion takes place while the piston is completing its intake cycle and transitioning to its compression cycle. The result of such extremely early lighting of the air/fuel mixture, which the upward traveling piston is trying to compress, is excess heat and pressure—and sometimes engine failure.

Some race engines, especially those with fixed timing, are prone to an entirely different type of crossfire. The errant spark will travel to the previously fired cylinder because the exhaust gasses in the cylinder provide a low resistance path. While this type of crossfire is not destructive, it does reduce power output. With the advent of high energy ignitions, the potential for crossfire has increased dramatically, but by taking the proper steps, such problems can be eliminated.

The Path of Least Resistance

Electricity is funny stuff—it seems to have a knack for determining where it

The big blocks installed in late-model trucks are computer controlled, which means there are no springs or weights in the distributor. The spark curve is controlled by a computer chip. Hypertech offers high performance chips for all late model big blocks.

To change chips, all you have to do is move the access cover on the ECM out of the way, pull the stock chip out and insert a replacement in the same position. ECM configuration varies from year to year, but the chip changing procedure is the same.

shouldn't be and then finding a way to get there. Of course, as long as it's flowing to the wrong place, it isn't getting to the right one. That may be too simplistic an explanation, but the fact of the matter is that electrical current, like a politician running for office, always takes the path of least resistance. And as energy (and consequently voltage) levels are increased, so too is the current's ability to open up new paths. The situation is somewhat akin to that of an old high pressure hydraulic line which has developed a number of weak points. Even though the pressure system is fitted with a relief valve (which represents the spark plug), as pressure increases, it is entirely possible that one of the weak spots will break before the valve opens. When this occurs, the entire line will be emptied through the break, rather than flowing through the relief valve.

Similarly, when a "break" occurs in the ignition system, none of the current reaches the spark plug; voltage is the electrical equivalent of pressure and it must be contained. If a wire's insulation is too thin, has cracked, split or burned away, it will allow the current flowing through it to take an alternate path which does not lead to the spark plug.

One of the advantages of a high energy ignition system is that it has sufficient power to jump across a relatively wide plug gap—.045 to .060 in. as opposed to the .030 to .035-in. opening required with a conventional system. Widening the gap has the same effect as increasing the pressure setting of a relief valve—when flow is restricted (the electrical term is resistance) internal pressure increases. And if a path of lesser resistance exists, either fluid or electricity will take it.

It is for precisely this reason that Chevrolet began using spark plug wires measuring 8mm in diameter (7mm wire was used formerly) on all engines fitted with high energy ignitions. Thinner wires were simply incapable of containing the "higher pressure" produced by electronic ignitions, over long periods of time.

Spacing Things Out

Another change necessitated by high energy ignition systems was in distributor cap configuration. Normally, the rotor tip is properly aligned with the distributor cap terminals when vacuum advance is at or near its highest level, as in a highway cruise condition. Under such conditions, the manifold vacuum causes the advance mechanism to rotate (advance) the magnetic pickup (or points in a standard system) such that when it triggers a spark, the rotor tip and appropriate distributor cap terminal are properly aligned. Since a typical passenger car engine spends most of its life in cruise mode, this arrangement is quite logical as it minimizes the distance the spark has to travel between rotor tip and terminal. But under full throttle or heavy load conditions, when manifold vacuum is too low to actuate the (vacuum) advance unit, and resistance at the plug gap is greatest, the rotor is no longer properly aligned (or phased) and crossfire can easily result if a distributor cap has closely spaced terminals. Improperly phased rotors increase the possibility of crossfire within the cap.

Solutions—This problem can be solved by fitting a larger diameter cap which allows the terminals to be spaced further from each other. Therefore, even if a rotor is out of phase, the distance between its tip and the adjacent terminal raises resistance to a point above that represented by the terminal to which current should be transferred. The path of least resistance then becomes the right one, and the potential for crossfire within the cap is all but eliminated—unless rotor misalignment is excessive.

Narrowing of the rotor tip is another means of reducing the possibility of crossfire within the cap. Grinding or filing the leading edge of the rotor tip increases the distance between it and the next terminal in the firing order. Filing a rotor tip's leading edge also delays the arrival of the rotor at the desired terminal, so you'd do well to check spark timing if you modify the rotor tip.

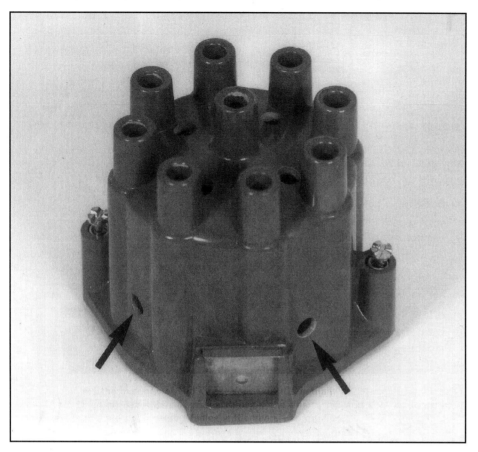

With a conventionally sized distributor cap, ventilation (to allow ionized air to escape) may be necessary to eliminate crossfire. When drilling holes in a cap, be extremely careful or you may find yourself thumbing a ride to the parts store. Vented caps are available from MSD.

with fins on their top surface keep the air inside a cap stirred up and also tend to reduce ionization problems. However, it may be necessary to vent the cap by drilling holes in it. This allows fresh air to enter, displacing the charged air inside. But it is advisable only for race cars or vehicles rarely driven in inclement weather, as moisture can easily enter the distributor.

Inductive Crossfire

Another form of crossfire, and one that is rarely understood, is caused by inductance. If you remember how a coil operates—current flowing through the primary winding creates a magnetic field that wraps itself around both the primary and secondary windings, inducing a voltage and consequently current though the two windings never touch—you're on the road to understanding inductive crossfire.

It usually occurs in the adjacent firing cylinders of a V-8 engine—numbers 5 and 7 on a big-block Chevrolet—where the two plug wires in question run close together over a relatively long distance. Inductive crossfire is especially prevalent in wires with solid-metal cores.

In effect, the two wires become a transformer much like a coil. As current flows through the "primary" (the first of the two cylinders to fire) it builds a magnetic field that wraps itself around the adjacent wire and induces a voltage in the "secondary." This results in a weak spark reaching the plug in the corresponding cylinder. The cure is to maintain adequate spacing between wires (use non-metallic wire separators), avoid running wires parallel to one another over a long distance, and to install helical core plug wires. In a helical or wire-wound spark plug wire, the conductor is spiral or helical wound around a non-conductive core. By winding the conductor in a spiral, the magnetic field is disrupted, eliminating the possibility of inductive crossfire. ■

In many instances, it isn't possible or desirable to install a large diameter HEI distributor. It is for such situations that the MSD Cap-A-Dapt was designed. In addition to the cap and adapter, the Cap-A-Dapt kit also features a special two-piece rotor which can be adjusted to obtain proper phasing. Cap-A-Dapt kits are available for standard Chevrolet, Accel and Mallory distributors. But regardless of the cap or rotor configuration, use high quality parts. High performance caps and rotors, such as those available from Accel, Mallory and MSD have a higher dielectric strength than their stock counterparts, so they do a better job of spark containment.

All Charged Up

As a spark jumps the air gap between the rotor tip and distributor terminal (a small gap is normal as it allows current to be routed to each terminal without metal-to-metal contact), it charges or ionizes the particles of air through which it travels. However, if the gap is too large, an excess amount of air is ionized. It is entirely possible that the air won't lose its charge before the next plug firing (especially at higher engine speeds) and before long, all the air inside the cap is electrically charged. When a spark occurs under this circumstance, it can and will jump anywhere—except to the right terminal since it offers the highest resistance, which is caused by cylinder pressure.

Ionization—Ionization of the air within the cap is usually a problem only with small diameter distributors. It can be reduced by installing an Alkyd cap, (usually tan, brown, red or blue in color) keeping it clean and free of carbon tracks and ensuring proper rotor phasing. Rotors

9

NITROUS OXIDE & SUPERCHARGING

NITROUS OXIDE

Nitrous oxide is a chemical compound composed of two nitrogen atoms and one oxygen atom (N_2O), and by weight it contains 36% oxygen. Nitrous oxide won't burn by itself, but what it does bring to an internal combustion party is a lot of oxygen, which is an essential ingredient in the combustion process. Also known as "laughing gas," nitrous oxide has been used as an anesthetic for quite some time.

Joseph Priestly (the English scientist who discovered oxygen) identified nitrous oxide in 1772, but it wasn't until nearly two centuries later—during World War II—that its power-increasing properties were applied to internal combustion engines. The Germans reportedly were the first to install nitrous oxide on their fighter planes and the Allies soon followed.

Current nitrous oxide systems are worlds apart from those used on aircraft and early automotive engines. Many of the horror stories about nitrous oxide causing engine damage resulted not from problems with nitrous oxide itself, but

Spray a dose of nitrous and two things are bound to happen–people laugh and engines growl. Also known as laughing gas, nitrous oxide injection functions as a chemical supercharger when fed into the intake tract. At the moment nitrous vaporizes, it is –128 degrees F and can drop temperatures in the intake tract by up to 70 degrees. (Photo courtesy NOS)

Charles Carpenter, the "grandfather of Pro Modified," revolutionized drag racing when he stuffed a big block in a '55 Chevy, added a healthy shot of nitrous and blasted into the sevens. Carpenter always puts on a great nitrous-powered show, in spite of his advanced years.

from poorly designed systems that were either destined to malfunction, or simply weren't designed to maintain the proper ratio of nitrous oxide to fuel.

As opposed to more traditional engine modifications (cams, heads, carbs, headers, etc.), nitrous oxide requires no engine disassembly and has no impact on fuel economy or exhaust emissions when not in use. And should a nitrous-equipped car be sold, the basic system can be easily removed and transferred to another vehicle with the right adaptive hardware.

Basic Nitrous Systems

Although it doesn't pressurize the intake tract, a nitrous oxide system can be thought of as a "chemical supercharger." The most basic nitrous oxide system consists of an injector plate, a supply tank with manual on/off valve, the lines and fittings to connect the two, mounting hardware and electrical switches to activate the system. The injector plate contains two spray bars (nozzles) and is easily installed beneath the carburetor or fuel injection throttle body. In a basic system, calibration is fixed to deliver the precise amounts of nitrous oxide and supplemental fuel needed to boost

horsepower a given amount. More sophisticated systems contain replaceable jets, which allow power output to be increased or decreased. Most adjustable single four-barrel street systems offer power increases ranging from 100 to 175 horsepower. Race systems designed for single four-barrel big blocks deliver 150 to 200 extra horsepower. Direct-port

nitrous oxide injection systems can be mounted externally, or concealed beneath the intake manifold. These systems can be calibrated to provide up to 300 horsepower—provided engine displacement and port size are adequate.

Operation—Inside the storage tank or bottle (which must be properly mounted so that the internal siphon tube angles down), nitrous oxide liquid lives in a high pressure environment—approximately 900 psi (actual pressure varies according to ambient temperature). As it exits the solenoid, nitrous enters a low-pressure area (inside the intake manifold). At and/or below atmospheric pressure, the liquid will vaporize, at which point there will be a severe drop in temperature; at the moment that liquid turns to vapor, nitrous temperature is minus 128-deg. F. One of the reasons that injector plate systems (placed beneath the carburetor or fuel injection throttle body) work so well is that the nitrous cools the entire contents of the intake manifold. Port injectors, being located much closer to the valves, offer less of a cooling effect, but pump more nitrous oxide directly into the intake ports.

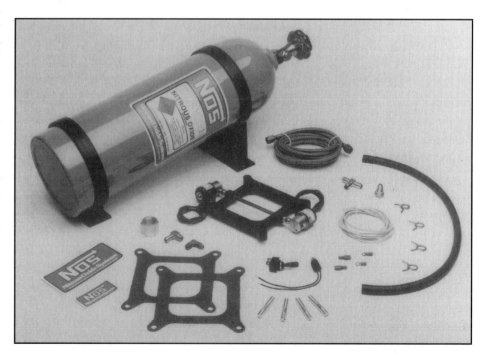

A typical nitrous kit contains a supply bottle, solenoids, fuel and nitrous lines, mounting hardware, activation switches and an injector plate that fits beneath the carburetor or fuel-injection throttle body.

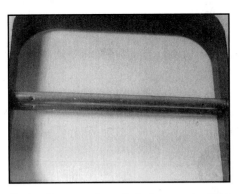

Basic nitrous systems include a spacer that fits between the carb and intake manifold and contains two spray bars–one for nitrous, the other for fuel. There's nothing terribly sophisticated about spray bars, just a couple of tubes with holes in them. However, the holes have to be oriented correctly (pointing towards the intake manifold, NOT the carb) and of sufficient diameter. Metering of nitrous and fuel is handled by jets, not the holes in the spray bars.

Direct port systems can be plumbed beneath the manifold, where they're hidden from view, or mounted on top to serve notice to the competition. This show system is more intricate than a typically direct port configuration, but it adds an exotic appearance–in addition to about 250 horsepower.

Increasing Horsepower

Nitrous oxide injection systems increase horsepower through two distinct means. As a gas flowing into the intake tract, nitrous oxide is an oxygen-bearing compound containing two parts nitrogen and one part oxygen. Since it's injected (under high pressure) directly into the intake manifold, an engine is fed more oxygen than it could receive by drawing air through the carburetors or fuel injection throttle body. This is the chemical supercharging aspect of nitrous oxide; provided additional fuel is also brought to the party, increasing the amount of oxygen that an engine consumes translates into greater potential power output.

Cooling Effects—The second power-producing facet of nitrous oxide's personality is its cooling effect. Being at a sub-zero temperature when it enters the intake tract, nitrous cools everything around it, including the air and fuel that has been drawn in through the carburetor or throttle body. As the temperature of air drops, it becomes denser, thereby increasing the number of oxygen molecules in a given volume of air space. The number of nitrogen molecules is also increased, but is of no significance since nitrogen does not participate in the combustion process. So even if nitrous oxide did not support combustion, its cooling effect would still increase power output.

Fuel Requirements

The fact that nitrous oxide delivers a substantial shot of oxygen necessitates that fuel also be injected through a special circuit that is precisely calibrated. By weight, the theoretical optimum ratio of nitrous oxide to gasoline is about 9.5:1. But as a matter of practice, this ratio is usually altered to about 8.75 parts of nitrous for each part of gas. This slightly richer ratio helps prevent combustion temperatures from getting out of hand. It's rather obvious then that jetting of the nitrous system's fuel circuit is critical. If fuel flow is inadequate, the overall air/fuel mixture will be excessively lean. That's a serious problem, because a nitrous system is activated under maximum load conditions—the worst possible time to feed an engine a mixture that is either too rich or too lean (with nitrous, both can be deadly). Problems ranging from poor performance to severe detonation and terminal engine damage are frequently the result of nothing more than an inadequate fuel delivery system. The vehicle's fuel pump and plumbing must be capable of meeting the demands of the carburetor/fuel injection and the nitrous system simultaneously. To guard against lean mixture problems, a fuel monitor should be installed that automatically shuts off the flow of nitrous if fuel pressure drops below a predetermined level.

Keep in mind that the nitrous systems installed on race cars are worlds apart from those used on street engines. According to Mike Hedgecock of Eagle Racing Engines, who builds a wide variety of nitrous race engines (including the big blocks for Robbie Vandergriff's 6-second, 200-mile-per-hour '57 Chevy):

"Whether you're running a street system or a race system, detonation is the thing you've got to watch out for. With a race engine, it's just so much more critical because you're running a ton more nitrous. But it's also serious in a street engine. I can guarantee that if you don't have an adequate fuel supply system, you'll fry a motor."

Two-stage systems are available in a variety of designs, including a spray bar/direct port combination like this. The spray bars handle the first stage which is usually jetted to produce from 50-175 horsepower so the tires don't go up in smoke when a car is launched. Once everything is hooked up and traction isn't as much of a problem, the direct port second stage is activated for an even greater power increase.

Mike also noted that adequate ignition plays a major role in the quest for maximum horsepower, especially with dual- or triple-stage nitrous systems. Any time you increase cylinder pressure, through any means, it increases the load on the ignition system. Any engine with nitrous—even a small 75-100 horsepower system—should have a solid high energy ignition system.

Although horror stories still abound, nitrous oxide injection systems offer safe and reliable horsepower—if they're properly installed. You cannot put enough emphasis on the fuel delivery side of a nitrous system. The system needs to maintain at least 4.5 psi of fuel pressure under all operating conditions, including maximum rpm in high gear. Nitrous oxide has taken a bad rap from street enthusiasts because they're frying motors with it. But in 99% of the cases, you can trace the problem to an improper installation. Grimes Automotive has developed a low pressure switch arrangement that can be wired up to either turn on an "idiot light" or shut off

the nitrous if fuel pressure drops below 4.5 psi. Some nitrous companies say that pressure can drop as low as 4 psi, and that's true—if your fuel system is absolutely perfect and your pressure gauge is dead-nuts accurate. But it is not uncommon for gauges to be as much as a pound off, and if they ever drop to 4 psi while the nitrous is activated and the engine is under maximum load, your

engine is history.

While a dependable high-volume fuel pump is an essential part of a nitrous system, it doesn't necessarily guarantee adequate fuel delivery. Some people install a high-volume fuel pump and connect it to a quarter-inch fuel line that has to run 15 feet to the engine and wonder why they have fuel delivery problems. That's one example of an improper installation. Even for a mild street engine, a 3/8-in. (or -6 AN) fuel line is needed at the very least; race cars call for a 1/2-in. (-8 AN) or larger fuel line.

Bottle Pressure

Nitrous bottle pressure is another factor that can cause problems. Although pressure usually isn't critical in a street installation (because things aren't being pushed to the limit), it can have a critical impact on a race engine. Surprisingly, even seasoned racers frequently overlook bottle pressure. According to Mike Hedgecock, pressure is most critical and has to be consistent because pressure and jetting are what control the amount of nitrous that goes into the engine. Normally, pressure will increase during the day as temperatures creep up, and drop at night when it cools off. Too many racers worry about (nitrous system) jet

Most full-on race systems mounted on tunnel ram manifolds are of the direct port persuasion and are plumbed externally. However, systems such as the one on the left, which is a plate version for use with twin Holley Dominator carbs, are also common. By comparison, the two-stage system on the right has spray bars mounted inside the manifold plenum.

Bottle pressure affects nitrous/fuel ratio and temperature affects nitrous pressure. When consistency is a major consideration, a bottle warmer is frequently installed to keep temperature constant. A bottle blanket can also be added to retain heat.

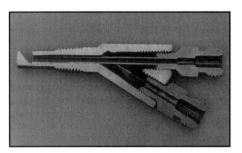

The "Fogger" nozzle is really two nozzles in one. Fuel flows through the tube running down the center while nitrous is brought in around it. As the nitrous vaporizes it improves fuel atomization. Some two-stage race systems incorporate individual nozzles in each runner and spray bars in the plenum. This type of system is most frequently installed on big blocks, but can be applied to large small blocks as well.

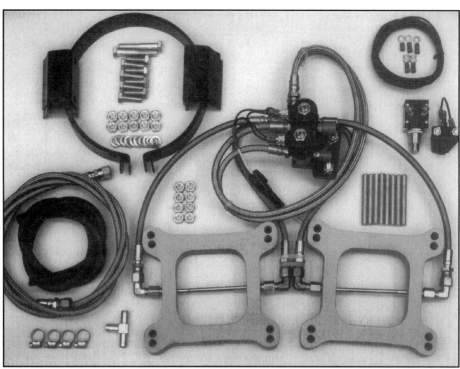

A complete system should include all the required fuel and nitrous lines, solenoids, clamps, fittings, electrical wiring and connectors and bottle mounting hardware. Typically, a five or 10 pound bottle of nitrous is also included.

size and don't have the faintest idea what their bottle pressure is. That's like worrying about plug gap when you don't know where the timing is set. And it can be the end of your engine. If the pressure is up, and you don't adjust the fuel, you can get into a lean condition that's bad enough to cause severe detonation.

Camshafts

Another key to maximizing performance and minimizing problems with nitrous oxide is to use common sense when building or modifying the engine. The most sensible approach when building a street engine is to select a camshaft that delivers strong low-speed and mid-range torque for everyday driving. That will assure crisp throttle response, good fuel economy and

driveability. Then the nitrous system can be called upon to really wake things up when it's needed.

Race Engines—Camming a race engine for use with nitrous also requires a bit of thought. If you plan to use "the bottle" only after the car has been launched (possibly in high gear only) a cam must be selected with that in mind. A car won't produce very impressive elapsed times if it's a slug until the nitrous system is activated.

Other Considerations

Beyond that, be sure to select a system produced by a reputable manufacturer; the money you save by buying an off-brand can be real expensive if you destroy an engine because of a nitrous system malfunction. Installation is usually a simple matter of following the manufacturers' instructions. Be sure to mount the bottle properly (away from engine heat), keep the nitrous and fuel lines away from the exhaust pipes, and make sure your electrical connections are correct.

Limits—Being reasonable is another prerequisite; you can only put so much nitrous through any given engine because every intake port has a flow limitation. A given engine can be forced to consume only so much nitrous. Once the bounds of good judgment are exceeded, you've created an accident that's waiting to happen. Carburetors meter fuel in response to a vacuum signal that's communicated through the intake manifold to the discharge nozzles. Injecting too much nitrous into the manifold can kill this signal, thereby reducing the amount of fuel metered by the carburetor, causing a lean condition. Racers using too many stages of nitrous set on "kill" have learned this expensive lesson the hard way—by destroying engines.

Mike Hedgecock has conclusively proven that excessive nitrous flow pays few horsepower dividends and is unnecessary. Rather than using three or four individual stages, Hedgecock equips his killer unlimited Pro Modified big blocks with a single- or two-stage system.

IHRA Top Sportsman is another class where big block Chevy power reigns supreme. This altered employs all the latest tricks, including a sheet metal intake manifold plumbed with a direct port nitrous system, for 7-second quarter-mile performance.

The cars that are powered by his engines are typically among the fastest qualifiers and most consistent performers at a race, so his philosophy has proven merit. Hedgecock states:

"If you can get into a nitrous overkill situation with a big block, just think what that means when you hook nitrous up to a street engine. The engine is smaller and so are the ports so you have to keep these limitations in mind. On a street engine that's 454 cubic inches or larger, stick to

a system rated at 200 horsepower or less; on a typical race engine, you can use an adjustable system that can be jetted up to about 350 horsepower."

The bottom line is that nitrous oxide systems deliver more horsepower per dollar than any other piece of speed equipment. They are also very reliable—there's no risk of engine damage so long as the system is calibrated and installed correctly. The only drawback is that the supply bottle must be refilled periodically

All solenoids are not the same. Internal passages can vary according to manufacturer and application and bigger isn't always better. If the passage on the supply side of the nitrous solenoid is too large, the solenoid may be prone to sticking closed because it can't overcome the nitrous pressure. Fluid enters through the outer passage and exits in the center.

at a cost of about $3.00 per pound.

SUPERCHARGING

Even if a supercharger didn't add an ounce of horsepower to an engine, it would still have merit. If nothing else, a 6-71 GMC blower makes any big block sound like it's pumping out more horsepower than the space shuttle. But as anyone who has driven a car powered by a supercharged engine can attest, blowers do a whole lot more than add looks and sound.

GMC

When General Motors Corporation (GMC) began manufacturing superchargers for its inline 6-cylinder diesel truck, bus and industrial engines back in the Thirties, no one had the faintest inkling that these units would one day be reworked for use on race engines. The first GM diesel was the 6-71; the designation refers to six cylinders each with a volume of 71 cubic inches. Over the years, GMC has produced 3-71, 4-71, 6-71 inline and 6V-71, 8V-71 blowers, the latter two being used on V-engines.

The 6-71 version is most commonly used on big-block Chevy engines, although some power maniacs have wrestled 8-71 and 10-71 blowers on top of 454+ cubic-inch small blocks. The 8-71 uses 8V-71 rotors mounted in an aftermarket case; the original 8V-71 case doesn't lend itself to use on an automotive V-8 engine. A 10-71 blower is built entirely of aftermarket components. The primary difference between each of these blowers is length; an 8-71 is one inch longer than a 6-71; a 10-71 is one inch longer than an 8-71 and a 12-71 (used only in alcohol and fuel applications) is one inch longer than a 10-71.

Roots Type—All GMC-type blowers are of the Roots type; all Roots-type blowers are termed positive displacement. The basic design, which incorporates two rotors, was first patented by the Roots Brothers in the mid-1800s. GMC blowers are obviously a far cry from the original Roots configuration, but still share the label, as does any multi-rotor supercharger.

The first use of GMC blowers as a means of increasing the power of automotive engines dates back to the late Forties. Most installations were relatively crude affairs, but they worked—sometimes all too well. Racers of the day didn't have adequate knowledge of fuels and many an engine expired as a result of too much boost and not enough octane. However, by the early Sixties, most of the bugs had been worked out and GMC blowers (commonly called "Jimmies") had become fairly common sights at drag strips across the country. And by the 1980s, enthusiasm for the look, sound and power produced by "Jimmy" blowers had spread to all types of street cars and boats. The tremendous popularity of GMC blowers prompted companies like B&M and Weiand Automotive to develop their own positive displacement blowers specifically for street and marine applications.

How it Works

Superchargers increase horsepower by literally forcing increased volumes of air and fuel into the cylinders. In a normally

Mounting a supercharger on top of a big block doesn't do anything but make a good thing better. The sound of a thumping 454 with a blower on top will even send chills down the spine of a Ford lover. There may not be a true substitute for cubic inches, but a blower comes mighty close.

aspirated engine, power output increases as air temperature drops because the cooler the air, the more dense it is, which means that more air (and the oxygen it contains) is drawn into the cylinders than normal. Instead of having to rely on atmospheric conditions to increase the volume of air entering the cylinders, a supercharged engine is force fed.

Regardless of the way it's achieved, increased cylinder filling translates directly to increased power output. By mechanically stuffing the cylinders with air and fuel, a supercharger makes it

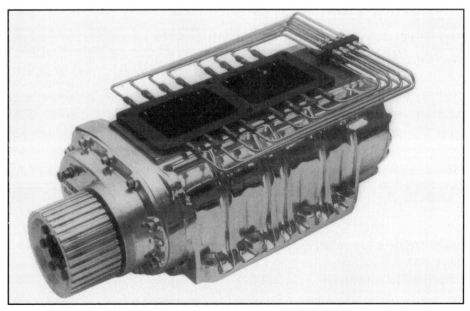

You can cook up a one-two power punch by adding nitrous oxide injection to a supercharger. Most systems discharge through a plate that fits between the carburetor adapter and blower body.

possible to achieve power levels not possible under normal atmospheric conditions; the more air/fuel mixture that's rammed into an engine, the more power it produces—up to a point.

Drive Ratio & Boost

Boost is the determining factor. Whereas a naturally aspirated engine operates with some amount of manifold vacuum, a blown engine has measurable positive pressure (stated in psi) in its intake tract once engine speed reaches a certain point. The drive ratio is largely what determines the amount of boost that a blower will produce. When a supercharger spins slower than the engine, it is said to be underdriven; if it rotates faster than engine speed, it's overdriven. Drive ratio is only one of the factors that determine boost. Valve timing, compression ratio and clearances within the blower itself are also part of the equation. Consequently, the correlation between drive ratio and the amount of boost pressure produced is not always consistent; 3% underdrive may result in 5 pounds of boost on one engine and 8 pounds on another of the same displacement.

Pulleys—Most drive systems incorporate pulley sizes that allow drive ratio to be altered in steps of 3%; tooth count is used to determine drive ratio and each time the count is altered by one tooth, the ratio changes 3%. As an example, many big-block Chevy street supercharger kits are supplied with 33-tooth bottom and 37-tooth top pulleys, which produce a 12% underdrive ratio. Switching to a 34-tooth bottom pulley alters the ratio to 9% underdrive. Whether it's the top pulley (on the blower) or bottom pulley (on the crankshaft) the effect on drive ratio is the same.

The beauty of this system is that top and bottom pulleys are interchangeable, so a quick switch from underdrive to overdrive can be made by just swapping

Jim Oddy's 526-cubic inch big-block powered Pro Modified Corvette ultimately did receive a real paint job, but even in primer, the car turned in record-breaking performances. The big 14-71 blower on top combined with Oddy's engine building and tuning expertise made life tough for the competition.

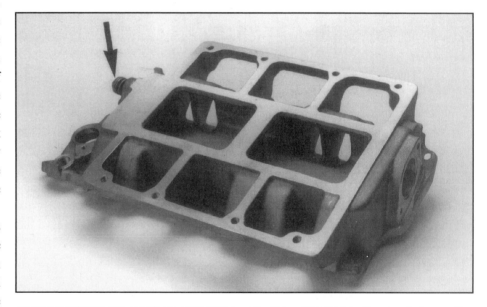

Blower manifolds are relatively straightforward affairs that bridge the gap between the blower's case and an engine's cylinder heads. The manifolds also contain a spring loaded pop-off valve (arrow) that opens in the event that manifold pressure reaches too high a level.

pulleys. Drive ratio is computed by dividing the number of teeth in the bottom pulley by the tooth count of the top pulley, as expressed in the formula:

$$\text{Drive Ratio} = \frac{\text{Bottom Pulley Tooth Count}}{\text{Top Pulley Tooth Count}}$$

Using the kit mentioned above, you'd divide 33 by 37, which gives you .89. This means the top pulley spins at 89% of the bottom pulley speed or that it is spinning 11% slower. A figure of 12% rather than 11% is normally used for simplicity. When the pulleys are switched, the equation becomes 37 divided by 33, which translates to 1.12 or 112% or 12% overdrive (rounding will also alter actual ratios slightly). Generally, for each change in top or bottom pulley tooth count (which alters drive ratio by 3%) there's a one to two psi change in boost pressure.

Blower drive ratio can be altered by changing the top, bottom or both pulleys. Top and bottom pulleys can be interchanged on most 6-71 drive systems, making it very easy to switch from underdrive to overdrive.

B&M offers several versions of its street supercharger. The larger a blower's capacity, the more boost it can produce on a given engine. The standard B&M big-block blower is designed to deliver boost levels between 5 and 7 psi.

Belts—Any particular drive ratio can be achieved through a number of pulley combinations. A 12% overdrive or underdrive ratio can be achieved with either a 32/36-, 33/37-, 34/38- or 35/39-tooth pulley combination. However, from a practical standpoint, wherever possible, it's preferable to switch to a larger pulley or pulleys (rather than smaller) when making a ratio change because belt speed is reduced—thereby increasing belt life. As an example, if you wanted to switch from a 12% underdrive to 9% underdrive, the preferred choice is to install a 38/35 combination rather than a 37/34. However, if the existing combination for 12% underdrive was 37/33, it would only be necessary to change the bottom pulley to arrive at 9% underdrive. From an economic standpoint, that's a better choice.

However, sometimes it isn't possible to change only one pulley unless a different length belt is also used, so the economics of each situation have to be weighed.

Fortunately, there's a good deal of belt tension adjustment on most drive systems, so a wide variety of drive ratios can be accommodated with a single belt. Belt length for big-block 6-71 blower installations is generally 56, 57, 58.5 or 60 inches; these lengths will cover total tooth counts (top and bottom pulley tooth counts added together) of 64-78.

When it comes to building supercharged street and race engines, Jim Oddy has a reputation that's hard to beat. Oddy, who operates Oddy's Automotive (651 Bullis Road, Elma, NY 14059, 716/674-2500) has the distinction of owning the world's quickest "doorslammer." His Pro Modified Corvette recorded a 1/4-mile elapsed time of 6.51 seconds at 205.98 mph.

Oddy also builds a number of blown big blocks for street, race and marine applications and he's developed some interesting combinations. According to Oddy:

"You just can't beat a 6-71 for a street engine. You can easily make over 800 horsepower from a 454 on unleaded premium with 10 pounds of boost. But what we generally advise is for someone to start out with a combination that limits boost to 5 or 6 pounds. There's a learning curve that you have to go through to find the type of gas, gear ratio, timing, valve adjustment and converter the engine likes. By limiting boost to 5-6 pounds, you probably won't hurt anything if you're off because you won't be on the borderline of detonation. Then, after everything is right, you can bump the boost up and make more horsepower—safely."

Race Motors—Race motors are different; they're on "kill" all the time. So while Oddy limits the boost of his street engines to 10 psi or less, a race engine will crank up 22-25 psi. The extra boost may not do much for longevity, but it does wonders for horsepower. Blown big

129

Since the drive pulley is attached to the vibration damper, it's a good practice to install a high performance damper. As boost levels increase so does stress on the damper hub. Stock dampers have a tendency to crack. This Fluidampr has been modified to include six pulley bolt holes so a drive pulley can be bolted directly to it.

Blower Drive Service offers a complete selection of supercharger manifolds for big blocks. The company offers both race and street manifolds and complete GMC blower systems.

blocks fitted with 8-71 blowers are approaching 3-hp per cubic inch on gasoline. In a race engine, the advantage of the 8-71 over the 6-71 is two-fold. First, the larger blower can be run slower and still make the same amount of boost. Secondly, it builds boost quicker, so it brings the power up quicker too. Total power potential is also greater with a larger blower (Oddy has also done some 10-71 big blocks), but as with anything, there are limits. By overdriving the blower to extremes, you'll only gain power up to a point, because the air will become heated too much. Also, the faster the blower is driven, the more torque is siphoned off the engine to drive it. So

somewhere along the line you reach a point of diminishing returns.

Air inlet temperature is a key thing that no one talks about, but it makes a tremendous difference. If the temperature of the air exiting the blower can be reduced by 70 deg., for example, an increase of 70 horsepower is possible. An intercooler is the only way to do that, but they've been banned by most racing organizations.

Fuel Systems—As a general rule, you should never go beyond a 1:1 drive ratio (into overdrive) if you're running pump gas; when you start cranking in boost, you need race gas in the tank. It is also most critical that the fuel system be adequate. You should run -8 AN line (1/2 in.) from the fuel tank to the mechanical fuel pump, and -6 AN lines (3/8 in.) from the pump to the carburetors. It's also advisable to use both a high-volume mechanical fuel pump and an electric pump (the electric pump pumps to the mechanical pump). If the electric pump fails, you won't get stuck, because the mechanical pump will still be operating. Use a mechanical pump that is rated at about 11 psi and a regulator to maintain a constant 8 psi; to avoid fuel delivery short-fall, the system should be able to maintain 8 psi at the carburetors, under all operating conditions.

Ignition Timing—Ignition timing is also critical with a supercharged engine. Typically, total timing is limited to 28-30 deg. because research has shown that the blower builds so much cylinder pressure that the engine doesn't like a lot of timing. Too much spark advance is the biggest engine killer when there's a supercharger in the picture because it just beats the bearing and rings to death. Dyno testing has proven that maximum power is produced with 28-30 deg. Even on a race engine, running race gas, total spark advance rarely goes beyond 32 deg. That's one of the keys to making a blown motor live. If everything is done right, there's no reason that a blown street

motor shouldn't last for over 100,000 miles. In reality, most street-driven vehicles don't get into boost that often. If you were driving on "kill" all the time, things would be different.

Marine engines present a slightly different situation because they run under loads that are more similar to those encountered by race engines. However, the same considerations apply; if boost, spark lead and fuel octane are all properly matched, a marine engine should run trouble-free for several seasons.

Even though street engines have limited boost, cylinder pressures and combustion temperatures get high enough to warrant extremely cold spark plugs. Oddy generally uses Champion plugs with a 57, 59 or 60 heat range. These are cold race plugs, so the ignition needs to be hot to avoid fouling. Oddy feels that you'd need an MSD-6A box at the very least to keep the plugs clean. Forget any type of point-triggered ignition—unless an electronic module (like an MSD 6A or 6AL) is incorporated in the system—because it won't provide a hot enough spark to keep the engine running.

Dampers—Another component that engine builders like Hedgecock and Oddy feel very strongly about is the vibration damper. When a supercharged engine is operating under boost, it puts significantly higher loads on the crankshaft and bearings than a naturally aspirated one. Most blown race engines are notorious for getting only a handful of runs on a set of bearings. A number of years ago, Oddy was experiencing typically short bearing life on his race engines so he began experimenting with the viscous vibration damper manufactured by Fluidampr. He noticed an immediate improvement in bearing life—instead of the bearings looking like trash after 10 runs or less, they lasted for over 30 runs and still looked like new. That experience prompted him to modify Fluidamprs specifically for supercharged engines. These modifications include

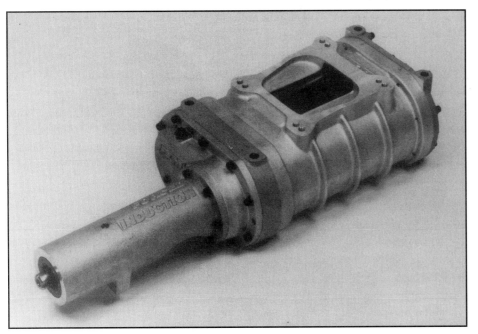

Aftermarket dampers like those produced by B&M and Weiand are very similar in construction to an original 6-71. The pulley is attached to a shaft that spins a pair of gears which drive the rotors. Depending on the application, the rotors may have Teflon tips.

drilling and tapping the necessary holes so a standard blower pulley (with six bolt holes) can be installed, and cutting a second keyway (1/4 in. wide). The additional keyway prevents the damper from spinning on the crankshaft in the event that the blower "sneezes" (kicks back).

Even on a street engine, a high performance damper should be used. Point one is that every engine needs a damper as opposed to a hub. Point two is that stock cast-iron dampers have a tendency to crack when used on supercharged engines. As horsepower increases, so does the need for adequate torsional vibration control, so just about every knowledgeable engine builder strongly advises the use of a high performance vibration damper on any supercharged engine.

Cylinder Heads

Obviously, cylinder heads are of vital importance in any high horsepower big block. For street engines, as well as some race engines, Oddy prefers Dart Merlin heads, and adds some trick port and combustion chamber rework. Compared to aluminum, the cast-iron Merlin heads are relatively inexpensive, but more importantly, they have excellent flow capacity, strength and durability.

Aftermarket vs. 6-71

The primary drawback of a 6-71 style blower is its expense and its size. Which is precisely the reason that B&M and Weiand developed their own Roots-type blowers. B&M's Powerchargers (formerly called Forced Induction) and Weiand's Pro Street and Pro Marine superchargers are smaller than a 6-71 and are designed specifically for use on automotive engines. These blowers have a carburetor mounting flange cast integrally in the blower housing and bolt to special intake manifolds which allow for a very low profile. The complete blower, with carburetor, will fit beneath the hoods of many cars and pickups.

Since the aftermarket blowers are relatively small, they must be turned at comparatively high rpm to develop boost. Both B&M and Weiand supply their street blowers with drive ratios in a range of 2:1. In 6-71 parlance, that translates to 100% overdrive, but even at these drive ratios, these blowers produce only 4-6 psi; even though they're relatively efficient, the comparatively small size of the B&M and Weiand blowers makes high drive ratios necessary. As more food for thought, consider that drive ratios ranging from 1.60:1 to 2.44:1 are available and they translate to overdrive ratios of up to 144%.

The size relationship of a 6-71 compared to these smaller aftermarket blowers provides an insight into the reason for the extreme differences in drive ratio. A 6-71 has a displacement of 411 cid. Weiand's Pro Street big block blowers have a displacement of 177 cid; B&M's Powerchargers for big blocks displace 174 and 250 cid respectively. But in spite of their size, the high drive ratios make it possible for these blowers to produce a reasonable amount of boost.

Limitations—Both the B&M and Weiand street blowers are designed to produce 5-6 pounds of boost (or up to 10 pounds with a Powercharger 250) on stock and mildly modified engines. They perform well in these type of applications, but problems frequently arise when attempts are made to push boost beyond design parameters. Both brands of blowers utilize a drive system that incorporates a ribbed, rather than a cog belt as found on a 6-71 installation. If you try to build too much boost, the belt will slip. The idler arrangement also contributes to belt slippage because the direction in which tension is applied pushes the belt away from the top pulley. Consequently, the belt doesn't get a good wrap around the pulley, which contributes to slippage. All blower drive systems have a similar idler mounting arrangement, but the larger blowers utilize a cog belt, so slippage is never a problem.

That may sound like an indictment of these superchargers; it's not. When operated within their design parameters, the B&M and Weiand blowers both perform very well and can increase

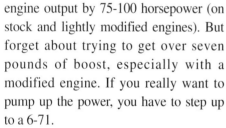

Whether it's supercharged or nitrous oxide-injected, a big block needs adequate fuel delivery to make maximum power. A high quality fuel pressure gauge is an absolute requirement to make sure fuel starvation doesn't occur. Keep in mind that a pressure gauge doesn't monitor volume, so if the fuel lines are too small, pressure will be way up, but the engine can still run out of fuel. If a mechanical or electric pump is to be used, it must have sufficient output to avoid fuel starvation. Installation of an electric pump is usually the best way to avoid problems.

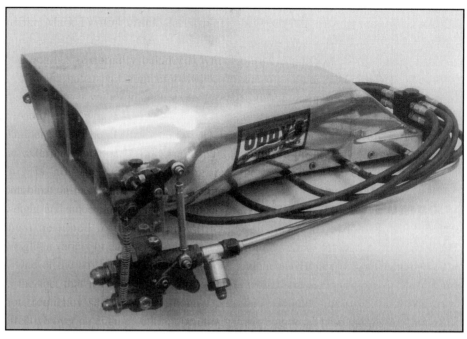

When a supercharged big block is fuel injected, the fuel delivery system can be incorporated in the "bug catcher." Fuel is discharged from the base which bolts directly to the blower delivered.

engine output by 75-100 horsepower (on stock and lightly modified engines). But forget about trying to get over seven pounds of boost, especially with a modified engine. If you really want to pump up the power, you have to step up to a 6-71.

Several companies offer 6-71 street blower kits, and a variety of 6-71 and 8-71 race blower assemblies. In addition to Weiand, Blower Drive Service (12140 Washington Blvd., Whittier, CA 90606, 213/693-4302), Dyer's Machine Service (7665 W. 63rd St., Summit, IL 60501, 708/496-8100), Littlefield Blowers (6840 Orangethorpe, Buena Park, CA 90620, 714/739-2275), and Mooneyham Blowers (13406 Lakewood Blvd., Bellflower, CA 90706, 213/634-5192), offer kits. B&M offers its own version of the 6-71, called the MegaBlower. As opposed to incorporating a remanufactured 6-71, the MegaBlower, which has a displacement of 420 cubic inches, is built entirely of new components designed and manufactured by B&M. Both street and marine versions are offered.

Centrifugal Blowers—Centrifugal

blowers, such as those produced by Paxton (929 Olympic Blvd., Santa Monica, CA 90404, 213/452-8093) and Vortech Engineering (5351 Bonsai Ave., Moorpark, CA 93021, 805/529-9330) also offer interesting power augmenting possibilities. Centrifugal blowers take air in at their center and force it out an orifice in the housing. In operation, a centrifugal blower uses an impeller, rather than overlapping rotors, to create boost. Centrifugal blowers are relatively small, but that's a double-edged sword. While they do fit beneath the hood of just about any car, they don't move the large volumes of air characteristic of a Roots blower. Consequently, they aren't well suited to big blocks. Besides, power-crazed hot rodders prefer the massive appearance and distinctive sound of a 6-71, which is another reason centrifugal blowers haven't gained much popularity with the big-block Chevy fraternity.

Another consideration that has limited the popularity of centrifugal blowers is that they don't build boost as rapidly as a Roots type. Rather than quickly building pressure and maintaining it as rpm increases, a centrifugal blower increases

boost at an exponential rate—doubling rpm increases boost by a factor of four. However, since a street engine can withstand only so much boost, blower drive ratio must be set to provide a particular boost level at a specific rpm. Consequently, at lower engine speeds, boost drops off significantly. On the other hand, this can be a blessing—limiting boost at lower speeds creates fewer traction problems.

Turbos

Turbochargers are essentially centrifugal blowers operated by exhaust gasses rather than mechanically. Although several manufacturers made a big push several years ago, turbos have never achieved widespread popularity. Complex installations, turbo lag and incompatibility with other types of performance equipment are a few of the causes of turbocharging's demise as popular add-on power boosters. That isn't meant to imply that turbocharging isn't practical, only that aftermarket systems aren't very popular. ■

10

HEADERS & EXHAUST

HEADERS

When tubular exhaust manifolds (the formal name for headers), were introduced, they were generally of the "Tri-Y" design. In this configuration, four relatively short primary tubes are connected in pairs, each of which leads into a larger diameter secondary tube. The two secondary tubes are then joined further downstream in a collector. As a result of primary tube pairing, adjacent firing cylinders are separated, at least until the exhaust gasses reach the collector. In fabricating a Tri-Y header, three individual "Y" connections are made, hence the name.

The stepped 4-2-1 arrangement of the pipes proved especially conducive to increased horsepower in the lower and middle rpm ranges. The Tri-Y system worked well into the late Sixties, until drag racing engines began peaking at considerably higher speeds. At this point, the four-tube, tuned, "equal length" header began to achieve more popularity. Although the Tri-Y arrangement, which bolsters low-speed and mid-range performance, is superior for most street and some race applications, it has been largely abandoned in the face of overwhelming demand for the individual tube variety. Tri-Y headers are harder to build and don't look as "racy" as the four-tube variety so they have two strikes against them. However, anyone looking for an increase in mid-range torque would do well to experiment with a set of

The quiet before the storm–Larry Lombardo gets ready to launch Bill Jenkins's 1979 Pro Stock Camaro. Jenkins has always paid particular attention to exhaust systems, one of the reasons his engines have always produced so much power.

Boat headers take a slightly different exit route than their automotive counterparts, but their function is the same–to route exhaust gasses out of the heads as efficiently as possible.

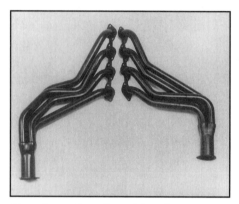

Chassis configuration determines a great deal about the length and routing of header primary tubes. Trucks have spacious engine compartments and plenty of room under the floor boards, so primary tube length can usually be as long as needed. These Hedman headers are designed for 1978-'87 C/10 pickups.

Tri-Y headers (which may require jetting and timing changes).

Four-Tube Headers

Although some header companies still offer Tri-Y headers, the majority of commercially available headers are comprised of separate tubes leading from a cylinder head port to a common collector. But from one manufacturer to another, there can be significant differences in the routes taken between the two termination points. Considering that all the tubes must end at a given length from the back of the block or other fore/aft reference point, it can be seen that the rear-most tube must travel a more tortuous route if it is to be the same length as the forward-most tube.

With a true race header, the fabricator will move heaven, earth, his mother-in-law and other immovable objects attempting to keep the lengths of all tubes within a tolerance of one to two inches. In fact, with some engine/chassis combinations, clearance is so tight that equal length can be approached only by routing a tube from one bank into the collector on the opposite side. Needless to say, installation of these headers must be done by a registered contortionist or masochist, but fortunately, big-block Chevys rarely present such problems when installed in a production chassis.

Dedication to near-perfect equality of length may be appropriate for some applications, but it's probably more of a case of ego on the part of the header designer. According to Keith Ferrell, general manager of Hedman South and Jr. Manufacturing, "We've gotten a lot of feedback from racers that their engines produce more power with unequal length headers. Sure, they need to be close in length—each tube should be within six or eight inches of the others in overall length—but when you put a collector on the end of a header, it changes the whole picture."

On street-driven vehicles and boats, tolerances of far greater proportions are maintained. Much of any length differential will be negated by the effect of an exhaust pipe and muffler being bolted to the output end of the collector. In any event, a street engine operates over a relatively broad rpm band so even though pipe length may vary considerably, the discrepancy will not be particularly detrimental if all pipes "tune" within the engine's normal rpm range.

Tubing Size

Diameter—Diameter is one of the most important factors with headers. If primary tube size is too large, both performance and fuel economy losses will be realized. In the days of oil "shortages," header manufacturers responded to the strong demand for mileage improving equipment by producing big block headers with primary tube diameters as small as 1-5/8 in. By comparison, in times when the demand for horsepower reigns supreme, street headers for big blocks are generally fabricated from tubing measuring 1-3/4- or 2-in. in diameter. As a general rule of thumb, as engine size and/or normal operating rpm decrease, there should be a concomitant reduction in header tube diameter. It is for precisely this reason that some manufacturers list more than one part number (for a particular vehicle) when a single model would seem to be sufficient; each is designed for a particular application.

As an example, the Hedman catalog lists a number of different part numbers for early-model Chevelles, Corvettes and Camaros with big-block engines. Displacements ranged from 396 to 454 cid, so it stands to reason that a single

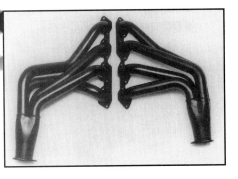

There isn't much room in a Corvette engine compartment, especially when it houses a big block, so street headers are on the short side. These headers employ 2-in diameter primary tubes which merge in a 3-in. collector.

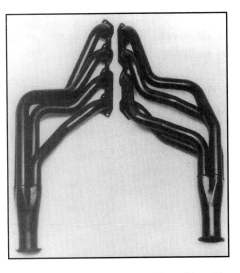

If you've got a '64-'77 Chevelle with a big block inside, your headers will look like this. Long, large diameter tubes help engine breathing which translates to high horsepower.

header for each chassis isn't adequate. For street/strip applications, a 2-1/8-in. or even 2-1/4-in. diameter might be appropriate, and for full-tilt, take-no-prisoners type of racing, the diameter of primary header tubes may be as large as 2-5/8-in. But when the same engine/chassis combination is pressed into highway service, one would be better advised to install a set of headers with 1-3/4-in. or 1-7/8-in. tubes. And for pure economy driving, a diameter of no larger than 1-3/4 in. is in order. What all this boils down to is that header tube diameter and length must be matched to a specific application for the best results.

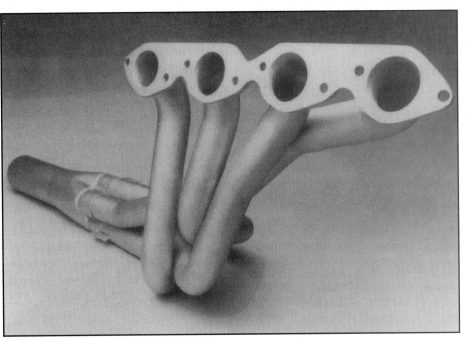

Race headers make fewer compromises than their street counterparts, so they have longer primary tubes and larger and longer collectors. Primary tube diameters for race headers range from 2-in to 2-5/8-in. in diameter.

Collector length is another consideration. Depending on the application, it can vary from 6 to 8 in. for 4- and 5-speed drag race applications to over four feet for oval track cars. Collector diameter generally varies from 3-1/2-in to 5-in, depending on engine size and operating rpm. In all cases, on cars with full length exhaust systems, a crossover pipe that connects the collectors will increase power.

BIBS—When selecting a set of headers, most people fall victim to BIBS—Bigger Is Better Syndrome. BIBS leads people to believe that if a set of 1-3/4-in. tube headers is good, a set with 2-in. tubes must be better and 2-1/4 in. header tubes must be pure heaven. Nothing could be further from the truth.

When primary tube diameter is too large, velocity is reduced and the header loses much of its scavenging capability. In a sense, this creates greater back pressure, because the slight vacuum created by a column of gas moving at high velocity is absent. With properly sized primary tubes—or even tubes that are slightly too small—exhaust gasses from each cycle help scavenge gasses

from the following cycle. In turn, this action tends to improve the fuel metering signal that reaches the carburetor. So in spite of the commonly held belief that installing a set of headers requires a richer mixture, if the headers are correctly sized, a leaner mixture may be required to compensate for a stronger signal.

Length—What about length? Big-block headers vary from 25 in. to over 40 in. in primary tube length; collector length ranges from 12 to 48 in. As with diameter, header length should be matched to engine size and operating rpm. Even if tube and collector diameter are ideally matched to engine displacement, if the primary tubes and/or collectors are too short, maximum scavenging occurs at too high an engine speed to be of any use. On the other hand, if header tube and collector length are too long they'll restrict flow, particularly at higher engine speeds. So the key is to determine the ideal diameter/length combination for a particular engine operated within a specific rpm range. Whether it's a street machine, drag race or oval track car, truck, tractor or boat, the volume of exhaust produced by the

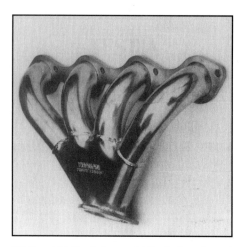

Stick a big block in an old Ford chassis and you have what's normally known as an interference fit. To minimize header installation problems, Hedman offers "Tight Tubes," a "shortie" style header with a flat collector.

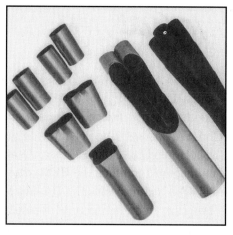

The best way to determine optimum header length is to use the vehicle on which they'll be installed as a test bed. Several companies offer kits that allow primary tube and collector length to be easily adjusted.

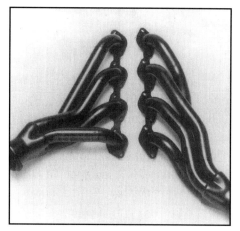

Unless major surgery is performed, 1967-81 Camaros don't offer an abundance of room for headers. As a result, the primary tubes aren't very long. Race headers have a completely different configuration that isn't too practical for the street.

engine is what determines header dimensions. A 396 cid race engine that turns 9000 rpm will produce more exhaust gas volume than a 454 cid street engine that never sees the high side of 5000 rpm.

Unfortunately, the ideal header may not fit the chassis in which the engine is installed; space limitations dictate that Corvette headers are shorter than Camaro, Nova, Chevelle or truck headers. Side-mounted exhausts can sometimes be used to extend header length, but there may be few other alternatives with an under-chassis exit aside from a set of custom-built headers.

Material

From the practical, as opposed to theoretical, standpoint, material is a major consideration. In days of old, all header tubing was 18 gauge (.049 in.) mild steel while the flange plate was cut from 1/4-in. thick material. A header so constructed usually offers sufficient strength and durability to provide years of good service, but in the damper regions of the country, the effects of rust and general deterioration can end header life in a hurry. When improved durability is required, headers made of thicker (16 or 14 gauge) material or stainless steel are

available as are chrome-plated or aluminum-coated models. However, in many cases, these special construction techniques (which obviously increase costs) aren't applied across the board so they may not be available for your particular application. Or they may not be desirable. If properly cleaned and coated with high temperature paint, race car headers will last almost indefinitely. That being the case, headers made from heavy gauge material offer nothing more than extra weight—except in a few circumstances; race cars that run for long periods of time may need heavier headers to avoid fracturing. In fact, reinforcing brackets may be required.

Header Coatings

One of the best ways to prevent rust and corrosion from turning headers into a set of bag pipes is to have them coated. Most header manufacturers offer a coating service, or uncoated headers can be sent to one of several coating companies. Jet Hot Header Coatings, (800/432-3379), Performance Coatings (404/478-2775), HPC (800/456-4721) and Polymer Dynamics (713/694-3296) all offer header coating services.

The most popular color for header coatings is a silver/aluminum one that has

an almost chrome-like luster. Several other colors are also available. Irrespective of color selection, headers should be coated inside and out to minimize the effects of moisture.

Tuning

Unquestionably, by tuning header length for maximum exhaust scavenging at a particular engine speed, there's a considerable amount of power to be gained. But before you go spending money like a politician, take a hard look at standard production headers. Some models offer adjustable primary tubes and collector extensions can be easily made from appropriately sized tubing. Many times, a few modifications made to an existing header are all that's required for maximum horsepower. On the other hand, you may not be so lucky, and a custom set of headers may be the only way to handle the competition. In either case, do enough experimenting to get a handle on the dimensions of the ideal header for your car. Many custom header fabricators are excellent craftsmen, but don't know as much about exhaust tuning as they do about brain surgery. Their opinions may be of little value. However, a header maker who has worked with racers and owners of high performance

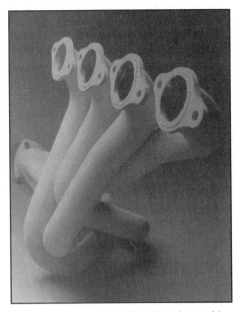

Heat, moisture and steel produce iron oxide—otherwise known as rust. To prevent it, many header manufacturers offer various coatings. These headers are coated with powdered aluminum, which results in a relatively rough surface. Most companies now use a smooth coating that has an almost chrome-like appearance.

With no body or chassis pieces to get in the way, Super Modified cars can accommodate just about any style of header. Even though these engines run at 6000 to 6500 rpm, most are equipped with headers like this which are relatively long.

street vehicle owners has probably built many different sizes of headers for your type of car, and may be an invaluable source of information.

Another consideration—on any vehicle equipped with a muffler, header length and diameter may not be all that critical. A muffler and exhaust system will negate much of any improvement derived from optimizing header configuration. This doesn't imply that such optimization is worthless, only that when a muffler is involved, the final performance achieved by optimizing header length and diameter will not justify the expense of designing and building a custom set of headers. A properly sized standard production header will deliver the best price/performance ratio. Any engine that will have its exhaust gasses routed through a muffler should be fitted with standard production headers.

Jetting & Timing—Any significant change made in the exhaust system brings with it a potential requirement to adjust the intake mixture and/or ignition timing. Switching from cast-iron exhaust

manifolds to tubular headers results in less residual exhaust gas being left in the combustion chambers. This can create the need for a slight change in jetting. Similarly, a change in header diameter or length may also require recalibration of the intake mixture. Many times a "trick" set of headers is written off because it doesn't improve performance, or worse, decreases it. However, the real culprit may be the racer who failed to experiment with jetting and timing.

EGO—One of the advantages of computerized engine controls is that the exhaust gas oxygen (EGO) sensor "reads" the exhaust content and supplies the control module with the data necessary to correctly recalibrate the air/fuel ratio. In some vehicles, it may be necessary to switch to a heated EGO sensor, because if it is relocated too far from the cylinder head, the exhaust will cool off too much to bring it up to operating temperature.

One way to keep the heat up for proper EGO sensor and possibly catalytic converter operation is to insulate the headers with a thermal coating or a special heat-insulating fabric tape. Most of the top Winston Cup engine builders

use one—or both—of these materials.

Headers that radiate less heat also make more power, because as exhaust gasses cool, they lose velocity. One of the advantages that cast-iron headers offer is that they retain more heat than tubular headers. Unfortunately, they have so much mass, that they become underhood heaters, which has a negative effect on power. Thermo-Tec of Berea, OH, markets header-insulating fabric in 50-foot rolls. Also note that some header guarantees are void if headers are wrapped with an insulating material.

Alternative Designs

AR Headers—While header technology has largely remained unchanged over the years, anti-reversion (AR) and stepped headers are two relatively recent developments. Developed and patented by an engineer named Jim Feuling, the AR header is designed to improve mileage and economy by reducing exhaust dilution of the incoming air/fuel mixture. This is accomplished by inserting a cone at the point where the header tube meets the flange. Since reversion pulses travel

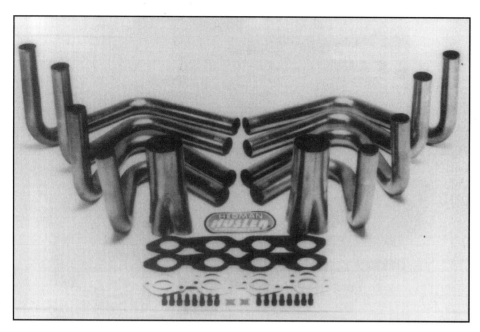

If you're real ambitious, you can build your own headers from a kit like this one from Hedman. It features 2-in diameter tubes and a 3-1/2-in collector.

A dragster is a header maker's dream because there's nothing in the way of the tubes, which allows for a great deal of design latitude. One advantage is that the distance between the flange and first bend can be made longer than with passenger car headers, and that improves flow characteristics.

along the wall of the tube, the cone, which is of slightly smaller diameter, traps them, thereby preventing entry into the combustion chamber. AR headers are produced by Cyclone and Blackjack under a licensing agreement with Feuling. Although they have performed well in a number of instances, it appears that they require different valve timing and air/fuel calibrations than conventional headers to produce

maximum power. Consequently, they never achieved the widespread popularity that was expected when they were introduced.

One of the problems may be that the anti-reversion principle works too well. By killing the reverse pressure waves that normally invade the combustion chamber, the scavenging effect of the gasses traveling through the header tube is increased to the point that it can

"vacuum" a portion of the incoming air/fuel mixture right through the combustion chamber. This problem is noticeable primarily with a dual-pattern camshaft with exhaust duration exceeding intake duration by 8 deg. or more.

By eliminating the flow of reverse pulses into the combustion chamber, AR headers keep the intake side of the engine "pure" (free of exhaust pulses). Consequently, a stronger metering signal is presented to the carburetor, necessitating smaller jets to achieve a given air/fuel ratio (compared to the same engine with conventional headers). Aside from tuning considerations, it should be noted that AR headers are designed to work with a crossover pipe connecting the collectors.

Some engine builders attempt to achieve an anti-reversion effect by installing headers with tube openings that are slightly larger than the port openings. One advantage to this approach is that conventional headers are cheaper than AR models and are also available in a wider variety of configurations. However, header flange/port mismatching does not function as effectively as AR cones.

Stepped Headers—Garden variety four-tube headers employ the same diameter tubing from the header flange to the collector. Stepped headers integrate two sizes of tubing. Depending on the design, the step may be up or down—1-3/4-in. tubes may step up to a 2-in. diameter, or 2-in. tubes may step down to 1-3/4-in. diameter. The direction of the step depends on the effect trying to be achieved. Headers that step up in diameter tend to function as extensions of the exhaust ports. As such, the velocity that exhaust gasses achieve in the port is maintained in the first part of the primary tube.

When tube size steps down, the first stage of the primary tube has a comparatively large capacity, so it will accept a large volume of exhaust gas. As

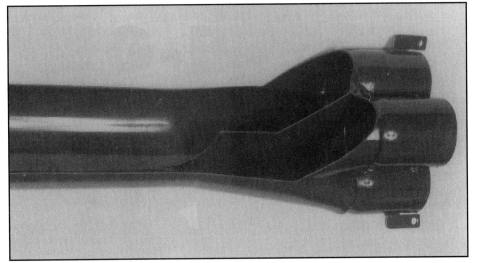

Several racers have found a performance improvement after installing a Flowmaster scavenger/collector. This four-two-one collector can be used on both race and street engines to improve mid-range torque.

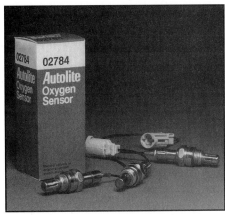

The exhaust gas oxygen sensor doesn't "light off" until it reaches normal operating temperature. When headers are installed, it may be necessary to replace the original EGO sensor with a preheated model; the further the sensor is from the cylinder head, the longer it takes to reach temperature.

the gasses move away from the cylinder head they cool, so they can be contained in a smaller diameter tube without it becoming a restriction. Stepping down in tube diameter allows the use of larger tubing at the port mouth than might otherwise be possible, if room limitations preclude the use of large diameter tubing all the way to the collector.

Most of the stepped headers in use are of the step-up variety. Compared to a conventional header, they tend to broaden the torque curve. Stepped headers are used on drag as well as oval track and road race engines.

180-Deg. Headers—Another variation on the standard header theme is the 180-deg. arrangement. Conventional headers, which bring the four tubes from the cylinders on each bank into a common collector, don't provide for even spacing between pulses. With the big block's 1-8-4-3-6-5-7-2 firing order, cylinder 1 (on the left bank) fires, then 90-deg. later cylinder 8 fires, followed by another 90 deg. before cylinder 4 fires. So the crankshaft has rotated 270 deg. before the next cylinder on the left bank fires. By comparison, there's only 90 deg. separating the firing of cylinders 4 and 8 on the right bank. Throughout the firing order, the interval between firings of

cylinders on the same bank is inconsistent and can be 90, 180 or 270 deg.

By comparison, 180-deg. headers bring primary tubes together based on firing order, not the side of the engine on which they're located. So the primary tubes from cylinders number 1, 4, 6 and 7 are brought into one collector while the tubes from cylinders 8, 3, 5 and 2 are brought into the other.

Although 180-deg. headers do offer a performance improvement in some applications, they are so cumbersome to install that they aren't widely used, except in some classes of oval track and road race cars.

Headers & the EPA

All was wonderful in the world of headers until November 1990, when the EPA added a few amendments to the Clean Air Act. These amendments make it illegal for anyone to make any changes to an engine if those changes involve disabling, removing or rendering inoperative any emissions-control device. Consequently, the only headers that can be legally installed on a 1968 or later (1966 or later in California) street-driven vehicle are those that have been certified by the EPA or exempted by the California Air Resources Board (CARB).

The EPA regulations pertain to virtually every piece of engine equipment that has anything to do with exhaust emissions. However, an exhaust system is an obvious focal point, for both regulators and inspectors.

Ultimately, the EPA regulations mean that only emissions-legal headers may be installed in vehicles registered in those areas of the country where vehicles are tested for exhaust emissions. Several companies have already been granted CARB exemptions (which the EPA accepts for the 49 other states). As time goes on, the number of legal headers will increase, but so will the price; "Smog" headers tend to be fabricated from heavier gauge tubing, and most also include fittings for connecting an air pump. This type of header is more expensive to produce, which is reflected in the cost.

CATALYTIC CONVERTERS & MUFFLERS

Whenever headers are installed, it's standard practice to add dual exhaust (if the vehicle isn't already so equipped) and low-restriction mufflers. While you can pretty well do what you wish with the mufflers and exhaust pipes, the law

Monolithic-type catalytic converters create surprisingly little back pressure. The honeycomb element is coated with metals like rhodium which react with hydrocarbons, carbon monoxide and oxides of nitrogen and convert them into compounds that aren't as harmful to the environment.

High efficiency catalytic converters like the Random Technology Super High Flow Converter reduce back pressure yet comply with EPA and CARB requirements. This model features 3-in diameter inlet and outlet tubes.

requires that a catalytic converter must remain in place if the vehicle was originally equipped with one. In fact, a catalytic converter can be replaced with an aftermarket model only if the vehicle has over 50,000 miles and the original converter is not operating properly. If a vehicle was originally equipped with a single converter, dual converters may not be installed unless an engine that was originally supplied with dual converters is installed.

In the meantime, the best way to achieve acceptable emissions levels while keeping horsepower at the highest possible level is with a high performance catalytic converter such as the Super High Flow model from Random Technology (404-978-0264). These converters feature 3-in. diameter inlet and outlet tubes and special construction to minimize unnecessary flow restriction.

Random also offers a special converter that may be bolted directly to a header collector. This converter is designed specifically for vehicles that were not originally equipped with a catalytic converter. With emissions requirements becoming more stringent, and applying to vehicles that were previously exempt from inspection, it may be necessary to

consider installing a catalytic converter. If that becomes necessary, fear not, horsepower losses are minimal. In addition, Walker/DynoMax also offers a high performance unit.

Converter Operation

For a catalytic converter to function properly, it must reach its "light-off" temperature, which is approximately 500-600 deg., quickly. Location is obviously a consideration and the closer a converter is to the exhaust ports, the quicker it will light off. Once it reaches normal operating temperatures, a catalytic converter will operate in the vicinity of 900-1200 deg. So in addition to location, heat radiance must also be considered to avoid causing under-car fires.

Type—A vehicle may be equipped with either a "two-way" or "three-way" converter. In a two-way type, unburned hydrocarbons and carbon monoxide serve as "fuel" for a combustion process that oxidizes these compounds. Hydrocarbons (HC) passing across a platinum catalyst are convinced to combine with oxygen to form water (H_2O). The platinum catalyst also convinces carbon monoxide (CO) to hook up with oxygen, in which case it becomes carbon dioxide. A palladium

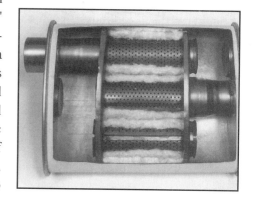

A typical "turbo" style muffler incorporates three tubes, perforated tubes and thermal packing. However, construction varies considerably as does back pressure, noise level and durability.

catalyst is also included to stabilize the compounds that have been oxidized.

A three-way converter functions in the same manner as a two-way, but also has a rhodium catalyst that affects nitrogen oxides. As opposed to an oxidizing catalyst, rhodium is a reducer—instead of

A blast from the bast–Ken Veney's 1972 Vega injected Funny Car powered by a 481 cid fuel-injected big block. Note the header which includes a long collector.

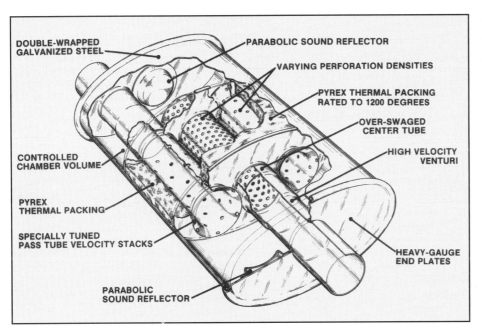

DOUBLE-WRAPPED GALVANIZED STEEL

PARABOLIC SOUND REFLECTOR

VARYING PERFORATION DENSITIES

PYREX THERMAL PACKING RATED TO 1200 DEGREES

OVER-SWAGED CENTER TUBE

HIGH VELOCITY VENTURI

CONTROLLED CHAMBER VOLUME

PYREX THERMAL PACKING

SPECIALLY TUNED PASS TUBE VELOCITY STACKS

HEAVY-GAUGE END PLATES

PARABOLIC SOUND REFLECTOR

A typical turbo-style muffler features large diameter perforated tubes and high temperature packing to control sound. Some models also incorporate sound reflectors and special chamber sizing to control sound while maintaining maximum flow capacity.

causing a compound to combine with oxygen, it causes oxygen to separate from another chemical. In this case, rhodium causes nitrogen oxides to break down into free nitrogen and oxygen.

Tampering—Keep in mind that even if you're working on a race car, it doesn't necessarily mean you can kiss off the EPA regulations. The anti-tampering rules apply to all vehicles. If you purchase a car that was factory-equipped with a catalytic converter, it is illegal to remove that converter or any other piece of emissions-control equipment. To be completely legal, it's necessary to apply to the EPA for an exemption. Of course, a race car is never subjected to an emissions inspection, so the chances of being "apprehended" are pretty slim. However, you might be in for a rough time when you sell the car if everything isn't perfectly legal with respect to the catalytic converter and other emissions-control equipment.

Another point to consider regarding catalytic converters is that in addition to neutralizing environmentally harmful components of engine exhaust, they also dampen exhaust noise levels. Consequently, mufflers that might be too noisy for a conventional exhaust system may be acceptable when used in conjunction with catalytic converters. There have even been some cases where sound muffling was left totally to the converters.

But in most instances, a pair of low-restriction "turbo" style mufflers with either 2-1/4- or 2-1/2-in. inlets and outlets, connected to appropriately sized exhaust and tailpipes, are in order. The end goal is to devise the lowest restriction exhaust system that provides adequate sound control. Flowmaster, Borla and Walker/DynoMax mufflers, with 2-1/2-in. or 3-in. inlets and outlets, are among the lowest restriction models available. ■

11

OIL SYSTEMS

Ask 10 different engine builders which brand or type of oil is best, and you'll likely get 10 different answers—and start an argument. But irrespective of brand or grade preference, everyone will agree that lubricating oil isn't much good unless it is delivered, at sufficient volume, throughout an engine. Oil has been called, among other things, an engine's life blood, so the system that delivers it must be adequate for whatever operating conditions are at hand.

Obviously, the next question is, "What's an adequate oiling system?" Again, individual opinion will vary, but there's something else to be considered; the specific engine and its intended application. The optimum system for a full-tilt drag race engine isn't necessarily the best bet for an oval track engine. And neither of these race systems may be particularly suitable for a street or marine big block.

OIL SYSTEMS

One of the big-block Chevy's most notable strong points is its oiling system. Whereas many Brand X engines require all types of special paraphernalia for any type of high performance work, you have to get into pretty severe operating conditions before a big block needs anything very special to bolster its lubrication system. In fact, some milder race engines operate very successfully with nothing more than a few modifications to the stock oiling system.

Conversely, when horsepower levels top 600 and normal operating speed exceeds 6000 rpm—or when severe g-forces lead to oil starvation—special components must be installed to ensure an adequate flow of oil. The best engine insurance you can buy is a top-notch lubrication system filled with "SH" grade synthetic oil. However, as an oiling

It may only run under power for six seconds at a time, but if an alcohol dragster engine isn't fed an ample volume of oil, it will reach the finish line in modular form. Irrespective of the application, if an engine is making horsepower, it must be well lubricated.

In a dry sump system, oil is held in a remotely mounted tank, not in the oil pan. A dry sump oil pump consists of three or four pumps bolted together to form a single unit. Each stage is simply a single pump with a specific purpose. The scavenge stages draw oil and air out of the pan, the pressure stage pushes oil through the block just as it does in a wet sump system. This is a gerotor type pump from Peterson Fluid Systems.

system becomes more exotic, it also becomes more costly, so it's necessary to strike a happy medium between cost and capabilities.

Oil systems for internal combustion engines fall within one of two categories—wet sump or dry sump. The sump is traditionally the lowest part of a lubrication system—the place to which oil will ultimately return after making a tour through the engine. If the oil reservoir is maintained in the sump—or oil pan—the system is described as a "wet" sump. On the other hand, if the reservoir is held in a remotely located tank, the system is called a "dry" sump. Each design offers particular advantages and disadvantages.

Dry Sump Systems

In a dry sump system, oil is sucked out of the pan by the scavenge stages of the oil pump; consequently the tank doesn't need to be at the lowest point of the system. Dry sump systems are more sophisticated than their wet sump brethren so naturally, they're more expensive. They also move a lot more oil which means the power required to drive

them is greater. On the plus side of the ledger, with an adequate supply of oil in the tank, even the highest g-forces (encountered during acceleration, braking and cornering) will not pull oil away from the pump pickup so momentary oil starvation is avoided—unless the drive belt breaks. Although a dry sump system is de rigeur on most types of race cars, it isn't an absolute necessity in all instances.

There's no doubt a dry sump system is the best way to go, but you also have to think about whether you really need one. If you run high rpm's for hours at a time, you need a dry sump system. But if you're running short features, and competing for a $250 purse, it doesn't make much sense to buy a $1,000 oil pump versus a $40 oil pump. You have to win an awful lot of races to pay for that oil pump. Whether or not you need a dry sump system depends on how hard you run the engine and for how long.

Operation—Dry sump systems are not without drawbacks, but obviously, they offer several notable advantages as justification for their increased cost. The primary among these is consistency of operation. Most dry sump systems

contain three stages—two scavenge stages to pull oil out of the pan and one pressure stage to keep oil flowing to vital parts (four and five stage pumps are sometimes used in road and oval track racing). Oil drawn out by the scavenge stages is returned to an external tank which is constructed to separate any air drawn in with the oil before it can reach the inlet to the pressure pump.

Multiple scavenge stages assure that little if any oil will remain inside the pan and deaeration of the oil in the tank prevents momentary losses of lubrication. But some engine builders feel that the advantages of a dry sump are too costly when weighed against the power required to drive them. On the other hand, keeping oil away from the crankshaft allows more power to be delivered to the flywheel and this offsets the power lost driving the pump.

To put things in perspective, consider what happens when you're driving a car and hit a puddle. The car momentarily slows down and the same thing happens when a crankshaft hits a puddle of oil. If you can keep a pan dry, you'll have more usable power. Certainly, it takes more power to turn a three-stage pump compared to a single stage model, but in a dry sump system, the two scavenge stages are sucking air much of the time, so it really isn't costing that much power.

Wet Sumps

In a wet sump system, the oil is returned to the oil pan after circulation via gravity. Automakers in Detroit and overseas have found that a well-designed wet sump oiling system is more than adequate for the average passenger-car engine. It's also relatively inexpensive to produce. And, although not as glamorous as a dry sump system, stock wet sump arrangements are the only choice for some classes of drag race and oval track competition—so say the rules. However, any wet sump system installed in a race engine should contain an oil pan with special baffling to prevent oil starvation during hard acceleration or cornering. For details, go to the section on Oil Pans.

OIL PUMPS

Wet or dry, a pump is needed to drive oil through the oiling system. The most commonly found oil pump is the gear type in which two spur gears mesh within a cast-iron housing. Power to drive the pump is supplied by the camshaft, through the distributor. An oil pump driveshaft transmits power from the distributor to the oil pump. Being driven by the camshaft, the oil pump turns at half engine speed. As the gears rotate, oil is drawn in through the pickup to the pump inlet and carried around the outside of each gear in the space between the teeth and housing. When the gears mesh in the center, oil is forced out from between the teeth into an outlet passage, producing oil pressure. The stock Chevy pump and all direct replacements are gear pumps.

Rotor Pump—A second type of pump is the gerotor or rotor-and-scroll type. This type of pump is available for

A stock-type big block pump is more than adequate for most high performance, street-driven engines. These pumps move a lot of oil, but they should be disassembled and inspected before installation.

big-block Chevys only as an external wet or dry sump pump. A gerotor oil pump employs a lobe-shaped inner gear meshing with a lobe shaped outer rotor to build oil pressure. The gear (which is driven, while the rotor goes along for the ride) has more lobes than the rotor so as it turns, it moves into and out of each rotor lobe. As the lobes separate, a slight vacuum is created, drawing oil in through the pump pickup. Continued rotation not only causes successive gear lobes to move back into a rotor lobe, but also turns the rotor so that the rejoining takes place on the outlet side of the pump housing. Thus, as the lobes mesh, they push oil through the outlet passage and into the engine.

High Volume Wet Pumps

Even though a number of manufacturers offer high volume oil pumps for the big-block Chevy, in most cases these are a waste of money. There's nothing wrong with a high volume pump but all too frequently, one is installed in an engine that doesn't warrant it. What results is excessive oil flow at all engine speeds, and that doesn't do much but consume excess horsepower and increase the possibility of spark scatter. Since the distributor drives the oil pump (in stock, internally mounted wet sump systems), varying resistance within the pump affects distributor shaft rotation. As the pump gears rotate, they cause a loading/unloading cycle which can cause spark timing to jump around or "scatter." Higher oil pressures and volumes are associated with a higher degree of spark scatter with distributor-driven oil pumps. Rapid distributor gear wear is another possibility of too much oil pressure.

All stock big-block Chevy oil pumps have two gears, each with 12 teeth. Standard pumps have gears measuring 1.19 in. long, high volume big-block pumps contain gears measuring 1.39-in. long. Chevrolet offers several high

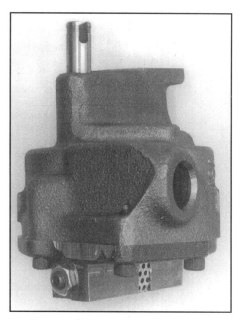

Special internal wet sump oil pumps are available from a variety of manufacturers. Unique features include pressure adjustment, oversized pickup tube hole anti-cavitation slots machined in the bottom cover.

volume oil pumps, including part number 3969870, which was originally used on the ZL-1 and LS-7 engines (for use with Corvette oil pan part no. 140913560); part number 475908, originally installed in LS-6 engines (for use with oil pan part no. 14081027); part number 10051105. The first two pumps include a pickup, while the last one does not.

If you plan to use an aftermarket oil pan, note that with part numbers 3969870 and 475908, the distance from the oil pump mounting surface to the bottom of the pickup is approximately 4.9-in.; oil pan depth must be appropriate. Also note that although many pumps originally designed for Mark IV engines may also be installed on Gen V blocks, pickups can vary significantly. Consequently, it's imperative that the pump, pickup and pan be trial-fitted before assembly. Also, some Mark IV pumps may not clear the Gen V rear main cap; it may be necessary to mill the bolt boss to achieve adequate clearance.

Building Pressure—If an engine is assembled with relatively wide bearing clearances, oil pressure may be lower than desirable. The easiest way to

144

An external wet sump pump is actually a single stage from a dry sump pump. An external line connects the inlet side to the oil pan and another line routes oil from the pump into the block.

crease pressure is to shim the pressure relief spring with washers. Unfortunately, unless you have "calibrated" washers, you won't know how much you've upped pressure. If too many washers are used, the piston will not uncover the relief port completely, which can lead to excessive pressure when the engine is started and the oil is cold. Even when a standard spring is used, some engine builders drill the bypass channel to a larger diameter to prevent excessive cold start oil pressures. Pressure can be so high that the oil filter will split or the gasket will be pushed out. Excessive distributor gear wear can also result from the high load.

External Wet Pump

Until fairly recently, wet sump systems always used an oil pump mounted in the stock location. Competition modifications typically involved nothing more than installation of a deeper-than-stock oil pan, a high pressure or high volume pump and an extended pump pickup. But where dry sump systems are unavailable, prohibited or too expensive, an externally mounted wet sump arrangement can be advantageous.

First of all, it allows the use of a full length windage tray because there's no pump hanging down in the pan. Other benefits are that ignition timing is more accurate because the distributor isn't driving the pump. Also, pressure can be adjusted very easily and the external mounting makes it much easier to prime an engine prior to initial start-up. It is often possible to run a lower oil level in the pan when an external wet sump pump is used because the pick-up is a fitting in the bottom of the oil pan.

Gerotor pumps are generally more efficient at moving oil, which means you can get the volume you need without having to use super high pressures. Aside from providing better insurance against oil starvation, gerotor pumps are reputed to require less horsepower to drive them.

Proponents of gear pumps dispute the claims made on the gerotor's behalf, but my personal experience with them has been very positive. In a series of dyno tests with a Peterson external wet sump, pressure was set at 55 psi. It never exceeded that figure, and never varied more than three psi from 1750 to 6000 rpm.

Dry Sump Pumps

As is the case with wet sump pumps, two types of multi-stage dry sump pumps are available—gear or rotor. Once again,

the superiority of each type is a matter of opinion. Weaver Brothers are the largest suppliers of dry sump oil pumps and they manufacture a gear type. On the other hand, many of the engine builders who use a gerotor type swear by them.

One of the considerations relative to pump type has nothing to do with efficiency—it has to do with digestion. Dry sump pumps have aluminum housings and when a piece of debris gets caught between the gear teeth and housing, the latter is generally destroyed. Conversely, with a rotor type pump, debris passes between the gear and rotor, both of which are steel, so the pump has a better chance of digesting it and remaining intact; damage isn't as great and it can be repaired by replacing a few components instead of the whole pump.

One of the major disadvantages to any system using an externally mounted oil pump is that the drive belt can break, or be thrown off, in which case oil pressure becomes a thing of the past. Such occurrences are rare, but they do happen,

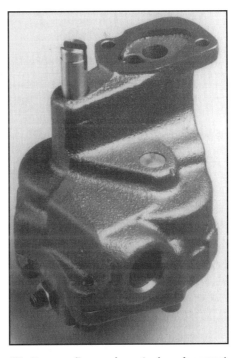

Whether an oil pump is a stock replacement or a high performance model, it should be disassembled and checked for proper gear to housing clearance. If clearance is excessive, or varies from front to back, pressure won't be consistent and can drop at precisely the wrong time.

This three-stage dry sump pump includes two scavenge stages to draw oil out of the pan, and one pressure stage to pump oil back to the engine. A four-stage pump has similar construction, but contains one more scavenge stage.

The oil pump is one thing, the pickup is another, and if there's nothing holding them together besides a standard press-fit, you may become acquainted with something else–engine failure. Always weld the pickup to the pump or use one that bolts in place.

so some type of safety measure is required to avoid running an engine with no oil pressure.

Pickups

The weakest link of a big block's oiling system is the oil pump pickup. In its stock form, the pickup tube is simply pressed into the oil pump's bottom cover. Although this arrangement may seem adequate, it isn't. Some form of positive retention is required. The most common method is to braze or tack-weld the pickup tube in place. To avoid heat generated during welding from warping critical components, it's advisable to remove the cover from the pump and to pull out the relief piston and spring before welding. It's also advisable to add a bracket from the pickup to the pump to provide extra support. The easiest type of bracket to fabricate is one that is attached by the same bolt that holds the pump to the block, or one that is held in place by one of the bottom cover bolts.

Construction—Regarding actual construction of the pickup, the most important consideration is controlling the vortex that develops as the pump draws oil out of the pan. If the pickup screen were simply a round, unbaffled affair, the incoming oil would "whirlpool" and

leave the pump sucking air. Consequently, all stock shaped pickups contain a baffle to prevent this occurrence. Many high performance baffles are square or rectangular in shape for the same reason.

When a special deep sump oil pan is installed, it's necessary to either use an extended pickup or to space the pump down from the block. If a pump spacer is used, the standard oil pump driveshaft will be too short, so a lengthened shaft must be installed. Spacer kits, such as those marketed by Moroso, include the necessary driveshaft and attaching hardware.

Whichever method is used, the end result should be the same—the pickup should be 1/4 to 3/8 in. from the pan's bottom surface. If it's too high, it may not be able to pick up sufficient oil; if it's too close to the pan, flow will be restricted.

Position—Another consideration is pickup position. For street and road race engines, the standard location is adequate. However, engines installed in drag race cars should have the pickup located toward the rear of the pan; oval track racing requires pickup placement towards the right side of the pan. In both applications, the philosophy is the same—place the pickup in the area of

greatest potential oil supply. That area is largely influenced by the g-forces generated during competition.

Clearance, Viscosity & Pressure

As applied to racing and high performance engines, either big or small block, the rule of thumb is that 10 psi of oil pressure should be maintained for each 1000 rpm. This is especially important in an engine with wide bearing clearances because there is so much internal hemorrhaging. Harold Elliot, who was Rusty Wallace's engine builder for several years (including 1989, when Wallace won the NASCAR Winston Cup championship) states:

"Our race engine bearing clearances are right at street car clearances. When some of our engine assemblers started a few years ago and saw that we fit main bearings up at .002 in. to .0025 in. and the rods at .0018 in. to .0022 in., they couldn't believe it because they didn't even fit street engines up that tight. But that's how efficient our oiling system is— we can run them that tight. The tighter the better, so long as you don't touch the bearings to the crank. People call me all the time and ask me what we fit our

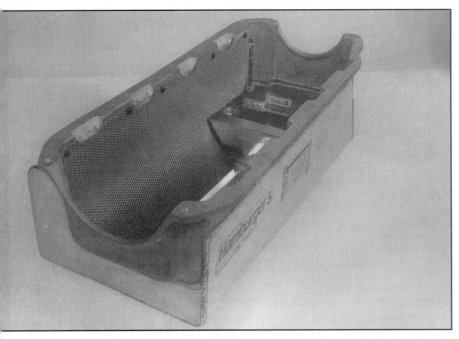

Most race-type high performance oil pans include a scraper, or wiper, and windage tray to keep oil away from the crankshaft. In this pan, both the scraper and windage tray run the whole length. The shallow depth of dry sump pans provides increased ground and chassis clearance.

bearings at and I know they think I'm *lyin', but our tightest is .0018 in. and our loosest is .0022 in. We don't throw off that much oil, so our recovery system doesn't have to work that hard. Generally, most of our stuff only passes 4-1/2 to 5 gallons per minute, so we don't have to recover that much and our scavenge stages don't have to work that hard."*

In combination with tight bearing clearances, Elliot uses polymer coated bearings and 5W-30 synthetic motor oil. And although Elliot worked primarily with small blocks, his recipe for a lubrication system is entirely applicable to a big block.

As with most automotive engine subsystems, a complete combination of parts and procedures must be developed to optimize performance. Use of lighter viscosity oil goes hand-in-hand with tighter bearing clearances. But just a few years ago, 5W-30 oils suitable for racing simply weren't available. In fact, it wasn't that long ago that straight 50 weight was considered mandatory in virtually any type of race engine. Tight bearing clearances wouldn't have been suitable

back then because oil flow would have been too restricted. On the other hand, when tight clearances are employed, there's no need for an oil pump with the capacity to fill an Olympic swimming pool in two hours.

However, all this oiling system philosophizing neglects one thing—the driver. In order for a finely tuned oiling

system to function properly, the oil must be brought to temperature before the engine is put under maximum load. And the oil and filter must be changed regularly. Some engine builders have found it necessary to set relatively wide bearing clearances because they know that the driver will do nothing more than unload the car at the track and hammer the throttle.

OIL PANS

Confusion and controversy surround this subject because a number of conflicting theories exist, yet each has merit. A configuration that provides superior performance in one application may severely compromise power in another. Therefore, one must subscribe to an open-minded approach, because as applications change, so does the ultimate oil pan design.

On a stock engine, an oil pan serves the perfunctory purpose of a holding tank. Oil is pumped out of the reservoir residing within, through the engine and returned. The shape of the pan is therefore dictated by engine skirt contour and the placement of chassis members.

With half of its oil pan cut away, this Gen V display engine provides a rat's eye view of the relationship of the pick-up to the pan and of the crankshaft to the windage tray. The tray should be located as close as possible to the crank, but the pickup must be about 3/8-in from the floor of the oil pan. If it's too close, oil flow will be restricted, if it's too far away, oil flow may be non-existent.

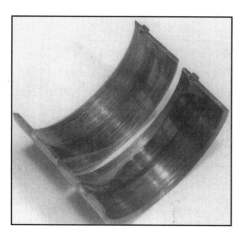

One of the first signs that the oiling system isn't adequate is excessive bearing wear. Note the scuff marks on these rod bearings. A few more laps and the bearings and crankshaft would have been severely damaged.

So long as a pan fits the engine in question, doesn't leak, doesn't contact any chassis parts and is reasonably efficient at preventing oil from scooting away from the pump pickup, it is deemed satisfactory.

Windage—High performance oil pans were initially designed to increase capacity (a four or five quart sump doesn't provide sufficient reserves to guard against oil starvation at high rpm) and provide improved containment of the oil reserve in the area of the pump pickup. But as the state-of-the-art progressed, windage became an equally important consideration as the fact was accepted that by keeping oil out of the path of a rotating crankshaft, power increases could be realized. Windage is now a point of universal concern, but even though knowledgeable racers, engine builders and oil pan manufacturers agree that it is advantageous to prevent oil from hanging around a spinning crankshaft, they don't concur upon how this is best done.

Dry Sump Pans

Obviously, if there is no oil in the pan, it can't interfere with the crankshaft. That's the philosophy behind a dry sump system. Two or three scavenge stages effectively vacuum out oil draining back to the pan (after having circulated through the engine) into an external reservoir. That would seem to imply that any type of pan is acceptable. But you know better than that—nothing is ever that simple.

As the crankshaft rotates, it moves the air around it much in the manner of a fan. The resulting envelope of swirling air carries quite a bit of force with it (the amount of which is partially determined by rpm) and it can literally draw oil up from the surface of a pan floor or windage tray and whip it into an air/oil emulsion. A dry sump pan must therefore be constructed to cause oil to flow rapidly to a collection area that is not affected by crank-generated whirlwinds. To do this with maximum effectiveness, a windage tray or baffle must be used with a complementary wiper.

Properly arranged inside the pan, the wiper/tray assembly will pull oil from the crankshaft and route it to an area below the tray. This prevents oil leaving the crankshaft from being drawn back into the whirling airstream before it can reach a scavenge port. The kick-out seen on some dry sump pans is also part of the anti-windage equation. The scraper and tray create a channel through which oil wiped from the reciprocating assembly flows. However, if the oil pan wall were not moved outward, flow into the collection area would be restricted and much of the oil scraped from the crank would remain on the tray surface and be swept up by the air whirling around the crank—precisely the condition that the pan/scraper/tray assembly was designed to minimize or eliminate.

Ideally, a full depth "kick-out" should run the entire length of a pan. However, use of a pan with full kick-out requires relocation of the starter and in some applications this is difficult or impossible. Pans with stepped kick-outs are a viable alternative as they are either compatible with a standard starter or require only a minor relocation of the starter.

Wet Sump Pans

In terms of windage treatment, the philosophies governing construction of dry sump oil pans apply to those in the wet sump category. The primary difference is that oil is much more troublesome when it's left in the pan rather than being removed to a remote storage tank. This is demonstrated by the fact that on a dyno (where no g-forces are affecting the oil) an engine will produce the same amount of power whether it's equipped with a wet-sump or dry sump

Many high performance oil pans are supplied with a mesh windage tray and scraper installed. Extended sumps increase capacity without adding depth, but will not clear crossmembers on some cars.

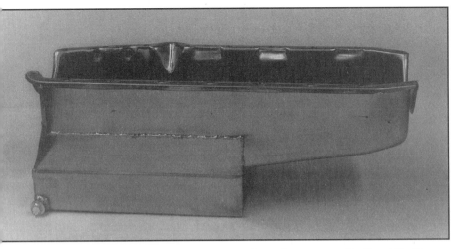

et sump pans are available in a variety of shapes, depending upon application. This Moroso n, with its winged bottom, offers increased capacity with no loss in ground clearance. It's itable for high performance street and road race engines.

stem. On a race track, a dry sump stem invariably proves to be superior.

The reason for this is quite simple. hen a vehicle accelerates, decelerates turns, the resulting g-forces imparted the oil push it up a wall of the pan. iven sufficient force, the oil will ctually find its way into a crankshaft's ath. Obviously, with several quarts of oil a wet sump pan, the problem is much ore acute than with a dry sump rrangement. However, irrespective of e sump configuration, as pan depth is creased, oil-induced power losses tend be minimized as the oil must travel rther to reach and interfere with the ciprocating assembly.

In addition to minimizing power losses lated to windage, a wet sump pan must lso ensure that oil stays in the area of the ump pickup under all operating onditions. It is for precisely this reason at the leading pan manufacturers offer il pans for specific applications. ypically, a drag race pan has no rovision to prevent side-to-side oil slosh ecause a car generates no lateral g- orces traveling in a straight line. Baffling therefore designed to prevent oil from limbing the rear pan wall (during cceleration) and from shooting forward way from the pickup (during braking). he latter consideration is especially mportant for cars competing in

categories with a break-out rule. Even though the engine may not be under power when the brakes are applied, it is still rotating at an elevated rpm. If the oil isn't effectively contained around the pickup, starvation can easily result.

Use of an oil pan designed only for drag racing on a car that is street driven may therefore be somewhat like signing a death warrant for the engine in question. Oil starvation will occur if the pan is so constructed that oil can easily migrate away from the pickup when lateral forces are applied (as in a turn). Many drag race

type pans can be used successfully on a street/strip car, but rather than risk lunching an engine, it is best to check that the pan is okay for such use before making a purchase.

Other specialized applications include oval track, road racing and marine. Pans intended for oval track use aren't suitable for anything else because their baffling is effective only when a car is turning left. Conversely, road race pans are applicable to cars that turn both left and right and most are quite suitable for street/strip use. However, they are typically more expensive than oil pans designed for high performance street or dual-purpose cars and offer comparatively little advantage in anything other than a full-on racing environment. Marine-style oil pans would be fine in a car except that they are full depth over their entire length and won't fit within most automotive frames.

Recommendations

With the myriad of styles and shapes in which oil pans are produced, deciding upon a particular model can be exasperating. However, there are several practical considerations that cut through the jungle of confusion:

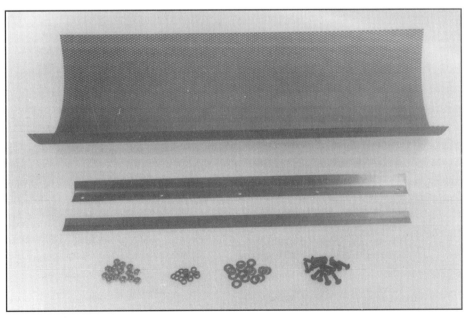

A universal windage tray and scraper kit allow you to take advantage of the latest in oil control technology, even with a stock oil pan. Both the scraper and tray must be custom fit to the crankshaft for maximum effectiveness.

The big blocks in Bill Kuhlmann's Pro Mod cars endure unbelievable stresses in a six-second, 200+ mile per hour run. The lubrication system has to perform flawlessly to prevent an engine failure. Sometimes even the best plans go awry.

Rules—In many classes, dry sump systems are not allowed. But even if the rules do allow a dry sump system, if your competitors race successfully with wet sump systems, you should be able to as well. The prize money has to be pretty good to justify the added expense.

Budget—The more exotic the oil pan, the higher its cost. There's no sense considering a $1,500 dry sump system if the budget won't allow an expenditure of more than $500.

Practicality—An oil pan must not only fit engine and chassis, it must afford a few inches of ground clearance. Some deep pans may be unacceptable because their proximity to the ground will make them a target for road debris or the pavement itself.

Operating Range—The greatest benefits from reduced windage-related power losses accrue at engine speeds in excess of 6000 rpm. If an engine is never taken beyond 6500-7000 rpm, benefits derived from a super exotic pan/tray/scraper assembly (compared to a deep pan with a simple tray) may be barely measurable.

For most applications, a dry sump system offers the best lubrication capabilities and minimal windage-related power loss. However, the expense of such

systems ($1,000-$2,000 depending upon equipment selected and prevailing pricing) puts them out of reach for many racers, which isn't all bad. In many instances, a good wet sump system is more than adequate. And, of course, there's always the debate over the additional power required to operate a multi-stage dry sump pump, more than offsetting the reduction in windage-related horsepower losses.

Winged Pans—With the idea behind a high performance wet sump pan being to keep the oil reservoir as far from the crankshaft as practical, recommendations usually lead to the deepest pan that will fit. In instances where additional depth cannot be accommodated, a "wing-bottom" pan is a viable alternative. Rather than being exceptionally deep, this type of pan flares out at the base, hence oil level is still lowered. In general, a deeper or larger capacity pan always helps whether you're running on a dyno or a race track because anything you can do to lower the oil level without reducing capacity is beneficial. While it isn't recommended, running a wet sump system one or two quarts low will usually produce a measurable power increase. However, a much safer way to accomplish the same thing is to install a

deep or wing-bottom oil pan.

Windage Tray—Even though expenses aren't always justified by the amount of performance improvement, any engine will benefit from a properly designed windage tray. The major power improvements occur at 6000 rpm and above, but there is something to be gained at lower engine speeds. For a number of years, the need for a windage tray was largely debated because some Chrysler racers used to run without a tray—but that was because they had special pans that were designed to serve as a tray. Lately, the trend is towards a semi-circular, Teflon-coated windage tray which minimizes oil puddling. Another school of thought holds that a screen-style tray is superior because oil can't puddle on it; with a screen or louvered tray, oil drains through it instead of laying on top of it.

With no definitive test results available, it is impossible to say whether a screen or solid windage tray is most effective. The primary difference in operating theory is that with a solid, semi-circular tray, the air mass rotating with and around the crankshaft is used to blow oil along the tray surface into a collection channel. Conversely, with a screen tray, oil immediately moves out of the crankshaft's path upon contacting the mesh. However, it has been argued that once the screening is saturated, the tray effectively becomes solid, allowing oil to puddle on its surface.

LS-7 Combo—For most street and street/bracket engines, an LS-7 pan and windage tray combination is right on target. Oil pan number 14091356 (five-quart capacity) includes a flat windage tray (part number 3967854), is relatively low in price and has been used quite successfully in a variety of high performance and race engines. (Four studs, part no. 3902885, are required to install the windage tray.) Originally designed for 1965-74 Corvette engines, this pan will not clear some Chevelle and

Racing filters like those offered by K&N have heavy-duty cases with a higher burst strength than a standard filter. The filtering medium is also specifically designed for high performance applications.

Camaro chassis. Alternatives are the four-quart LS-6 pan (part no. 14081027) or a custom pan such as those produced by Moroso.

For Gen V big blocks, the hot number is 10198998, a six-quart oil pan that's found on HO 454 and 502 engines. This pan is compatible with windage tray part no. 14097040, but it's not compatible with some Chevelle and Camaro chassis unless it's modified. High performance parts manufacturers like Hamburger, Milodon and Moroso also offer a variety of economically priced high performance oil pans and windage trays that are suitable for street engines. These manufacturers also offer a wide selection of race-type oil pans and matching windage trays.

While there may be considerable controversy as to the best method of reducing windage-related power losses, the fact that such losses do exist is irrefutable. And that means there just may be some free horsepower hiding in your oil pan.

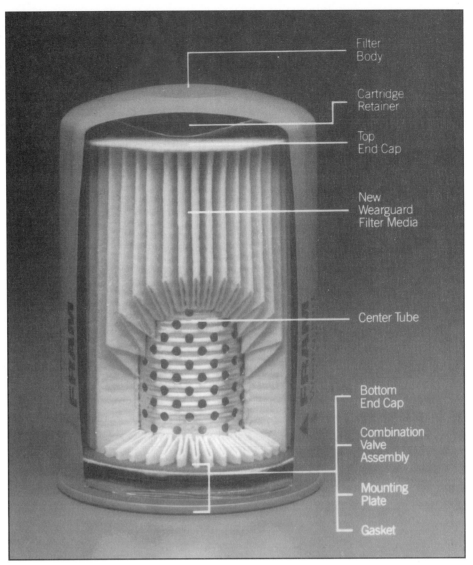

Standard filters have more internal parts than you might think. This cut-away of a Fram Wearguard filter shows that there's more there than meets the eye.

OIL FILTERS

There are oil filters and there are oil filters. For most engines, it's hard to go wrong with a brand-name filter like Fram, AC, Lee, Motorcraft or Purolator. In fact, some off-brand or private brand filters are actually produced by these manufacturers. In some cases, they're just as good, but lower in price because of reduced advertising and packaging costs. But as is the case with motor oil, individual brand preferences tend to be strong—even though documented evidence concerning performance differences is hard to find.

Racing Filters

Racing oil filters, marketed by companies like Fram, K&N and Moroso, are similar to standard filters in construction with one major exception—burst strength. Standard spin-on filters have a burst strength of 200 psi or less; racing filters are typically rated at over 400 psi. Racing filters also feature a thicker flange plate for improved gasket retention and a low restriction filtering medium with superior fuel resistance.

Screen Type—Another type of racing filter uses a mesh screen rather than a paper or fabric filtering element. Most engine builders prefer this type of filter, manufactured by System One and Oberg,

151

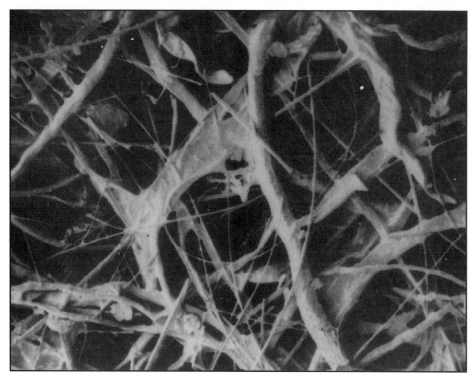

This may look like the makings of bird's nest soup, but it's actually a 220-time magnification of the media in an oil filter. As oil passes through, the fibers trap and hold contaminants. There's a piece of a big block bearing hiding in the fibers–can you find it?

because the screen is reusable and can be easily removed for inspection. Jim Oddy uses a System One filter on his Pro Modified big blocks and states:

"The first thing we do the Monday after a race is look at the oil filter. You'd be amazed at what you find in the filter. No matter how careful you are, you'll find pieces of silicone, lint and all kinds of other things. But as long as you don't find pieces of bearings, you're in good shape."

Bypass Valve

Although it may seem ludicrous that an oiling system would develop sufficient pressure to burst a standard filter, it does happen. Race engines are particularly adept at blowing up oil filters because the bypass valve is normally plugged to assure full filtration. Although the Chevy big block is supposed to be equipped with a "full flow" oil filter, much of the oil is normally bypassed. The stock filter adapter (part no. 3952301) that bolts to the block, and to which the filter attaches, contains a bypass valve that opens under

relatively low pressure. Theoretically, this valve serves to relieve excess pressure. But in real life, it's open almost all the time, and whatever oil flows through it bypasses the filter. Most race engine builders block the valve opening with an Allen plug so that all the oil must flow through the filter.

This arrangement is a double-edged sword. Although it assures maximum filtration, it also builds higher than normal pressures in the filter. However, pressure usually reaches the critical point only if an engine is run at high speed while the oil is still cold. If the crankcase is filled with a multi-viscosity oil, and common sense is used, pressure will never reach a level that will threaten oil filter integrity.

Remote Installation

In some instances, it may be desirable to install the oil filter remotely. This is commonly accomplished with an adapter that mounts in the oil filter cavity. A remote filter mount can then be plumbed to the adapter with flexible line. Some

filter mounts do not accept a standard Chevrolet filter, so you may end up having to use a (bite your tongue) Ford filter on your big block. There's no particular advantage to remote mounting except that it may make filter changing easier. However, some remote mounts have provisions for two filters, making for a quick and easy way to increase filtering capacity. Unfortunately, some dual-filter mounts accept only filters with internal bypass valves which means that much of the oil will circulate through without being filtered. If you plan to install a remote filter, look for a mount that does not have a bypass and accepts a non-bypassing type filter. AC's number 832 Chevy truck filter has been popular as a remote racing filter for many years.

OTHER CONSIDERATIONS

No, we're not done talking about the engine's lubrication system just yet. There are still several other items or factors you need to consider when designing or modifying your oiling system.

Temperature

When an engine runs under load, it generates a tremendous amount of heat. One of the most important functions of the oil is to remove this heat. But without a "radiator" the only component that can pull any amount of heat out of the oil is the pan. That's acceptable in many street cars because the engine rarely runs under full load, and when it does, it's only for brief periods. But any time a vehicle is used for towing, or operated continuously at wide open throttle, engine oil can easily exceed the maximum desirable operating temperature (270 deg.). Consequently, any type of competition engine, except for those used in drag racing, and most marine engines, can benefit from an oil cooler.

High performance Mark IV and Gen V cylinder blocks contained tapped holes designed to accept fittings to plumb an oil

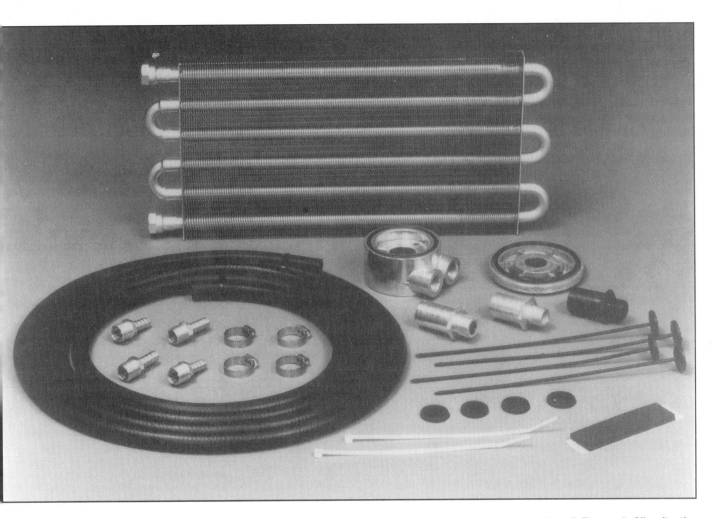

Aftermarket oil coolers are designed for easy installation and frequently include an adapter that mounts to the oil filter pad. Oil exits the adapter, flows through the oil cooler, then returns to the adapter. From there, it exits into the oil filter, which attaches to the bottom of the adapter. From the filter, it returns to the block.

cooler. It's also possible to plumb a cooler using the same type of adapter employed for connecting a remote oil filter. But if you race during cold weather, be sure that the oil isn't too cool before you hammer the throttle. Too often, a guy goes out to qualify and sits there for an hour waiting to run. As soon as the engine is fired, the oil temperature is high and the water temp is low. Just as soon as the oil passes over the block and cylinder heads— which are cold—the oil temperature comes down and the oil pressure goes up. That's the worst condition you can have. When the oil gets down to about 130 deg., you're only flowing half as much as you did at 220 deg. At 8000 rpm with an oil temperature of only 140 deg., the oil is bypassing and going back to the dry sump tank. It's not even going into the

engine. There might be oil pressure readings, but there isn't really any volume.

So the key is to make sure the oil is within the desired temperature range— not too hot and not too cool. In cold weather, it may be necessary to partially block airflow through the oil cooler to maintain adequate oil temperature. Ideally, oil temperature should not exceed 220 deg. during normal operation. If it does, an oil cooler should be installed. But don't be wooed into installing an oil cooler just because Winston Cup, Grand National, ARCA and other race cars of that ilk are so equipped. If your engine's oil temperature stays within the recommended range, an oil cooler is nothing more than excess weight. Of course, you'll never know if an oil cooler

is required unless you install an oil temperature gauge.

Oil Accumulators

On occasion, even the most carefully designed wet sump lubrication system can momentarily lose pressure. All it takes is for g-forces to pull the oil away from the pickup a few seconds and the pump winds up pumping air instead of oil. One safeguard against such an occurrence is an oil accumulator such as the Accusump which was introduced by Mecca Industries. An Accusump system is essentially a sealed tube with a floating piston inside. It is connected to the pressure side of the oil pump, so that whenever the engine is running, oil is pumped into one end of the tube, which forces the piston toward the tube's other

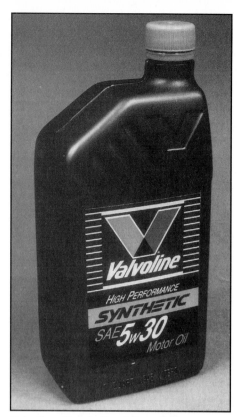

Valvoline offers both a full synthetic oil and a synthetic/mineral oil blend. The full synthetic is superior, but it is also more expensive.

to pressurize the oiling system immediately prior to start-up.

Oil

What's the best oil? That's an eternal question without an answer. Many people have very definite preferences and wouldn't be caught dead with anything other than their favorite brand of oil in their engine's crankcase. But the fact of life is that big-block Chevys have been raced successfully with just about any brand of oil you can think of in their respective crankcases.

Viscosity and applicability are of far more importance than brand identification. Motor oils have been improved dramatically in recent years, largely through the formulation of the additive package that's added to the base stock. The additive packages blended into racing oils offer superior performance under severe service operation. Specifically, they are more resistant to deterioration caused by extreme heat and pressure.

Viscosity—Then there's the matter of viscosity. For years, it was standard procedure to run SAE 40W or 50W oil in any type of race engine. But the additive packages developed in recent years have eliminated the need for "thick" oils. Even in the most demanding forms of competition, 20W-50 is about the heaviest weight oil now being used. 10W-30 mineral based and 5W-30 synthetic oils are also routinely used in all types of racing engines.

With the quality of oils now available,

Amongst professional engine builders, opinions differ as to which brand of motor oil is best. However, there's total agreement that a top quality oil--one that contains a strong additive package--should be used in any high performance engine. Synthetic oils like Red Line offer better engine protection and less friction than conventional mineral oils. Synthetics were once viewed as "snake oil," but they've proven themselves superior in all types of racing.

end. However, the chamber on the piston's back side is filled with air, so oil being pumped in compresses that air. With normal oil pressure on one side, and compressed air on the other, the piston remains stationary. However, should oil pressure drop below normal operating level, the compressed air behind the piston forces oil held in the Accusump cylinder into the engine, thereby preventing momentary oil starvation. By installing a manual valve in the line between the engine and accumulator cylinder, an Accusump can also be used

the hot tip is to run the lightest viscosity oil possible so long as adequate oil pressure can be maintained—the lighter the oil, the less power required to drive the oil pump. Old-time racers will disagree with that statement, but several Winston Cup teams race week after week with 5W-30 synthetic oil. ∎

12

EXTERNAL COMPONENTS

COOLING SYSTEM

If your big block maintains its cool under all conditions, a water pump is little more than an appendage stuck to the front of the engine. But high coolant temperatures and overheating are common problems, a water pump, like every other part of the cooling system, takes on new significance.

Overheating is rarely caused by a water pump. However, it can be a contributor in a marginal cooling system. Typically, overheating is brought on by insufficient airflow through the radiator, a collapsed radiator hose, a blocked radiator, a defective or inadequate pressure cap, a failed fan clutch or too little coolant capacity. While a killer water pump won't cure any of these problems, it can mean the difference between normal operating temperatures and overheating if cooling capacity is marginal.

Of course, if a water pump is to do its job properly, it must be spun at the correct speed. Stock pulleys are adequate in virtually all street applications, and underdrive pulleys (which slow down water pump and alternator speeds as a means of gaining horsepower) are also acceptable in most cases.

Thermostat

Depending upon ambient air temperature, either a 160- 180- or 195-deg. thermostat must also be installed. In some racing applications, it may be possible to install a 5/8 or 11/16-in.

Nothing is tougher on a race engine than a group of students learning how to drag race. So if the big block in this Drag Racing School dragster going to survive, the external components—as well as the internal parts—must be able to handle the work load.

Water pumps for big blocks are available in one of two configurations–a short pump was factory installed on 1969 and earlier engines and the long version, shown here, replaced it beginning in 1969.

NC 27262, 910/889-8789) utilize a ball/roller bearing combination that has approximately five times the load carrying capability of the standard bearings. The ball/roller assembly is used in conjunction with a special seal which is compatible with both water and anti-freeze. The seals in standard pumps will usually fail if only water is used in the cooling system; water doesn't lubricate as well as anti-freeze.

Cooling System Operation

Selecting the right water pump is one step in the quest for a trouble-free cooling system. But understanding system operation is even more important if you want your engine to keep its cool.

Howard Stewart of Stewart Components has been manufacturing racing water pumps for over eight years, and although the Stage III Stewart pump is superior to any other type, Howard was convinced that something better could be built. The biggest problem was that there was no reliable means of testing water pumps. So he designed a water pump dyno. As he explains:

diameter restrictor in place of a thermostat, but for the majority of street and race engines, use of a thermostat is highly recommended.

Water Pumps

Over the years, two styles of water pumps have been installed on big-block Chevy engines. Prior to 1969, a "short" pump was employed; engines produced in 1969 and later model years were fitted with a "long" pump. For racing and high performance engines, the short pump is generally preferred because it's more compact, slightly lighter and is available in aluminum as well as cast iron. However, if an engine is configured to accept a long water pump, an aluminum version can be installed through use of a spacer kit such as the one offered by Moroso under part number 63610.

Depending on the type and brand of water pump, either a cast-iron or stamped-steel impeller may be used. The cast-iron version is stronger and moves more water, so it is typically found in race-type water pumps. Some companies offer a steel plate that can be riveted to the vanes of a stamped-steel impeller.

Although great claims of increased cooling efficiency are made, testing has shown that this device has virtually no effect (see test results).

Bearings and seals can also differ from pump to pump. Standard pumps have two roller bearings whereas race pumps, such as those produced by Stewart Components (P.O. Box 5523, High Point,

Like everything else on a big block, the water pump is large and that means heavy. One way to trim a few pounds is with an aluminum pump such as this Stage 2 model from Stewart Components. In addition to reducing weight, this pump also increases longevity because it includes heavy duty shaft, bearings, impeller and hub. This pump also includes an adjustable cam stop.

Some race pumps are adjustable so belt tension can be maintained without an idler. This arrangement is typically used in conjunction with a short belt that runs only around the crankshaft and water pump pulleys.

"The only way you can get valid results is to test a water pump under the same conditions that it sees on an engine. The water has to be at normal operating temperature (180-200 deg.), you've got to have the same type of flow restrictions as you do in the block and heads and you also have to apply pressure to the entire system, just like a radiator cap does. These things all influence the amount of water that a pump moves, so if you don't duplicate engine conditions, you don't get valid test results."

Water Flow—Those test results proved to be very enlightening and served to dispel a number of cooling system myths that have existed for years. One long-standing myth that frequently leads people to the wrong conclusions concerns water flow. A common belief is that if water flow is too high, an engine will overheat because it isn't in the block long enough to carry heat away. This dates back to the days of the '55-'57 Chevys—when the thermostat was removed on these cars, overheating

would invariably result. The (incorrect) conclusion that most people came to was that removal of the thermostat allowed water flow to increase so much that it moved through the engine too quickly to provide adequate cooling.

In fact, what actually happens is that when the thermostat is removed from a cooling system with a vertical radiator, the point of highest pressure in the system moves to the radiator tank. Consequently, normal operating pressure exceeds the capacity of the radiator cap spring, so the cap opens and allows coolant to escape—even though the engine is not overheating. But it doesn't take long for coolant loss to reach the point where there isn't enough left in the system to provide sufficient cooling. So it appears that unrestricted flow leads to overheating, which causes coolant to escape. However, what really occurs is that normal pressure causes the cap to lift, which allows coolant to escape, which leads to overheating. As Stewart explains:

"It's easy to see why people came to the

incorrect conclusion; it took a lot of research and some sophisticated instrumentation to figure out what was really going on. And I know some people will still argue that less water flow will make an engine run cooler, but we've proven this is not correct. Every test we've run shows that with a properly designed cooling system, the higher the flow rate and the higher the system pressure, the cooler the engine runs."*

Pressure

In addition to a healthy flow of coolant, pressure is also useful in preventing a big block from overheating. Many racers install pressure caps rated at 22 psi. While that type of pressure may make radiator manufacturers cringe, it has proven very effective at keeping big-block cooling system temperatures in line.

Keith Dorton of Automotive Specialists, Inc., Concord, NC, has also determined that pressure and flow are required in ample amounts to keep an engine cool. Dorton's company builds all types of competition engines and he states:

"We invested in some high-dollar test equipment and did a limited study on water flow. We learned a lot, especially about water outlet configuration and now we record water flow in and out of every engine we run on the dyno. You need good water flow through the engine—we were turning the pump at 60% of engine speed and running into overheating problems. After we increased pump speed to 80%, the problems went away. We're also looking at running higher pressures. The old Nissan IMSA GTP cars that ran in the early 1990s had pressures averaging 40 or 50 psi, and they could run as high as 70 psi. I don't think our stuff could handle that much pressure, but I think that we could run more than the 15-18 psi we're running now and it would help."

One of the latest improvements in big-block water pumps is the DRV8 impeller from Stewart Components. Incorporated in all Stage IV pumps, it's CNC machined from 6061-T6 billet aluminum; this impeller almost doubles coolant flow while consuming less horsepower than conventional impellers.

One of the factors controlling water pump efficiency is the clearance between the impeller and housing. It should be tight—less than .100-in.

Cavitation—This brings up the subject of pulling water. Cavitation is largely blamed for all manner of cooling system inadequacies, but according to Stewart, it's simply not a factor in cooling, so long as the system is pressurized.

On the water pump dyno, you can hear when the impeller is cavitating, but you can't see it because it has so little effect on the flow curve. What happens during cavitation is that the impeller actually pulls the water apart and turns it into a vapor. That's why you can't pull water. But when you put pressure behind the water, it changes everything.

First of all, it raises the speed at which cavitation occurs and secondly, it allows the impeller to recover quickly—that's why the flow curve doesn't change that much. Some people think that when the impeller cavitates, it either stops moving water, or flow rate remains constant when you increase pump rpm. That may be true with no system pressure, but it's definitely not true when you have a pressurized cooling system. About all cavitation can do is cause the impeller tips to wear.

On the water pump dyno, the effects of system pressure are readily apparent—higher pressure translates directly to increased flow (see chart). Another factor that affects flow is the impeller clearance. One of the "secrets" of Stewart Components water pumps is that impeller clearance is precisely set in every pump. With most water pumps, production tolerances may exist, but judging by the end product, no one knows what they are. Howard Stewart tested three-vane impellers (stock impellers with every other vane removed), six-vane impellers, with curved and straight vanes, and did not record any increase in flow. The same results occurred when he pop-riveted the plate to the back of the impeller. But when he set the clearance properly on a stock pump, Stewart noticed a measurable increase in flow.

Horsepower Loss

But there's always a question about the horsepower cost incurred in the name of cooling efficiency. While there is a correlation between the volume of water pumped and the horsepower consumed doing it, the overall power loss is relatively insignificant. Besides measuring water flow, Stewart's water pump dyno also monitors power consumed driving the pump. Depending on the model, spinning a water pump at 8000 rpm (pump speed) requires between 6 and 11 horsepower. That's not much of a penalty to pay, especially when you consider that most water pumps are underdriven (by at least 30%), so power consumption would be less.

Stewart's water pump dyno is set up to measure total flow, as well as flow through the left side or right side only. This configuration allowed Stewart to confirm what only a handful of engine builders have known; in a big-block Chevy, one side of the engine frequently runs hotter than the other. In fact, the left side of a big block may have 30% less water pumped through it than the right side. The ramifications of this difference are far reaching. Not only in terms of tuning, but also in evaluating cooling system modifications. For example, when every other vane was removed from a Stewart Components Stage III pump, not only did total flow decline, but the left-to-right bias was skewed in the wrong direction. Although Stewart's Stage III pump (with a 43% left/57% right ratio) is more than adequate for the cooling demands of the majority of big blocks, a Stage IV pump has been introduced for maximum output endurance competition like Winston Cup. This pump includes a unique internal configuration, delivers equal flow to both sides of the engines and requires only 5.3 horsepower to drive at 8000 rpm pump speed.

Cooling Considerations

Due to the operating environment, street and drag race engines place considerably fewer demands on the cooling system. However, in all cases, the highest rated pressure cap available should be installed (assuming the radiator is in good condition). A pressure cap is merely a safety valve and has no function if the system is operating properly. Increased cap pressure assures optimum water flow through the engine.

This is especially true in vehicles with upright radiators, because the cap is exposed to maximum system pressure. Outlet restrictors can be used to concentrate pressure in the engine, rather than the radiator, but a cross-flow radiator is a much better arrangement as the pressure cap is on the suction side of the system.

Electric Motors—In the name of horsepower conservation, drag race engines typically do not drive the water pump off the crankshaft pulley. Instead, a small electric motor is used to spin the pump. Sharp racers have recently discovered that this system is like jumping over dollar bills to pick up pennies. The few horsepower saved by this arrangement is more than offset by the power lost due to the tuning requirements of an engine that isn't being cooled properly.

An electric motor doesn't spin the water pump fast enough to pressurize the block. Consequently water flow to the cylinder heads, particularly at the rear, is inadequate for proper cooling. In turn,

For many years, drag racers thought they were eliminating a large parasitic loss by using a small electric motor to turn the water pump. While this arrangement definitely reduces power losses compared to an engine-driven water pump, it doesn't move enough coolant to pressurize the block and properly cool the heads. This Pro Modified engine, built by Mike Hedgecock of Eagle Racing Engines, drives its water pump off the crankshaft for improved cooling and more tuning latitude.

ignition timing and air/fuel ratio must be adjusted to compensate. Even though drag race engines run for a relatively short time, they still develop enough heat to warrant a fully operational cooling system with a water pump spinning fast enough to pressurize the block. It's for precisely this reason that Mike Hedgecock of Eagle Racing Engines installs belt-driven water pumps on the record-setting big blocks he builds for Pro Modified racers like Brian Gahm and Scotty Cannon.

Reverse Flow—Then there's the question of flow direction. Reverse-flow cooling systems made a big splash a few years ago and while the theory may seem to have some validity, in practice, it seems to cause more problems than it cures. Stewart takes exception to the whole concept:

"You don't really need a reverse-flow cooling system because the block is a water manifold. You don't need to do much cooling down around the bottom of the cylinders. The holes in the head gasket are orifices or restrictions so when

the coolant in the block is pressurized (by the water pump) cooling is uniform from front to back. About the only thing wrong with a standard system is that coolant has to flow from the back of the cylinder head to the front, and that leads to higher temperatures at the front of the head. External water manifolds cure that problem. Look at it this way—an unrestricted Winston Cup engine puts out over 650 horsepower, runs at maximum rpm for three hours, and under normal conditions never overheats. How bad can conventional cooling system design be? With a big-block street car, the situation might be a little different because of engine speed. If a car is built that way fine, but otherwise, the expense of converting to a reverse-flow cooling system just doesn't seem justified."

Fans

Driving down the road at a speed of 30 mph or faster, an engine doesn't need a fan to keep it cool. But when traffic brings forward movement to a halt, even the coolest running big block will overheat. A fan hanging on the end of the

Installing underdrive pulleys on a late-model truck engine is relatively easy because a single serpentine belt is used to drive all front-mounted accessories.

water pump, or mounted to the radiator and driven electrically, is clearly necessary.

Much has been made of the power-robbing effect of engine driven fans. While that's definitely a consideration, it's hard to beat an original equipment fan mounted on a thermal fan clutch. Up to approximately 5000 rpm, this arrangement requires less than five horsepower to keep it spinning. Flex fans eat up considerably more horsepower.

The one problem with a stock-type fan and a clutch is that they are heavy. If an engine regularly sees more than 4000 rpm—even for short bursts—water pump

bearing failure will result in relatively short order.

By far, the best arrangement is to install an electric fan and completely remove the mechanically driven one. In some cases, if a large diameter fan (17 or 18 in.) can't be obtained, two smaller diameter units (12 to 14 in.) may be required. In all cases, special shielding may be required to direct airflow through the radiator. And for maximum cooling system effectiveness, the radiator should be completely sealed to the radiator support.

Radiators

Although a radiator isn't directly

connected to an engine, it does play a vital role in performance. Especially with big blocks which have overheating problems with irritating regularity.

The optimum radiator configuration required for adequate cooling still appears to be a mystery. And while it would appear that a three- or four-core radiator is the solution, that's clearly not the case in most vehicles. Consider that most big-block-powered street rods and street machines are equipped with extra thick radiators, yet most have cooling problems.

Conversely, look at the radiator in a stock car or truck. Typically, it's relatively thin, yet the engine that's behind it will idle all day long, with the air conditioning on, and not overheat. That certainly indicates that a thick radiator is not necessarily the best means of achieving adequate cooling.

As with most aspects of engine operation, a cooling system is a matter of compromises. If a system is to keep temperatures at desirable levels, a proper balance must be struck between radiator area, coolant flow velocity (through the radiator), system flow volume and air flow across the radiator surface. Many times an extra thick radiator is a cause of high coolant temperatures, rather than a cure, because it has such a large volume that flow inside becomes laminar. When that occurs, coolant doesn't transfer heat efficiently to the radiator.

Pulleys

For years, stock pulleys were deemed sufficient for race as well as street engines. Then, some enterprising individual noticed that the diameters selected by the factory for use on plain vanilla passenger cars weren't the hot tip for performance.

Underdrive pulleys have been around for years, but it wasn't until the advent of the single serpentine belt systems that they achieved widespread popularity. With a single belt system, the effects of a

Underdrive pulleys for serpentine systems are most frequently installed on the crankshaft and water pump. Alternator pulleys are also available. Both aluminum and steel pulleys are available; steel is preferable for durability.

Underdrive pulleys are available for conventional V-belt accessory drives. This polished aluminum set from March Performance not only improves acceleration, it enhances the engine's appearance.

Comparing the size of a stock crankshaft pulley (on the right) to an underdrive version makes it easy to see why the latter delivers a measurable performance improvement. In addition to slowing the speed of crank-driven accessories, the smaller diameter pulley is easier to accelerate because its mass is located closer to the crankshaft centerline.

The 468-cid big blocks that propel winged Super Modified cars, also known as "Asphalt Outlaws," burn alcohol, so their engines run relatively cool. However, since they produce over 700 horsepower, they still require a race-type water pump and properly sized drive pulleys.

pulley drive ratio change are more readily apparent, because the speed at which all accessories are driven is changed at one time. Switching to underdrive pulleys can improve quarter-mile times by up to .2 seconds. The most effective approach is to change the crankshaft, water pump and alternator pulleys. Many three-pulley kits allow the original belt to be retained.

Vibration Dampers

When the sanctioning bodies that govern organized drag racing outlawed stock vibration dampers (also called harmonic balancers) in most classes, they did so out of concern for safety. That raises concerns over the use of a stock vibration damper on a street car—especially one with a high performance engine. Do the safety considerations that apply to race engines also pertain to street powerplants? As it turns out, they do. Therefore it makes sense to consider installing a high performance damper on a street engine. However, safety is only one reason. More power and improved engine life are other potential advantages.

Stock Dampers

There's really nothing wrong with a stock vibration damper—except that it's designed for the engine in Aunt Martha's luxobarge which will never see daylight above 4000 rpm. At higher engine speeds, stock dampers have been known to fracture and ultimately explode. While such occurrences are rare on a street-driven vehicle, they do happen.

Cast-iron flywheels have the same tendency, which is why they are forbidden on high revving (race) engines. On a stock damper, the inertia ring is constructed of cast iron, hence the concern. Although acceptable for low rpm applications (where a change in materials would do little besides increase costs) cast iron has a nasty habit of fracturing when subjected to the high levels of centrifugal force generated by elevated engine speeds. Once the ring begins fracturing, pieces break off and are hurled outward. As you might imagine, when a few ounces of iron being spun at 6500 rpm break free, they hit like a blast from Dirty Harry's favorite handgun. A half-pound of iron on the outer ring of an 8-in. damper generates a force of 3182 pounds when spun at 7000 rpm. Although the probability of a stock inertia ring fracturing is remote, it's not out of the question.

Elastomer Strip—Of course, there are other considerations. Another weak point of a stock damper is the elastomer strip between the hub and inertia ring. This strip functions in the manner of a tightly wound spring. Vibrations are damped because the inertia ring, which seems to be solidly mounted to the inner hub, actually rotates forward and back on the hub in response to crankshaft vibrations. As the inertia ring works to and fro on the elastomer strip, it creates heat. All dampers function by converting vibration energy to heat.

Because it is rubber and therefore does not take kindly to heat, elastomer deteriorates when repeatedly exposed to high temperatures. Before long, the elastomer loses its grip and allows the inertia ring to slide forward or rearward, to rotate freely around the hub, or to fall

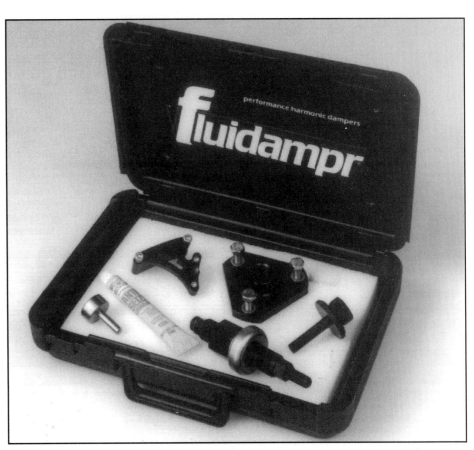

There's only one way to install a vibration damper and it does NOT include use of a hammer. Proper installation and removal tools are essential for long, trouble-free damper life. Fluidampr's Pro Installer kit includes everything needed.

off. Many times, ignition timing is found to be off because the inertia ring has moved from its original position. These types of damper failures do occur on high performance street engines with some amount of regularity; they occur more frequently on race engines. The harder an engine is run, and the higher the rpm, the more prone a stock damper is to failure.

Many of the high performance dampers that meet race organization specifications are actually nothing more than a stock-type damper with a steel rather than cast-iron inertia ring. Some brands of elastomer dampers are a bit cheaper than either friction or viscous types, and while they do eliminate the potential for inertia ring explosion, they are subject to the same heat-induced elastomer deterioration that plagues stock dampers. When the elastomer deteriorates, the damper must be scrapped. Some elastomer dampers are supposed to be rebuildable, but the jury is still out on the

feasibility of replacing the elastomer strip.

Viscous Dampers

Diesel engines have horrendous vibration problems and the viscous damper was developed specifically for this application. A number of years ago, Vibratech Performance, Buffalo, NY, the world's largest manufacturer of diesel vibration dampers, began producing Fluidampr viscous dampers for high performance street and race engines. With their superior damping capability, viscous dampers have mushroomed in popularity. In fact, they are now available through the Chevrolet and Goodwrench high performance parts programs.

The concept behind a viscous damper is actually quite simple. According to Fluidampr's Fred Roland:

"Thick silicone fluid is pressure-fed into the narrow gaps between the inertia ring

Viscous vibration dampers seem to be the preferred design with professional engine builders. This cutaway photo shows the inertia ring, which resides inside a hermetically sealed housing. The silicone fluid that surrounds it knots up in response to crankshaft vibration. Viscous high performance dampers such as this one from Fluidampr are available from a variety of sources, including GM Performance Parts.

All 396 and 427 big blocks are internally balanced from the factory, so the dampers for these engines do not have a counterweight. Most full-tilt race engines are also internally balanced, so they are equipped with a non-counterweighted vibration damper. This small diameter "Pro Stock" damper can be found on Chevy big-block-based engines built by Warren Johnson and other front runners.

On the other hand, 454 and 502 big blocks are externally balanced, so a vibration damper for these engines must have a counterweight. The term "externally balanced" simply means that some amount of counterweight is contained by the damper and/or flywheel. In an internally balanced engine, all the counterweight needed to offset the mass of the pistons and connecting rods is located on the crankshaft. Internal components of both types of engines must be individually balanced when an engine is built.

and its hermetically sealed housing. The inertia ring is not physically attached to the housing, and the silicone fluid provides a connection in much the same manner as transmission fluid is the link between the input and output sides of a torque converter. To carry the analogy a bit further, the silicone fluid's consistency determines its 'stall speed'—the point at which the fluid shears. The shearing action provides vibration damping."

During normal engine acceleration, the fluid offers enough resistance to keep the inertia ring spinning just slightly slower than crankshaft rpm. However, crankshaft vibration occurs in the range of 300 cycles per second, and when these high amplitude forces attempt to make the damper housing vibrate, the fluid "knots up" or wedges itself between the inertia ring and the housing. When this occurs, the mass of the inertia ring actively resists crankshaft vibration because of fluid action in the housing. But when vibration-induced crank movement

subsides, the inertia ring does not have to rebound to its original position. This allows the viscous damper to control vibrations at all engine speeds, which is advantageous.

Conversely, elastomer type dampers are frequency sensitive which means they offer maximum vibration damping only at a particular engine speed (where vibration frequency is within the range that the damper is tuned to control). Consequently, if the mass of the reciprocating assembly is changed (such as when aftermarket pistons or connecting rods are installed or when crankshaft stroke is changed), the damper's effectiveness will be diminished. By comparison, the intensity (amplitude) of the vibration, not its frequency, is the controlling factor with amplitude sensitive dampers. An amplitude sensitive damper will therefore offer maximum vibration damping at all engine speeds.

Do you need a high performance vibration damper? That depends upon

how your big block will be used. If you do any type of racing, or routinely run your engine at high speeds, or have added a blower or nitrous oxide, the answer is an unqualified yes. If you just drive your street engine hard on occasion, you can slide by with a stock damper—just be sure to inspect it occasionally.

While a high performance damper may seem like overkill for most street engines, sometimes it's more of a necessity than a luxury. Grimes Automotive sells a number of different types of complete reciprocating assemblies for high performance big-block engines and they've found that it doesn't really take that much of a change in connecting rod or piston weight to get to the point where the stock damper just doesn't control vibrations the way it should. This doesn't apply to an engine vibrating so bad that it jumps around, because you can't feel crankshaft vibration. But when you tear an engine down after 50,000 miles or so, you'll find pretty bad bearing wear and occasionally a cracked crankshaft. They recommend Fluidamprs with all of their balanced assemblies, especially when parts are mixed and matched, and especially on a supercharged engine because the hub won't crack like it does on a stock damper. One thing Grimes can tell you for sure is that in a race engine with a cast-iron crankshaft, you need something like a Fluidampr or the crank just won't live.

Now that high performance dampers have been on the market for several years, evidence is mounting that they do indeed provide superior vibration damping capability. And in many cases, they'll actually deliver a slight power improvement because reduced crankshaft vibration provides greater cam and ignition timing accuracy. The problem is that a damper's effect on power output isn't consistent from one engine to another. Sometimes a damper change will produce a noticeable power increase, other times it won't. However, in all cases, a high performance damper that controls crank vibration over the widest range of engine speeds always shows a reduction in bearing and crank wear. Consistency usually improves as well.

Selection

When selecting a vibration damper for a big block, keep in mind that 396, 402 and 427 engines are internally balanced while 454 and 502 engines are externally balanced. The difference between these two techniques is simply the matter of counterweight placement. With an internally balanced engine, all the counterweight is incorporated in the crankshaft; with external balancing, counterweight material is found in the crankshaft, and on the flywheel and vibration damper.

Chevrolet offers a variety of production-style dampers for big blocks. Part number 3879623 is intended for internally balanced 396, 402 and 427 engines; part number 14097024 is designed for externally balanced 4.00-in.

stroke Mark IV 454 crankshafts; part number 14097023 fits Gen V 454 and 502 engines (externally balanced) with steel crankshafts; part number 10101160 fits Gen V 454s with iron crankshafts.

Although it would seem that a single damper should be all that's required for an externally balanced 454 crankshaft, this is not the case. Each engine combination has a different reciprocating weight and since elastomer-type dampers must be tuned to that reciprocating weight, a variety of dampers is required.

One of the advantages of a Fluidampr is the fact that it is amplitude sensitive, not frequency sensitive. As such, it is effective over an engine's entire operating range and does not need to be tuned to a specific reciprocating assembly weight. The same Fluidampr (part no. 712105) is equally effective whether installed on a Mark IV or Gen V 454 or a 502.

Fuel Pumps

Much ado is made about fuel pumps on race engines, and for good reason. Fuel starvation is one of the most frequent causes of poor performance. Starvation means the carburetor doesn't receive, under some circumstances, enough fuel to keep the fuel bowls full. It doesn't mean the carb runs dry. Fuel starvation is rarely a problem with fuel-injected engines, because the high pressure fuel pumps that are required usually have sufficient capacity to handle an engine's needs.

Capacity—In drag racing, the rule of thumb is that an electric fuel pump should be able to output one gallon of gasoline (measured at the carburetor inlet) in 20 seconds or less. Mechanical fuel pumps are not usually adequate for serious drag engines—even though they can pump enough fuel to supply the demands of a 700-horsepower NASCAR Winston Cup engine.

The g-forces working against the fuel pump constitute a major difference

between drag racing and oval track fuel systems. With a mechanical pump located on the engine, it must pull fuel from the rear of the car; g-forces push fuel away from the pump inlet. On the other hand, an electric fuel pump is mounted at the rear of the car adjacent to the fuel tank. It therefore pushes fuel under pressure all the way to the carburetor.

High Capacity Pumps

High capacity fuel pumps are available from a variety of sources. For carbureted engines, a Holley or Carter high-volume mechanical fuel pump is usually more than adequate for street and oval track race engines. These pumps are frequently offered as Super Speedway models by carburetor specialists. Internally, they're the same as a standard high-volume pump, but they have oversized fittings heli-arc welded into place. Six-valve pumps rated at 130 gallons per hour (gph), and either 7 or 15 psi, are also available.

A variation on the mechanical pump is the belt-driven type that is frequently used with super high horsepower gasoline

For oval track racing and take-no-prisoners street driving, a high performance mechanical fuel pump is the weapon of choice. Several versions of this type of pump are available; this is a six-valve model.

A wheels-up launch is accompanied by a heavy g-force load. That presents unique problems for the fuel delivery system. Typically, an electric fuel pump, mounted at the rear, is required to ensure adequate fuel delivery.

and most alcohol-fired small blocks. Driven by a belt off the crankshaft, these pumps can deliver over 350 gallons per hour. They are usually plumbed to a bypass and fuel pressure varies with engine speed.

High capacity electric pumps vary widely in capacity; some street models are rated at 97 gph while maximum output race versions carry a 400+ gph rating. While some of the larger models constitute overkill for most big blocks, their capacity does offer some amount of insurance against fuel starvation.

Although race-type electric fuel pumps put out all kinds of volume, they don't have enough pressure for most types of fuel injection. Consequently, special pumps capable of producing over 50 psi are used with all TPI engines. Throttle body injection systems use lower pressures, but are still above the pressure ratings of electric pumps designed for carbureted engines.

Fuel Lines—Irrespective of the type of pump selected, it must be connected to adequately sized fuel lines. On a high performance street car, 3/8 in. or -6 line is generally adequate. Race cars call for 3/8 or 1/2 in. hard lines or -8 or -10 braided hose, depending on the application. In routing fuel lines, the important point to remember is that they should be kept away from all exhaust system components and any bends in rubber hoses should have a large radius. Many fuel starvation problems are caused by nothing more than a sharply bent rubber fuel line sucking closed.

Regulating Pressure—Although adequate volume is the key to avoiding fuel starvation, pressure is typically used to monitor fuel flow. That's because pressure is far easier to measure, and, if a given amount of pressure is maintained within a fuel line of a specific diameter, adequate flow is usually assured. Any fuel system that can maintain at least 4 psi of fuel pressure through 3/8-in. lines—at maximum engine speed and maximum load—is probably capable of keeping up with the demands of most big blocks. This assumes that there are no restrictions in the line. If a car is plumbed with adequately sized lines, but an undersized fitting is used at the carburetor, or in a fuel block, or a low capacity fuel filter is included, fuel starvation is a very real possibility. Also keep in mind that most pressure regulators are restrictive—which is the reason that some race cars are equipped with two or more pressure regulators.

That doesn't mean that a system should be run without a regulator. If it is, excessive fuel pressure at idle may literally blow the carburetor inlet needles off their seats and fuel may come pouring out the booster nozzles. Similarly, the fact that a fuel filter is a potential restriction doesn't mean it should be left out. Low restriction fuel filters are available from a variety of sources and should be included on any vehicle. ■

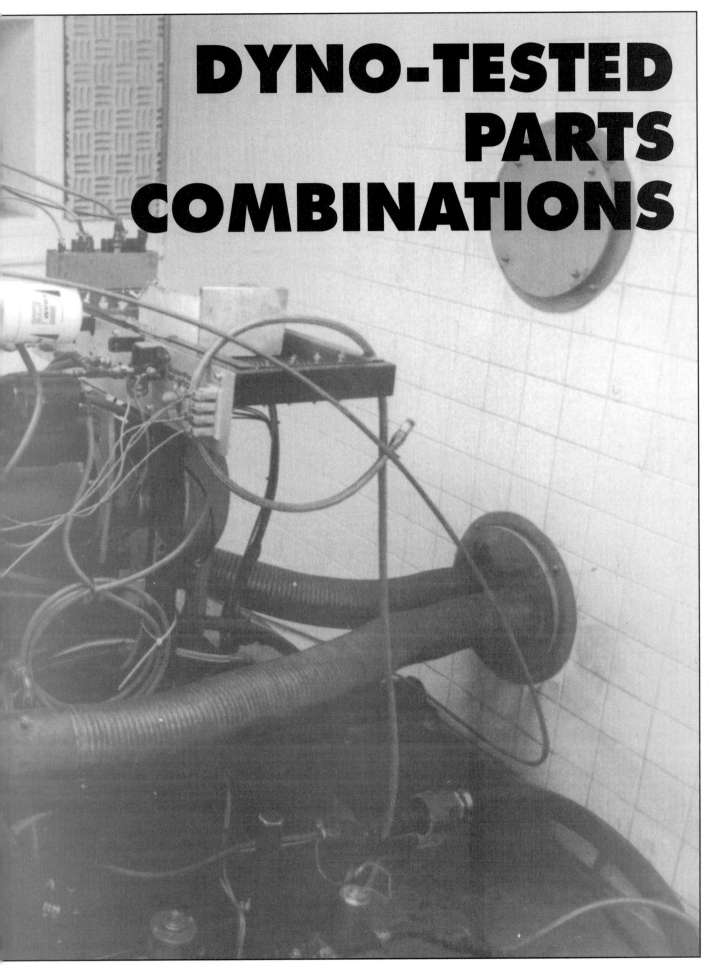

DYNO-TESTED PARTS COMBINATIONS

TEST A

ENGINE: 408 cid 396, bored to 4.15", stroke 3.75", 10:1 compression ratio, stock intake manifold, Holley 0-3310 carburetor (750 cfm), Comp Cams 325-hp Muscle Car Cam (280 AH12)

RPM	CBT	CBHp
3000	399	228
3500	414	276
4000	428	326
4500	433*	371
5000	414	394
5500	381	399*
6000	333	380

NOTES: Essentially a bored and blueprinted version of a stock 325-hp 396 engine, this test demonstrates the potential of a Sixties-era Muscle Car powerplant. The stock engine is handcuffed by a 565-cfm carburetor and an exceptionally mild camshaft. A larger carb and more aggressive camshaft raised horsepower to an impressive level. Torque readings are also exceptionally strong.

TEST B

ENGINE: 468 cid, 454 bored to 4.309", stroke: 4.00", 10:1 compression ratio, pocket ported oval port heads with 117cc chambers, Weiand 8013 intake manifold, 830-cfm Holley carb, MSD 6T ignition, Competition Cams 292 hydraulic camshaft (244/244 duration at .050" lift, .556" lift, 110-degree lobe separation)

RPM	CBT	CBHp
2500	424	202
3000	499	285
3500	506	337
4000	505	385
4500	511*	437
5000	507	482
5500	481	504*
6000	421	480

NOTES: It didn't take much besides a high performance camshaft, some cylinder head work and solid short block assembly procedures to coax over 500 horsepower from 468 cubic inches. This engine offers good drivability with over 400 lbs./ft. of torque at 2500 rpm, making it ideal for a boat, bracket car or street-driven vehicle. With only 10:1 compression ratio and a cam that has 244 degrees of duration at .050" lift, this engine has a low enough cylinder pressure to run happily on premium pump gas.

TEST C

ENGINE: 468 cid., 454 bored to 4.309", stroke 4.00", 10:1 com-pression ratio, pocket ported oval port heads with 117cc chambers, Weiand 8013 intake manifold, 830-cfm Holley carb, MSD 6T ignition, Competition Cams 306 mechanical camshaft (260/260 duration at .050" lift, .636" lift, 110-degree lobe separation)

RPM	CBT	CBHp
3500	490	327
4000	483	368
4500	497	426
5000	505*	481
5500	495	518
6000	456	521*
6500	410	507

NOTES: The same engine used in the previous test, but with a longer duration mechanical lifter cam and Edelbrock Torker II intake manifold. Notice how the cam/manifold change raised the horsepower peak to 6000 rpm, but reduced torque 16 lbs./ft. at 3500 rpm. The engine also wasn't happy running a wide open throttle much below 3500 rpm, proving once again that there are no free lunches. Typically, when cam duration is increased to raise horsepower, mid-range torque falls off. That's precisely what happened here.

TEST D

ENGINE: 468 cid, 454 bored to 4.309", stroke 4.00", 10:1 compres-sion ratio, pocket ported oval port heads with 117cc chambers, Dart single plane intake manifold, 830-cfm Holley carb, MSD 6T ignition, Competition Cams 288 Roller camshaft (244/244 duration at .050" lift, .631" lift, 110-degree lobe separation)

RPM	CBT	CBHp
3000	529	302
3500	535	357
4000	537	409
4500	558*	478
5000	555	528
5500	539	565
6000	503	574*
6500	445	550

NOTES: Camshafts designed for roller lifters open valves faster and keep them at maximum lift longer than their flat tappet-oriented counterparts. This test demonstrates that effect on horsepower. Aside from a camshaft and intake manifold change, engine specifications are the same as those in the previous test. But in this configuration, the engine produced 53 more horsepower and 53 more lbs./ft. of torque. Also note that with the roller cam's shorter duration (compared to the 306 mechanical grind) the engine would run happily at wide open throttle, under full load, at 3000 rpm.

TEST E

ENGINE: 468 cid, 454 bored to 4.310", stroke 4.00", 12:1 compres-sion ratio, fully ported rectangular port heads with 117cc chambers, Dart single-plane intake manifold, 1050-cfm Holley carb, MSD 7AL ignition, Competition Cams 312/319 roller cam

RPM	CBT	CBHp
3500	517	345
4000	507	386
4500	501	429
5000	537	512
5500	546*	572
6000	528	603
6500	495	613*
7000	457	609

NOTES: Throw serious parts at a 468 big block and it makes serious power. This engine is designed for Super Gas, Super Comp type drag racing, but would also be appropriate for use in a hot rod boat. Although the camshaft is fairly radical, note that the power peak is at 6500 rpm, which makes for excellent durability. With 517 lbs./ft. of torque at 3500 rpm, mid-range torque is excellent. However, owing to the combination of cam duration, cylinder head port volume and intake manifold configuration, this engine would prove balky if installed in a street-driven vehicle. But it would definitely pin you in the seat when you put the throttle down.

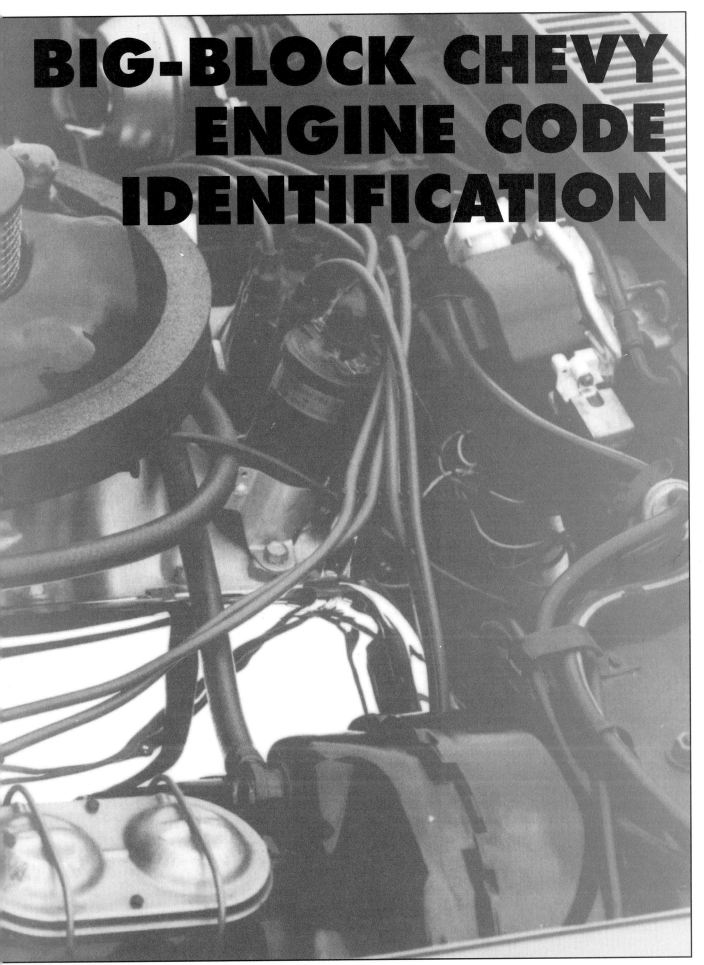

BIG-BLOCK CHEVY ENGINE CODE IDENTIFICATION

YEAR	ID CODE	MODEL	CID	HP	TRANS	NOTES
1965	IA	Chevrolet	396	325	mt	
1965	IC	Chevrolet	396	325	mt	ti
1965	IE	Chevrolet	396	425	mt	SHP
1965	IG	Chevrolet	396	325	PG	
1965	II	Chevrolet	396	325	PG	ti
1965	IV	Chevrolet	396	325	TH	
1965	IW	Chevrolet	396	325	TH	
1965	LB	Chevrolet	396	325	PG	
1965	LC	Chevrolet	396	325	TH	
1965	LF	Chevrolet	396	325	mt	
1965	IF	Corvette	396	425	mt	
1966	IA	Chevrolet	396	325	mt	
1966	IB	Chevrolet	396	325	mt	
1966	IC	Chevrolet	396	325	PG	AR
1966	ID	Chevrolet	427	425	mt	SHP
1966	IG	Chevrolet	396	325	PG	
1966	IH	Chevrolet	427	390	mt	
1966	II	Chevrolet	427	390	mt	AR
1966	IJ	Chevrolet	427	390	TH	
1966	IN	Chevrolet	396	325	TH	
1966	IO	Chevrolet	396	325	TH	
1966	IV	Chevrolet	396	325	TH	
1966	ED	Chevelle	396	325	mt	
1966	EF	Chevelle	396	360	mt	HP
1966	EG	Chevelle	396	375	mt	SHP
1966	EH	Chevelle	396	325	mt	
1966	EJ	Chevelle	396	360	mt	HP
1966	EK	Chevelle	396	325	PG	
1966	EL	Chevelle	396	360	PG	HP
1966	EM	Chevelle	396	325	PG	
1966	EN	Chevelle	396	360	PG	HP
1966	IK	Corvette	427	425	mt	SHP
1966	IL	Corvette	427	390	mt	
1966	IM	Corvette	427	390	mt	
1966	IP	Corvette	427	425	mt	SHP
1966	IQ	Corvette	427	390	PG	
1966	IR	Corvette	427	390	PG	AR
1967	EI	Camaro	396	350		HP

ABBREVIATIONS

AR—Air Injection Reactor system (smog pump)
CA—California emissions
HD—Heavy Duty
hdc—heavy duty clutch
HP—High Performance

PG—Powerglide
mt—manual trans, mt-3—3 speed
SHP—Special High Performance
TH—Turbo Hydramatic
ti—Transistor ignition

YEAR	ID CODE	MODEL	CID	HP	TRANS	NOTES
1967	EQ	Camaro	396	350	at	TH
1967	EY	Camaro	396	350		HP AR
1967	MQ	Camaro	396	375	mt	
1967	MR	Camaro	396	375	mt	
1967	MW	Camaro	396		mt	
1967	MX	Camaro	396			AR
1967	MY	Camaro	396	325	TH	
1967	MZ	Camaro	396	325	TH	
1967	IA	Chevrolet	396	325	mt	
1967	IB	Chevrolet	396	325	mt	AR
1967	IC	Chevrolet	396	325	PG	
1967	ID	Chevrolet	427	425	mt	SHP
1967	IE	Chevrolet	427	385	mt	Impala SS
1967	IF	Chevrolet	427	385	TH	AR Impala SS
1967	IG	Chevrolet	396	325	PG	AR
1967	IH	Chevrolet	427	385	mt	AR
1967	II	Chevrolet	427	385	mt	AR
1967	IJ	Chevrolet	427	385	TH	AR
1967	IK	Chevrolet	427	425	mt	AR SHP
1967	IN	Chevrolet	396	325	TH	AR
1967	IO	Chevrolet	427	385	TH	AR
1967	IS	Chevrolet	427	385	TH	AR Impala SS
1967	IV	Chevrolet	396	325	TH	AR
1967	IX	Chevrolet	427	385	mt	AR Impala SS
1967	ED	Chevelle	396	325	mt	
1967	EF	Chevelle	396	350	mt	HP
1967	EG	Chevelle	396	375	mt	SHP
1967	EH	Chevelle	396	325	mt	
1967	EJ	Chevelle	396	350	mt	HP
1967	EK	Chevelle	396	325	PG	
1967	EL	Chevelle	396	350	PG	HP
1967	EM	Chevelle	396	325	PG	
1967	EN	Chevelle	396	350	PG	HP
1967	ET	Chevelle	396	325	TH	
1967	EU	Chevelle	396	350	TH	HP
1967	EV	Chevelle	396	350	TH	HP
1967	EW	Chevelle	396	350	TH	HP
1967	EX	Chevelle	396	375	mt	SHP

ABBREVIATIONS

AR—Air Injection Reactor system (smog pump)
CA—California emissions
HD—Heavy Duty
hdc—heavy duty clutch

PG—Powerglide
mt—manual trans, mt-3—3 speed
SHP—Special High Performance
TH—Turbo Hydramatic

YEAR	ID CODE	MODEL	CID	HP	TRANS	NOTES
1967	IL	Corvette	427	390	mt	
1967	IM	Corvette	427	390	mt	
1967	IQ	Corvette	427	390	PG	
1967	IR	Corvette	427	390	PG	
1967	IT	Corvette	427	435	mt	SHP
1967	IU	Corvette	427	435	mt	SHP
1967	JA	Corvette	427	435	mt	SHP
1967	JC	Corvette	427	400	mt	
1967	JD	Corvette	427	400	PG	
1967	JE	Corvette	427	435	mt	SHP
1967	JF	Corvette	427	400	mt	
1967	JG	Corvette	427	400	PG	
1967	JH	Corvette	427	435	mt	SHP
1968	MQ	Chevy II	396	375	mt	HP
1968	MR	Chevy II	396	350	TH	HP
1968	MX	Chevy II	396	350	mt	HP
1968	MQ	Camaro	396	375	mt	
1968	MR	Camaro	396	350	TH	
1968	MT	Camaro	396	375	mt	
1968	MW	Camaro	396	325	mt & at	
1968	MX	Camaro	396	350	mt	
1968	MY	Camaro	396	325	TH	
1968	IA	Chevrolet	395	325	mt	
1968	IA	Chevrolet	427	425	mt	SPH
1968	IB	Chevrolet	427	385	TH	Police
1968	ID	Chevrolet	427	425	mt	SHP
1968	IE	Chevrolet	427	385	mt	
1968	IF	Chevrolet	396	325	TH	Police
1968	IG	Chevrolet	396	325	PG	
1968	IV	Chevrolet	396	325	TH	
1968	IH	Chevrolet	427	385	mt	
1968	IK	Chevrolet	396	325	mt-3	Police
1968	IJ	Chevrolet	427	385	TH	
1968	IN	Chevrolet	396	325	PG	Police
1968	IO	Chevrolet	427	425	mt	SHP
1968	IS	Chevrolet	427	385	TH	
1968	ED	Chevelle	396	325	mt	
1968	EF	Chevelle	396	350	mt	HP

ABBREVIATIONS

AR—Air Injection Reactor system (smog pump)
CA—California emissions
HD—Heavy Duty
hdc—heavy duty clutch

PG—Powerglide
mt—manual trans, mt-3—3 speed
SHP—Special High Performance
TH—Turbo Hydramatic

YEAR	ID CODE	MODEL	CID	HP	TRANS	NOTES
068	EG	Chevelle	396	375	mt	SHP
068	EK	Chevelle	396	325	PG	
068	EL	Chevelle	396	350	PG	HP
068	ET	Chevelle	396	325	TH	
068	EU	Chevelle	396	350	TH	HP
068	4W	Chevelle	396	350	at	
068	4U	Chevelle	396	350	mt	
068	4T	Chevelle	396	325	mt	
068	IL	Corvette	427	390	mt	
068	IM	Corvette	427	400	mt	HP
068	IO	Corvette	427	400	TH	HP
068	IQ	Corvette	427	390	TH	
068	IR	Corvette	427	435	mt	SHP
068	IT	Corvette	427	435	mt	SHP
068	IU	Corvette	427	435	mt	SHP
969	JF	Chevy II	396	350	mt	HP
969	JH	Chevy II	396	375	mt	SHP
969	JI	Chevy II	396	350	TH	HP
969	JL	Chevy II	396	375	TH	SHP
969	KA	Chevy II	396	350	mt	HP
969	KC	Chevy II	396	375	mt	SHP
969	JM	Chevy II	396		TH	
969	JU	Chevy II	396		PG	
969	KE	Chevy II	396		mt	
969	JB	Camaro	396	325	PG	
969	JF	Camaro	396	350	mt	HP
969	JG	Camaro	396	325	TH	
969	JH	Camaro	396	375	mt	SHP
969	JI	Camaro	396	350	TH	HP
969	JJ	Camaro	396	AH	mt	
969	JL	Camaro	396	375	TH	SHP
969	JM	Camaro	396		TH	alum hd
969	JU	Camaro	396	325	mt	
969	KA	Camaro	396	350	mt	HP
969	KC	Camaro	396	375	mt	SHP
969	KE	Camaro	396		mt	alum hd
969	CJB	Camaro	402		mt	alum hd
969	CJF	Camaro	402	350	mt	HP

ABBREVIATIONS

AR—Air Injection Reactor system (smog pump)
CA—California emissions
HD—Heavy Duty
hdc—heavy duty clutch

PG—Powerglide
mt—manual trans, mt-3—3 speed
SHP—Special High Performance
TH—Turbo Hydramatic

YEAR	ID CODE	MODEL	CID	HP	TRANS	NOTES
1969	CJG	Camaro	402	325	TH	
1969	CJH	Camaro	402	375	mt	SHP
1969	CJI	Camaro	402	350	TH	HP
1969	CJL	Camaro	402	375	TH	SHP
1969	CJU	Camaro	402	325	mt	
1969	JN	Chevrolet	396	265	mt	
1969	JO	Chevrolet	396	265	TH	Police
1969	JP	Chevrolet	396	265		Police
1969	JQ	Chevrolet	396	265	TH	
1969	JR	Chevrolet	396	265	mt	Police, hdc
1969	JT	Chevrolet	396	265	mt	hdc
1969	LA	Chevrolet	427	390	mt	HP
1969	LB	Chevrolet	427	335	mt	
1969	LC	Chevrolet	427	390	TH	HP
1969	LD	Chevrolet	427	425	mt	SHP
1969	LE	Chevrolet	427	335	TH	
1969	LF	Chevrolet	427	390	TH	HP Police
1969	LG	Chevrolet	427	390	mt	HP Police
1969	LH	Chevrolet	427	390	mt	HP
1969	LI	Chevrolet	427	335	TH	
1969	LJ	Chevrolet	427	335	TH	Police
1969	LK	Chevrolet	427	335	mt	Police
1969	LS	Chevrolet	427	425	TH	SHP
1969	LY	Chevrolet	427	335	mt	Police
1969	LZ(	Chevrolet	427	390	mt	HP Police
1969	MA	Chevrolet	427	335	mt	
1969	MB	Chevrolet	427	390	mt	HP Police
1969	MC	Chevrolet	427	390	mt	HP
1969	MD	Chevrolet	427	425	mt	SHP
1969	JA	Chevelle	396	325	mt	
1969	JC	Chevelle	396	350	mt	HP
1969	JD	Chevelle	396	375	mt	SHP
1969	JE	Chevelle	396	350	TH	HP
1969	JK	Chevelle	396	325	TH	
1969	JV	Chevelle	396	325	mt	
1969	KB	Chevelle	396	350	mt	HP
1969	KD	Chevelle	396	375	mt	SHP
1969	KF	Chevelle	396	375	TH	SHP

ABBREVIATIONS

AR—Air Injection Reactor system (smog pump)
CA—California emissions
HD—Heavy Duty
hdc—heavy duty clutch

PG—Powerglide
mt—manual trans, mt-3—3 speed
SHP—Special High Performance
TH—Turbo Hydramatic

YEAR	ID CODE	MODEL	CID	HP	TRANS	NOTES
1969	KG	Chevelle	396		mt	alum hd
1969	KH	Chevelle	396		TH	alum hd
1969	KI	Chevelle	396		mt	alum hd
1969	CJA	Chevelle	402	325	mt	
1969	CJC	Chevelle	402	350	mt	HP
1969	CJD	Chevelle	402	375	mt	SHP
1969	CJE	Chevelle	402	350	TH	HP
1969	CJF	Chevelle	402	375	TH	SHP
1969	CJK	Chevelle	402	325	TH	
1969	CJV	Chevelle	402	325	mt	
1969	LL	Corvette	427	390	TH	HP
1969	LM	Corvette	427	390	mt	HP
1969	LN	Corvette	427	400	TH	HP
1969	LO	Corvette	427	430	mt	HD
1969	LP	Corvette	427	435	mt	alum hd
1969	LQ	Corvette	427	400	mt	HP
1969	LR	Corvette	427	435	mt	SHP
1969	LT	Corvette	427	435	mt	SHP
1969	LU	Corvette	427	435	mt	alum hd
1969	LV	Corvette	427	430	TH	HD
1969	LW	Corvette	427	435	TH	alum hd
1969	LX	Corvette	427	435	TH	SHD
1969	ME	Corvette	427	430	mt	
1969	MG	Corvette	427	430	at	
1969	MH	Corvette	427	390	mt	
1969	MI	Corvette	427	390	at	
1969	MJ	Corvette	427	400	at	
1969	MK	Corvette	427	400	mt	
1969	MR	Corvette	427	430	mt	
1969	MS	Corvette	427			Questionable
1970	CKO	Chevy II	396	375	mt	SHP
1970	CKP	Chevy II	396	375	TH	SHP
1970	CKQ	Chevy II	396	375	mt	SHP
1970	CKT	Chevy II	396	375	mt	SHP
1970	CKU	Chevy II	396	375	mt	SHP
1970	CTW	Chevy II	396	350	TH	HP
1970	CTX	Chevy II	396	350	mt	HP
1970	CTW	Chevy II	396	375	TH	SHP

ABBREVIATIONS

AR—Air Injection Reactor system (smog pump)
CA—California emissions
HD—Heavy Duty
hdc—heavy duty clutch

PG—Powerglide
mt—manual trans, mt-3—3 speed
SHP—Special High Performance
TH—Turbo Hydramatic

YEAR	ID CODE	MODEL	CID	HP	TRANS	NOTES
1970	CTZ	Chevy II	396	350	mt	HP
1970	CJF	Camaro	396	350	mt	
1970	CJH	Camaro	396	375	mt	
1970	CJI	Camaro	396	350	TH	
1970	CJL	Camaro	396	375	TH	
1970	CKO	Camaro	396	375	mt	SHP
1970	CTW	Camaro	396	350	TH	HP
1970	CTX	Camaro	396	350	mt	HP
1970	CTY	Camaro	396	375	TH	SHP
1970	CGS	Chevrolet	454	345	mt	Police
1970	CGT	Chevrolet	454	390	mt	HP Police
1970	CGU	Chevrolet	454	390	mt	HP
1970	CGV	Chevrolet	454	345	mt	
1970	CKO	Chevelle	396	375	mt	SHP
1970	CKP	Chevelle	396	375	TH	SHP, alum hd
1970	CKQ	Chevelle	396	375	mt	SHP
1970	CKT	Chevelle	396	375	mt	SHP
1970	CKU	Chevelle	396	375	mt	SHP
1970	CRN	Chevelle	454	360	mt	HP
1970	CRQ	Chevelle	454	360	TH	HP
1970	CRR	Chevelle	454	450	TH	SHP
1970	CRS	Chevelle	454	450	TH	SHP, alum hd
1970	CRT	Chevelle	454	360	mt	HP
1970	CTW	Chevelle	396	350	TH	HP
1970	CTX	Chevelle	396	350	mt	HP
1970	CTY	Chevelle	396	375	TH	SHP
1970	CTZ	Chevelle	396	350	mt	HP
1970	CRV	Chevelle	454	450	mt	HP
1970	CGW	Corvette	454	390	TH	HP
1970	CRI	Corvette	454	390	mt	HP, ti
1970	CRJ	Corvette	454	390	TH	ti
1970	CZL	Corvette	454	465	mt	HD
1970	CZN	Corvette	454	465	TH	HD
1970	CZU	Corvette	454	390	mt	HP
1971	CLA	Monte Carlo	396	300	mt	
1971	CLA	Monte Carlo	402	300	mt	
1971	CLB	Monte Carlo	396	300	TH	
1971	CLB	Monte Carlo	402	300	TH	

ABBREVIATIONS

AR—Air Injection Reactor system (smog pump)
CA—California emissions
HD—Heavy Duty
hdc—heavy duty clutch

PG—Powerglide
mt—manual trans, mt-3—3 speed
SHP—Special High Performance
TH—Turbo Hydramatic

YEAR	ID CODE	MODEL	CID	HP	TRANS	NOTES
1971	CLL	Monte Carlo	396	300	mt	
1971	CLL	Monte Carlo	402	300	mt	
1971	CLP	Monte Carlo	396	300	TH	
1971	CLP	Monte Carlo	402	300	TH	
1971	CLS	Monte Carlo	396	300	mt	
1971	CLS	Monte Carlo	402	300	mt	
1971	CPA	Monte Carlo	454	365	mt	
1971	CPD	Monte Carlo	454	365	mt	
1971	CPG	Monte Carlo	454	365	mt	
1971	CLC	Camaro	396	300	mt	
1971	CLC	Camaro	402	300	mt	
1971	CLD	Camaro	396	300	TH	
1971	CLD	Camaro	402	300	TH	
1971	CLP	Chevrolet	396	300	TH	
1971	CLP	Chevrolet	402	300	TH	
1971	CLR	Chevrolet	396	300	mt	
1971	CLR	Chevrolet	402	300	mt	
1971	CPD	Chevrolet	454	365	mt	
1971	CPG	Chevrolet	454	365	mt	
1971	CLA	Chevelle	396	300	mt	
1971	CLA	Chevelle	402	300	mt	
1971	CLB	Chevelle	396	300	TH	
1971	CLB	Chevelle	402	300	TH	
1971	CLL	Chevelle	396	300	mt	
1971	CLL	Chevelle	402	300	mt	
1971	CLP	Chevelle	396	300	TH	
1971	CLP	Chevelle	402	300	TH	
1971	CLR	Chevelle	396	300	mt	
1971	CLR	Chevelle	402	300	mt	
1971	CLS	Chevelle	396	300	mt	
1971	CLS	Chevelle	402	300	mt	
1971	CPA	Chevelle	454	365	mt	
1971	CPD	Chevelle	454	365	mt	
1971	CPG	Chevelle	454	365	mt	
1971	CPP	Chevelle	454	425	mt	
1971	CPR	Chevelle	454	425	TH	
1971	CPH	Corvette	454	365	mt	
1971	CPJ	Corvette	454	365	TH	

ABBREVIATIONS

AR—Air Injection Reactor system (smog pump)
CA—California emissions
HD—Heavy Duty
hdc—heavy duty clutch

PG—Powerglide
mt—manual trans, mt-3—3 speed
SHP—Special High Performance
TH—Turbo Hydramatic

YEAR	ID CODE	MODEL	CID	HP	TRANS	NOTES
1971	CPW	Corvette	454	425	mt	
1971	CPX	Corvette	454	425	TH	
1972	CLA	Camaro	396	240	mt	
1972	CLA	Camaro	402	240	mt	
1972	CLB	Camaro	396	240	TH	
1972	CLB	Camaro	402	240	TH	
1972	CTA	Camaro	396	240	mt	AR
1972	CTA	Camaro	402	240	mt	AR
1972	CTB	Camaro	396	240	TH	AR
1972	CTB	Camaro	402	240	TH	AR
1972	CLB	Monte Carlo	396	210	TH	
1972	CLB	Monte Carlo	402	210	TH	
1972	CPD	Monte Carlo	454	270	TH	
1972	CRW	Monte Carlo	454	270	TH	AR
1972	CTJ	Monte Carlo	396	210	TH	
1972	CTJ	Monte Carlo	402	210	TH	
1972	CLB	Chevrolet	396	210	mt	
1972	CLB	Chevrolet	402	210	mt	
1972	CLR	Chevrolet	396	210	mt	
1972	CLR	Chevrolet	402	210	mt	
1972	CPD	Chevrolet	454	270	TH	
1972	CPG	Chevrolet	454	270	TH	
1972	CRW	Chevrolet	454	270	TH	AR
1972	CRY	Chevrolet	454	270	TH	AR
1972	CTB	Chevrolet	396	210	mt	AR
1972	CTB	Chevrolet	402	210	mt	AR
1972	CTJ	Chevrolet	396	210	mt	AR
1972	CTJ	Chevrolet	402	210	mt	AR
1972	CLA	Chevelle	396	240	mt	
1972	CLA	Chevelle	402	240	mt	
1972	CLB	Chevelle	396	240	TH	
1972	CLB	Chevelle	402	240	TH	
1972	CLS	Chevelle	396	240	mt	
1972	CLS	Chevelle	402	240	mt	
1972	CPA	Chevelle	454	270	mt	
1972	CPD	Chevelle	454	270	TH	
1972	CRX	Chevelle	454	270	mt	AR
1972	CRW	Chevelle	454	270	TH	AR

ABBREVIATIONS

AR—Air Injection Reactor system (smog pump)
CA—California emissions
HD—Heavy Duty
hdc—heavy duty clutch

PG—Powerglide
mt—manual trans, mt-3—3 speed
SHP—Special High Performance
TH—Turbo Hydramatic

YEAR	ID CODE	MODEL	CID	HP	TRANS	NOTES
1972	CTA	Chevelle	396	240	mt	AR
1972	CTA	Chevelle	402	240	mt	AR
1972	CTB	Chevelle	396	240	TH	AR
1972	CTB	Chevelle	402	240	TH	AR
1972	CTH	Chevelle	396	240	mt	AR
1972	CTH	Chevelle	402	240	mt	AR
1972	CTJ	Chevelle	396	240	TH	AR
1972	CTJ	Chevelle	402	240	TH	AR
1972	CPH	Corvette	454	270	mt	
1972	CPJ	Corvette	454	270	TH	
1972	CSR	Corvette	454	270	mt	AR
1972	CSS	Corvette	454	270	TH	AR
1973	CWB	Monte Carlo	454	245	TH	
1973	CWD	Monte Carlo	454	245	TH	CA
1973	CWD	Chevrolet	454	250	TH	CA
1973	CWJ	Chevrolet	454	250	TH	CA
1973	CWK	Chevrolet	454	250	TH	
1973	CWL	Chevrolet	454	250	TH	
1973	CWA	Chevelle	454	250	mt	
1973	CWB	Chevelle	454	250	TH	
1973	CWC	Chevelle	454	250	mt	CA
1973	CWD	Chevelle	454	250	TH	CA
1973	CWM	Corvette	454	275	mt	
1973	CWR	Corvette	454`	275	at	
1973	CWS	Corvette	454	275	at	CA
1973	CWT	Corvette	454	275	mt	CA
1974	CWD	Monte Carlo	454	235	TH	
1974	CWX	Monte Carlo	454	235	TH	
1974	CXR	Monte Carlo	454	235	TH	
1974	CXS	Monte Carlo	454	235	TH	
1974	CWU	Chevrolet	454	235	TH	Police
1974	CWW	Chevrolet	454	235	TH	CA Police
1974	CWY	Chevrolet	454	235	TH	CA
1974	CXA	Chevrolet	454	235	TH	CA
1974	CXB	Chevrolet	454	235	TH	CA
1974	CXC	Chevrolet	454	235	TH	CA
1974	CXT	Chevrolet	454	235	TH	
1974	CXU	Chevrolet	454	235	TH	

ABBREVIATIONS

AR—Air Injection Reactor system (smog pump)
CA—California emissions
HD—Heavy Duty
hdc—heavy duty clutch

PG—Powerglide
mt—manual trans, mt-3—3 speed
SHP—Special High Performance
TH—Turbo Hydramatic

YEAR	ID CODE	MODEL	CID	HP	TRANS	NOTES
1974	CWA	Chevelle	454	235	mt	
1974	CWD	Chevelle	454	235	TH	CA
1974	CWX	Chevelle	454	235	TH	
1974	CXM	Chevelle	454	235	mt	
1974	CXR	Chevelle	454	235	TH	
1974	CXS	Chevelle	454	235	TH	
1974	CWM	Corvette	454	270	mt	
1974	CWR	Corvette	454	270	TH	
1974	CWS	Corvette	454	270	TH	CA
1974	CWT	Corvette	454	270	mt	
1975	CXW	Chevelle	454	215	TH	
1975	CXK	Chevrolet	454	215	TH	
1975	CXL	Chevrolet	454	215	TH	
1975	CXX	Chevrolet	454	215	TH	
1975	CXY	Chevrolet	454	215	TH	
1976	CXX	Chevrolet	454	225	TH	LS4

ABBREVIATIONS

AR—Air Injection Reactor system (smog pump)
CA—California emissions
HD—Heavy Duty
hdc—heavy duty clutch

PG—Powerglide
mt—manual trans, mt-3—3 speed
SHP—Special High Performance
TH—Turbo Hydramatic

INDEX

ABOUT THE AUTHOR

Photo by Jim Monteith, **Country House Studios.**

Dave Emanuel began his career in automotive journalism in 1970 when his first article was published in *"Car Craft"* magazine. Since then, his byline has appeared on over 1,000 feature articles in magazines such as *Hot Rod, Super Chevy, Stock Car Racing, Super Stock, Popular Hot Rodding, Road & Track, Motor Trend, Corvette Fever, Muscle Car Review, Home Mechanix, 4-Wheel & Off-Road,* and *Automobile Quarterly.* He has also written six books and appears on the television program *Road Test Magazine* which airs on The Nashville Network (TNN).

A thorough knowledge of a subject is required before an author can write authoritatively about it and Dave gained his knowledge about automobiles the old-fashioned way—he broke them. It wasn't long after he began driving legally that Dave made his first visits to a drag strip, first as a spectator, then as a competitor. After several years of racing experience, the marriage of journalism and automobiles came about when Dave set a track record and decided to chronicle his efforts. After dabbling in journalism on a part-time basis for several years, Dave decided to abandon his job as a computer systems analyst and began writing full time.

In a relatively short time, he established himself as one of the country's leading automotive journalists. Although he has done road tests, product reviews, personality profiles and features, he is best known for his technical articles and books. He brings a unique perspective to these through combination of personal relationships with a number of the most successful race engine builders in the nation, and extensive hands-on experience. ∎